# CONSCRIPTS OF MODERNITY

DAVID SCOTT

# Conscripts of Modernity

## The Tragedy of Colonial Enlightenment

DUKE UNIVERSITY PRESS

Durham & London 2004

© 2004 Duke University Press

All rights reserved

Printed in the United States

of America on acid-free paper ♾

Designed by Rebecca M. Giménez

Typeset in Quadraat by Tseng Information

Systems. Library of Congress Cataloging-

in-Publication Data appear on the

last printed page of

this book.

FOR RITTY

There is always, when reading

great masterpieces of the past, a difference in

the emphasis of the author and the reader.

C. L. R. JAMES, *Mariners, Renegades*

*and Castaways*

# Contents

# Prologue

Milton has a great phrase; he says: "A good book is the precious life-blood of
a master's spirit." But it is more than that. It is the result of the circumstances
of the age playing upon a mentality and the circumstances of people who are
central to it.

## I

My most general concern in this book is with the conceptual problem
of political presents and with how reconstructed pasts and anticipated
futures are thought out in relation to them. More specifically, my principal concern is with our own postcolonial present, our present after the
collapse of the social and political hopes that went into the anticolonial imagining and postcolonial making of national sovereignties. This
is our present, as I have put it elsewhere, *after* Bandung.[1] My concern
is with the relation between this (as it seems to me) dead-end present
and, on the one hand, the old utopian futures that inspired and for a
long time sustained it and, on the other, an imagined idiom of future
futures that might reanimate this present and even engender in it new
and unexpected horizons of transformative possibility.

What are the critical conceptual resources needed for this exercise?
There is today no clear answer to this question. In many parts of the
once-colonized world (not least in the one that forms the geopolitical
background—if not the specific object—of this book, the Caribbean),
the bankruptcy of postcolonial regimes is palpable in the extreme. Where
in the early decades of new nationhood an earnestly progressive ideology (radical nationalisms, Marxisms, Fanonian liberationisms, indige-
nous socialisms, or what have you) aimed at giving point to the relation between where we have come from, where we are, and where we
might be going, these days even the nostalgia for what the late Guya-

nese poet Martin Carter memorably called "a free community of valid persons" is met with cynical contempt and sometimes with worse.[2] The acute paralysis of will and sheer vacancy of imagination, the rampant corruption and vicious authoritarianism, the instrumental self-interest and showy self-congratulation are all themselves symptoms of a more profound predicament that has, at least in part, to do with the anxiety of exhaustion. The New Nations project has run out of vital sources of energy for creativity, and what we are left with is an exercise of power bereft of any pretense of the exercise of vision. And consequently, almost everywhere, the anticolonial utopias have gradually withered into postcolonial nightmares.

I think we live in tragic times. This, however, is not merely because our world is assailed by one moral and social catastrophe after another. It is rather because, in Hamlet's memorable phrase, our time is "out of joint." The old languages of moral-political vision and hope are no longer in sync with the world they were meant to describe and normatively criticize. The result is that our time is suffering from what Raymond Williams (in his discussion of modern tragedy) aptly described as "the loss of hope; the slowly settling loss of any acceptable future."[3] But if what is at stake in critically thinking through this postcolonial present is not simply the naming of yet another horizon, and the fixing of the teleological plot that takes us there from here, still, what is at stake is something like a refusal to be seduced and immobilized by the facile normalization of the present. This is the theme of my deliberations here.

SOME YEARS AGO I published a book, *Refashioning Futures*, in which I sought to sketch out some of my disquiet about the ways in which colonialism was being constructed and theorized as a *conceptual* problem for our postcolonial present. That disquiet had several interconnected dimensions, but one of them—one upon which I want to fasten our attention in this book, *Conscripts of Modernity*—had to do with the assumptions made about the present in relation to which pasts are reconstructed and represented for contemporary inquiry. We are all, after Michel Foucault, historians of the present, but it seemed to me that very little systematic consideration, if any, was being given to *what* present it is that the past was being reimagined *for*. Of course, the rationale for the postcolonial reinterrogation and recharacterization of the colonial past (which began in earnest in the 1980s, at least in the North Atlantic academy) has rightly been that it will enable some critical purchase on the present. But what present was this supposed to be that the past was being called upon to illuminate, and, moreover, in relation to what prospect—what hope—what expectation? In the conceptual reorientation that has characterized the intervention of postcolonial theory over the past two decades, the precise nature of the relation between pasts, presents, and futures has rarely ever been specified and conceptually problematized. It has tended, rather, to be assumed, to be taken for granted.

Postcolonial theorists have made a considerable name for themselves by criticizing their predecessors, the anticolonial nationalists, for their essentialism—that is, for holding conceptions of nation, race, identity, history, and so on that assume (in the well-known phrase) a metaphysics of presence, a stable ground of explication and justification. It has been easy for these theorists, armed with social constructionism, to demonstrate the error in these conceptions and to appear in turn to hold more theoretically sophisticated understandings of the past and its relation to the present.[4] I have never entirely disagreed with this postcolonial dissatisfaction (nor with the attitude of hermeneutical suspicion with which it is articulated), but my worry has been that in adopting this kind of critical approach postcolonial theorists have often unwittingly made an essentialist mistake of their own. These critics have sometimes assumed that the questions to which the anticolonial nationalists addressed themselves—questions about their presents and their connection to their pasts and their hoped-for futures—were the same as the ones that organize their own contemporary concerns and preoccupations. The postcolonial assumption, in other words, has often been that the anticolonial nationalists merely had bad (i.e., essentialist or metaphysical) answers to good (or anyway, standardly formulated) questions. This is what I think is mistaken; it has appeared to me to be but another version of the essentialism they have so incisively criticized. In this instance, the metaphysics of antiessentialism has been to assume that it is postcolonial *answers*—rather than postcolonial questions—that require historicization, deconstruction, and reformulation. My view is precisely the reverse of this: it is our postcolonial *questions* and not our answers that demand our critical attention. In my view, an adequate interrogation of the present (postcolonial or otherwise) depends upon identifying the *difference* between the questions that animated former presents and those that animate our own.

In spelling out this disquiet I have sought to elaborate a conception of the temporality of what I call "problem-spaces." This is a concept that will also be central to this book's concerns, and it will be helpful, therefore, to say again what I mean by it, why I find it handy, and what I mean it to do.[5] A "problem-space," in my usage, is meant first of all to demarcate a discursive context, a context of language. But it is more than a cognitively intelligible arrangement of concepts, ideas, images, meanings, and so on—though it is certainly this. It is a context of argument and, therefore, one of *intervention*. A problem-space, in other words, is an ensemble of questions and answers around which a horizon of identifiable stakes (conceptual as well as ideological-political stakes) hangs. That is to say, what defines this discursive context are not only the particular problems that get posed as problems as such (the problem of "race," say), but the particular questions that seem worth asking and the kinds of answers that seem worth having. Notice, then, that a problem-space is very much a context of dispute, a context of rival views, a context, if you like, of knowledge and power. But from within the terms of any given problem-space what is in dispute, what the argument is effectively about, is not itself being argued over. Notice also that a problem-space necessarily has a *temporal* dimension or, rather, is a fundamentally temporal concept. Problem-spaces alter historically because problems are not timeless and do not have everlasting shapes. In new historical conditions old questions may lose their salience, their bite, and so lead the range of old answers that once attached to them to appear lifeless, quaint, not so much wrong as irrelevant. In such conditions the old paths between questions and answers do not necessarily disappear; their cognitive connections may remain visible and intelligible as the norm or the convention, but the paths now go nowhere because the stakes involved in walking them have dissolved. This is why for me the idea of a problem-space is connected to the idea that criticism has always to be *strategic* inasmuch as in judging its purchase criticism ought always to seek to clarify whether and to what extent the questions it is trying to answer continue to be questions worth having answers to. And, therefore, what this idea of a problem-space does is to oblige us to frame the criticism of the present in terms of the strategic value of responding—or evading response—to the conventions of the language-game we find ourselves participants in.

This way of coming at the problem of criticism's construal of the relation between colonial pasts and the postcolonial present, as I explain in *Refashioning Futures*, is one I derive in large part from the Hegelian philosopher R. G. Collingwood and his more Wittgensteinian disciple, Quentin Skinner. I come back in the following chapter to their work and my uses of it, but there is another salient formulation of the problem of historical investigation from which I have learned a great deal and which bears preliminary consideration here—not least because of the points of contact between it and the question-and-answer approach of Collingwood and Skinner, and also because it is explicitly concerned with some of the problems of time and revolutionary thought that are going to engage my attention in this book. I am thinking of the work of Bernard Yack, in particular his very remarkable book, *The Longing for Total Revolution*.[6] Published about two decades ago, Yack's book is animated by a certain skepticism regarding the specific shape of modern social and political discontent and the radical hopes and expectations and demands that have often been derived from that discontent. These radical hopes and expectations and demands, Yack suggested, have been infused by a distinctive desire for social transformation, a desire he felicitously calls "a longing for total revolution." In Yack's view, however, these radical hopes and expectations and demands are philosophically incoherent as well as practically impossible, and only a comprehensive revision of our understanding of the philosophical sources of the discontent that inspires them can begin to clarify our contemporary predicaments, and open out possible cognitive-political paths beyond them. Now, I may not share the ideological hopes that inspire Yack's political position (they are largely liberal hopes, so far as I can tell), but I think that the framing conceptual move he urges is an instructive and enabling one, and I should like to commend it.[7] As he suggests, many studies of revolutionary discontent have failed to adequately understand the role of new concepts in *generating* social discontent. This is because they have mistakenly focused on the way these concepts define *alternatives* to the present social limitations *rather* than on the way they shape our understanding of these limitations themselves. Notice the orientation of Yack's approach, its family resemblance to Collingwood's question-and-answer logic: it is the conceptualization of the *obstacles* to be overcome that interests him, not the seeming virtues of the proffered alternatives. Or, to put it otherwise, for Yack, the analytical purchase of the latter cannot be understood without a genealogy of the former. In short, historicizing past hopes (such as anticolonial ones) ought to entail an analysis less of the transformative projects themselves than of the way those hopes reflect a certain understanding of the problem to be overcome; in Yack's language, the way the sources of discontent or the obstacles to satisfaction are conceived and defined.

ANTICOLONIALISM HAS BEEN a classic instance of the modern longing for total revolution. In some of the texts that define its ethos and aspiration—Aimé Césaire's *Discourse on Colonialism*, for instance, or Frantz Fanon's *The Wretched of the Earth*—colonialism is conceived largely as a totalizing structure of brutality, violence, objectification, racism, and exclusion that the anticolonial revolution was supposed to overcome. Colonialism was principally described as a *negative* structure of limiting and stultifying power to which the anticolonialists were obliged to respond with a positive and regenerative counter-power. I am not concerned to doubt the justification of this view. My worry, however, has been that in challenging the anticolonialist's answers rather than their questions postcolonialism has uncritically taken over this Fanonian image of colonialism. So that, paradoxically, although postcolonial theorists have elaborated postcolonial answers (by which I mean have employed a familiar poststructuralist apparatus to demonstrate the instability of the concepts their predecessors took for granted) they have continued to assume an anticolonial picture of the *problem* of colonialism. That is to say, the conception of colonialism that postcolonialism has constructed and made the target of its analytical focus has continued to bear the distinctive traces of anticolonialism's conceptual preoccupations. And consequently postcolonialism has continued to be concerned with exposing the *negative* structure of colonialism's power and with demonstrating the colonized's agency in resisting or overcoming these conditions. In this book I should like to urge us away from this preoccupation.

My argument, of course, is *not* that colonialism was not a structure of violence and brutality. I have no doubt that it was (and that it continues to be where it persists). My argument is that (as Yack suggests) the way one defines an alternative *depends* on the way one has conceived the problem. And therefore, reconceiving alternatives depends in significant part on reconceiving the object of discontent and thus the longing that stimulates the desire for an alternative. The view I wish to commend is that it is not the anticolonial nationalist's answers that have needed changing so much as the postcolonial theorist's questions that needed dissolving. To put this proposition another way: it is the old object of our anticolonial discontent that stands in need of reformulation. We need, in other words, to give up constructing an image of colonialism that demands from us an attitude of anticolonial longing, a longing for anticolonial revolution. It seems to me that a more fruitful approach to the historical appreciation of prior understandings of the relation between pasts, presents, and futures is to think of different historical conjunctures as constituting different conceptual-ideological problem-spaces, and to think of these problem-spaces less as generators of new propositions than as generators of new questions and new demands. Consequently, what is important is to read historically not just for the answers that this or that theorist has produced but for the questions that are more or less the epistemological conditions for those answers.

Part of what is at stake here, clearly, is the problem of *narrative*, because the relation between pasts, presents, and futures is a relation constituted in narrative discourse. In this book, I have been particularly inspired by Hayden White's metahistorical intervention in debates about the writing of history, and specifically his argument for an understanding of the "content of the form" of historical narrative. If the forms of narrative, White suggests, have built into their linguistic structures different myth-models or story-potentials, and if different stories organize the relation between past, present, and future differently, it may be important to inquire into the relation between the poetic form and the conceptual and ideological content of historical discourse. Historically minded criticisms of colonialism seem to me to have something to learn from this idea. Does anticolonialism depend upon a certain way of telling the story about the past, present, and future? I mean this question in a narratological sense. Is the narrative connecting pasts, presents, and futures distinctively constructed within anticolonial texts? Or to put it slightly differently: Does the political point of anticolonialism depend on constructing colonialism as a particular kind of conceptual and ideological object? Does the moral point of anticolonialism depend on constructing colonialism as a particular kind of obstacle to be overcome? Does the purchase or salience of anticolonialism depend on a certain narrative form, a certain rhythm, and a certain conception of temporality? Does the anticolonial demand for a certain kind of postcolonial future oblige its histories to produce certain kinds of pasts?

I am going to suggest that anticolonial stories about past, present, and future have typically been emplotted in a distinctive narrative form, one with a distinctive story-potential: that of *Romance*. They have tended to be narratives of overcoming, often narratives of vindication; they have tended to enact a distinctive rhythm and pacing, a distinctive direction, and to tell stories of salvation and redemption. They have largely depended upon a certain (utopian) horizon toward which the emancipationist history is imagined to be moving. I do not take this conceptual framework to be a mistake. However, in the wake of the global historico-political and cognitive shifts that have taken place in the past decade or two, I have a doubt about the continued critical salience of this narrative form and its underlying mythos. Indeed, my wager in this book is that the problem about postcolonial futures—how we go about reimagining what we might become of what we have so far made—cannot be recast without recasting the problem about colonial pasts. My undertaking here is aimed at offering one approach to such an inquiry.[8]

MANY YEARS AGO, Talal Asad published a short essay in honor of the anthropologist Stanley Diamond. The essay was entitled, "Conscripts of Western Civilization."[9] Diamond, in the great tradition of radical Boasians (from Edward Sapir to Paul Radin), was a protagonist of the idea of Western civilization as a destructive force reordering the worlds of non-European peoples, and of anthropology as a "civilized discipline" shaped by and self-reflexively responding to that destruction.[10] Writing against the assumption that "acculturation" could be conceived of without reference to the project of European colonialism, Diamond argued:

> In fact, acculturation has always been a matter of conquest. Either civilization directly shatters a primitive culture that happens to stand in its historical right of way; or a primitive social economy, in the grip of a civilized market, becomes so attenuated and weakened that it can no longer contain the traditional culture. In both cases, refugees from the foundering groups may adopt the standards of the more potent society in order to survive as individuals. But these are conscripts of civilization, not volunteers.[11]

Asad's essay is framed by this arresting passage, but he develops the insight with a significantly different emphasis, and point. For Asad too, all non-Western societies ("primitive" and otherwise) are being "destroyed and remade" by the political, economic, and ideological forces "unleashed" by European modernity, but he sets aside Diamond's humanist and Romantic nostalgia for the "primitive" as well as the perspective of moral critique that stresses the "survival" of the conquered. Asad's point is neither that authentic difference is disappearing or surviving, but that difference, such as it is, is increasingly obliged to respond to—and be managed by—the categories brought into play by European modernity. Culture, as he says, may always be invented, but the rise of the modern imperial world has irrevocably altered the conditions of that invention.[12] Therefore, while Asad shares with Diamond the starting point that non-Europeans were conscripted to modernity's project—were, that is, coercively obliged to render themselves its objects and its agents—what bears inquiry in his view is the complex character of the varied powers that secured those conditions and their effects.

As will be only too clear to the reader, I have been profoundly inspired by the angle of this approach to thinking about modernity and historical change.[13] It seems to me to offer a way of remapping the problematic in which the relation between colonial pasts and the postcolonial present is conceived. Or, to put it another way (and connecting Asad to Collingwood and Skinner on one hand and Yack on the other), it offers a way of altering the question about the colonial past (the cognitive-political problem about colonialism) that is deemed useful for the criticism of the postcolonial present.

II

It is this concern with a criticism of the postcolonial present, with rethinking the narratological relation between colonial pasts and postcolonial futures, that provides the occasion for reconsidering what is undoubtedly one of the seminal anticolonial histories of the twentieth century, The Black Jacobins by C. L. R. James. The Black Jacobins is surely one of the great inaugural texts of the discourse of anticolonialism. Written by a black colonial intellectual in the middle of a life of incipient Trotskyist and anticolonial engagement in London in the interwar years of the 1930s, it is an enduring work about a transforming moment in Caribbean and, indeed, world history: the Haitian Revolution of 1791–1804. As is well known, The Black Jacobins is the revolutionary story of the self-emancipation of New World slaves. It records, in turn, the violence accompanying the capture and transportation of the slaves across the Middle Passage and the depraved social conditions in which they lived and worked on the sugar plantations; the location of slave-grown sugar in the emergence of a global economy; the dependence of French capital on slave labor; the colonial reverberations of the French Revolution; the slave revolt initiated by Boukman in the summer of 1791; and the dramatic rise to eminence of Toussaint of Bréda and his supreme leadership over the rebellious forces. Indeed, most of all it is the political biography of this enlightened and inspiring leader—Toussaint—who mythologized himself as "L'Ouverture," the Opening—and who gave vision to that heroic struggle for liberty. It is the story of his personality, his almost obsessive self-consciousness and willful determination, and his transformation from a man of decisive action into a man assailed by a crippling uncertainty that leads to his betrayal and eventual arrest and deportation into exile and death in France. In short, *The Black Jacobins* is a revolutionary epic. It is precisely the narrative history of a revolutionary struggle in which, from a particular present, a certain past is reconstructed and deployed in the service of imagining the direction in which an alternative future might be sought.

But if *The Black Jacobins* was written as a complex response to a complex demand for anticolonial overcoming (and thus participates in what Yack calls the longing for total revolution), it has largely continued to be read as though we ourselves transparently inhabit the problem-space out of which it was composed, as though the questions through which James's revolutionary narrative constituted a more or less compelling answer ought, necessarily, to continue to be ours. I want to express a strong doubt about this assumption and the kinds of historiographical argument that have followed from it. And yet (as we will see), part of what makes *The Black Jacobins* the exemplary and lasting work of historical criticism that it is, is the self-consciousness with which James connects the story of Toussaint Louverture to the vital stories of his— that is, James's—time. Doing so, he urges us to connect Toussaint to the vital stories of *our own* time. But being James, he does much more. He provides us with clues as to what, exactly, that connection might be.

In 1963 a new and revised edition of *The Black Jacobins* was issued in the United States by Vintage. This was an event. The book, originally published in 1938 (by Secker and Warburg in London and Dial in New York), had been out of print for many years. The new edition—a handy paperback—would help to bring James, and in particular this extraordinary early work of his, to the attention of later generations of readers (in the Caribbean and elsewhere) whose worlds might have been formed by different predicaments than his, but who might, nevertheless, be inspired by his vision. It is an important fact (about the book itself but also about the idea of history, black colonial history especially) that *The Black Jaco-*

*bins* has been continuously in print since then, and indeed a testimony to the belated stature of James himself that it has recently been reissued as a Penguin classic.[14]

It is well known of course that this 1963 reissue is not only a second but also a *revised* edition. It announces itself as such, after all. But it seems to have been very often assumed that the only, or at least the most important, revision consists of the appended essay, "From Toussaint L'Ouverture to Fidel Castro." This may be understandable, but it is mistaken. For besides this justly famous appendix (and the new footnotes scattered throughout the body of the main text) there is another set of revisions that are perhaps of even more far-reaching importance. These are the additions made to chapter 13, "The War of Independence," the last, the longest, and in many ways the most momentous chapter of *The Black Jacobins*. It is curious that as decisive as this chapter is for the overall dramatic action of James's history it has scarcely been recognized, much less discussed and properly appreciated, that the first seven paragraphs in the 1963 edition are fresh interpolations. They do not occur in the first edition of 1938. What is of particular significance to me, however, is not merely the occurrence of this unnoticed revision, but the fact that these seven paragraphs constitute a very profound meditation on tragedy. They are an explicit consideration of the tragedy of Toussaint Louverture specifically, and through him and his predicament, I am going to suggest, the larger tragedy of colonial enlightenment generally. This is the generative theme of my book.

JAMES'S INTRODUCTION OF the literary-philosophical problematic of tragedy into the broader questions of colonialism, revolution, civilization, and enlightenment is a move that offers, I think, a provocative point of departure from which to challenge the conventional Romantic organization of the narrative relation between pasts, presents, and futures. In a sense it allows us to consider Hayden White's point about the contrast between Romance and tragedy as modes of historical emplotment. James, as we will see, was a close and avid reader of tragedy, Athenian as well as early modern. For more than a decade before the appearance of the revised edition of *The Black Jacobins*, a period, as we know, of considerable alteration and reexamination of the contexts and preoccupations of his own life and work, James had in fact been worrying over the historical-critical problem of tragedy. We see this throughout the writings of the 1950s—the literary-critical essays (the work on *Hamlet*, in particular) and in greater elaboration in *American Civilization, Mariners, Renegades and Castaways*, and *Beyond a Boundary*.[15] James was most impressed by the problem of the historical moment of tragedy, those moments of large historical conflict in which new forms of thought and action are struggling relentlessly with old: Aeschylus in fifth-century Athens, Shakespeare in early modern England, Melville in nineteenth-century America. They all wrote in a time of historical upheaval or civilizational rupture. For James, these were moments not merely of transition, but moments when great historical forces were at irreconcilable odds with each other, in which the tensions between competing historical directions were at a particularly high pitch, and in which new kinds of subjects (James would have said new kinds of "personalities") were being thrown upon the historical stage, individuals embodying within their single selves the mighty conundrums and divisions of their age. In a very Hegelian way, therefore, James was particularly alert to the ways in which tragedy both constitutes and enables a distinctive reflection upon subjectivity in moments of historical crisis.

In more recent years, a number of scholars—classicists, philosophers, literary scholars, and political theorists among them—have turned their attention to exploring these (and other) critical resources of tragedy, some more affiliated with the Aristotelian reflection on the ethics of human action than with the Hegelian concern with the individual's embodiment of historical conflict. My own exploration of the problem of tragedy in *The Black Jacobins* is indebted to their work, especially that of Charles Segal, Martha Nussbaum, J. Peter Euben, Christopher Rocco, and Jean-Pierre Vernant and Pierre Vidal-Naquet.[16] In this work, variously articulated, of course, tragedy is seen as offering a literary-philosophical genre in which a number of the consequential theoretical shibboleths of our time are challenged. For these writers, tragedy offers the most searching reflection on human action, intention, and chance, with significant implications for how we think the connections among past, present, and future. Tragedy questions, for example, the view of human history as moving teleologically and transparently toward a determinate end, or as governed by a sovereign and omnisciently rational agent. These views of human history suppose that the past can be cleanly separated from the present, and that reason can be unambiguously disentangled from myth.

Tragedy raises doubts about the salience of the Platonist vision of the hyperrational ideal and the Kantian belief in the sufficiency and autonomy of the self. These conceptions of the subject and its actions depend upon a decisive blow being delivered to the poetic and to the idea of human being as dependent on or vulnerable to forces and powers not entirely within its rational control. Above all, tragedy is troubled by the hubris of enlightenment and civilization, power and knowledge. As we will see, however, the strategy of tragedy is not to dismiss out of hand the claims of reason, but to honor the contingent, the ambiguous, the paradoxical, and the unyielding in human affairs in such a way as to complicate our most cherished notions about the relation between identity and difference, reason and unreason, blindness and insight, action and responsibility, guilt and innocence. As Jean-Pierre Vernant and Pierre Vidal-Naquet eloquently put it in a fascinating passage:

> From a tragic point of view . . . , there are two aspects to action. It involves on the one hand reflection, weighing up the pros and cons, foreseeing as accurately as possible the means and the ends; on the other, placing one's stake on what is unknown and incomprehensible, risking oneself on a terrain that remains impenetrable, entering into a game with supernatural forces, not knowing whether, as they join with one, they will bring success or doom. Even for the most foreseeing of men, the most carefully thought out action is still a chancy appeal to the gods and only by their reply, and usually to one's cost, will one learn what it really involved and meant. It is only when the drama is over that actions take on their true significance and agents, through what they have in reality accomplished without realizing it, discover their true identity. So long as there has been no complete consummation, human affairs remain enigmas that are the more obscure the more the actors believe themselves sure of what they are doing and what they are.[17]

In short, tragedy sets before us the image of a man or woman obliged to act in a world in which values are unstable and ambiguous. And consequently, for tragedy the relation between past, present, and future is never a Romantic one in which history rides a triumphant and seamlessly progressive rhythm, but a broken series of paradoxes and reversals in which human action is ever open to unaccountable contingencies — and luck.[18]

I want to suggest that this is the understanding of action, history, and enlightenment that James's revisions to the second edition of The Black

*Jacobins* alert us to. The local stage upon which the dramatic action takes place is framed by the world-historical relation between New World slavery and modern civilization (their constitutive connection as well as their constitutive antagonism) and the irreparable breach opened by the French Revolution which altered forever the epistemic and political conditions in which thought and action were possible in the modern world. In this setting of profound social upheaval and historical conflict, James's great protagonist, Toussaint Louverture, is placed at a crossroads of absolute choice between options to which he is equally and completely committed (the freedom of the slaves on the one hand and the enlightenment of revolutionary France on the other) and in circumstances in which he must choose and yet cannot choose without fatal cost. Considered in this way, I think that the revised edition of *The Black Jacobins* urges us to take another—and a hard—look at the consoling (anticolonial) story we have told ourselves about colonialism and civilization, modernity and enlightenment, and especially the vindicationist narratives of emancipation that have animated our hopes for a world without dissatisfaction, injustice, and unhappiness. Read as a tragedy of colonial enlightenment, *The Black Jacobins* transgresses the now conventional Romance of revolutionary overcoming and offers us the elements of a critical story of our postcolonial time.

III

*The Black Jacobins* is a curiously understudied book. To be sure, since his death in May 1989, there is now a considerable—and rapidly growing— body of scholarship on C. L. R. James. And, as may be expected, most of this scholarship (much of it in the form of intellectual and political biography) passes through and acknowledges the inaugural importance of *The Black Jacobins*, both to the overall development of James's thought and to the development of anticolonial and radical black historiography.[19] But there has been little sustained discussion of this text itself.[20] Part of the reason, perhaps, has to do with the widely held view that James's best work comes later, in *American Civilization* (written between 1949 and 1950 but published posthumously in 1993) and *Beyond a Boundary* (published in 1963). I do not share this estimate, but I have no wish to dispute it. This is because my primary interest in *The Black Jacobins* is not James per se, though aspects of his intellectual and political biography will play a part in my investigations. Nor is this a study of James's thought as a whole, though again I will occasionally have to situate what I am saying in the wider context of his far-flung oeuvre. I am after something else than what these otherwise helpful forms of inquiry illuminate. My interest in The Black Jacobins is rather as an instance—a particularly insightful and provocative instance—of the problem of writing critical histories of the postcolonial present. In other words my aim is less to write about The Black Jacobins than to write through it.

It should also be clear, therefore, that I am not going to be interested in the fine historical details of the events that make up the Haitian Revolution. A number of distinguished scholars—David Geggus, Carolyn Fick, and Alex Dupuy among them—have offered revisionist histories of the revolution, and these have significantly altered our understanding of the sources, character, and consequences of that world-historical event.[21] Worthy as I consider it, I have nothing to contribute to that endeavor. Nor am I immediately concerned with the important historiographical question of the "silencing" of the revolution in colonialist discourse—though I touch on one aspect of it in the Epilogue. This is an issue of some significance, and in a book of admirable eloquence Michel-Rolph Trouillot has written impressively against this production—or produced elision—of that past.[22]

I am inspired by another way of coming at The Black Jacobins, one interested less in its status as social history than in the poetics that constitute its dramatic narrative about slavery and freedom, and the figuration that establishes the presence of its historical subject, the protagonist Toussaint Louverture. I am inspired, in short, by approaches that acknowledge the mythopoetic character of The Black Jacobins, that read it less for its facts than for its literary-political project. The earliest and best-known discussion of The Black Jacobins (of any significance, at least), the one offered by the novelist George Lamming in his long and magisterial essay on writing and empire, The Pleasures of Exile, is famously of this sort.[23] (The Pleasures of Exile is in many ways Lamming's salute to a then marginal and unremembered C. L. R. James.)[24] And in an unforgettable chapter, devoted to rehearsing the story of The Black Jacobins, Lamming refigures Toussaint Louverture in the image of Shakespeare's Caliban: Caliban, as he says, ordering history, resurrecting himself "from the natural prison of Prospero's regard." This interleaving of The Black Jacobins and The Tempest has been enormously compelling, partly because it captures so vividly the fact that the encounter between Africa and Europe in the New World was structured by power in such a way as to oblige the enslaved and dis-

placed African to learn—and learn to inhabit as much as learn to transform—Europe's natural and conceptual languages. "We shall never ex-
plode Prospero's old myth until we christen Language afresh; until we
show Language as the product of human endeavour; until we make available to all the result of certain enterprises undertaken by men who are
still regarded as the unfortunate descendants of languageless and deformed slaves."[25] I am, needless to say, deeply indebted to Lamming's
reading of Toussaint as Caliban appropriating language and remaking
history.[26] But there is, to my mind, side by side with the cursing Caliban,
another Shakespearean figure at work in *The Black Jacobins*, one connected
to James's tragic imagining of Toussaint, and one moreover that explicitly brings into the interpretive picture the whole problem of the *modern* world and the *modernist* subject. This is the (perhaps unlikely) figure
of Hamlet. I have already suggested James's fascination with Hamlet,
and I am going to argue that in his revisions to the 1963 edition James's
Toussaint is imagined not only as a newly languaged Caliban, but as a
modernist intellectual, suffering, like Hamlet, the modern fracturing of
thought and action.

The approach to *The Black Jacobins* that I am after in this book is also
close to the one offered by Kara Rabbitt in a fascinating (and insufficiently appreciated) essay published a number of years ago in a collection
devoted to James's intellectual legacy.[27] In this essay Rabbitt focuses her
attention on James's *figuring* of Toussaint Louverture. She is therefore as
attuned as I would like to be to the attention James pays to narration and
dramatization in *The Black Jacobins*, to his self-consciousness of literary
style in casting the story of Toussaint as he does, creating, as she puts it,
a "dramatic figure from a historical one."[28] Consequently Rabbitt is sensitive to the tensions between materialist analysis and portraiture, between history and literature, between science and art in *The Black Jacobins*.
As she says, "James is engaged in a tenuous, genre-challenging enterprise."[29] "Tenuous" is not the word I would use, but "genre-challenging"
is exactly right. Rabbitt is particularly attentive to James's self-conscious
use of Aristotle's conception of the poetics of tragic drama, and especially to his characterization of Toussaint as a "tragically flawed" hero—
though not surprisingly she seems unaware that at least the explicit reference to Aristotle and his theory of tragedy were additions to the 1963
edition. Be that as it may, however, Rabbitt recognizes James's desire
to imagine in his hero a mythological figure whose predicament points
beyond the details of his historical circumstances. As she says:

James appears to make full and conscious use of the Aristotelian tragic structure, allowing a mimesis of the historical events of the Haitian Revolution to point toward the universals regarding the fall of colonialism and repressive hegemonic systems. . . . At a more mundane level this allows James to assume, much like the classical dramaturgists, that the drama that took place on the historical stage of eighteenth century San Domingo is one intimately known to his readers, his task being thus to fill in the important details and to offer analyses of events rather than to provide a historical timeline.[30]

As I have already suggested, in his conceptualization of tragedy James's Aristotelian affiliations have to be set in relation to his Hegelian-Marxist understandings and commitments. But nevertheless, Rabbitt's observations regarding James's dramatic style and her remarks concerning his uses of myth and history are acutely insightful. And to this point she and I have intersecting concerns.

But in the end, Rabbitt and I have different, if not antithetical, overall purposes in our considerations of *The Black Jacobins*. Her critical project drives her in the direction of weighing up the pros and cons of James's narrative strategy, seeking to show where it fulfills and where it falls short of what she takes to be his proper revolutionary aims. These aims she reads elsewhere (that is, *outside* of the text of *The Black Jacobins* itself), especially in the later theoreticopolitical work of the 1940s that champions the self-emancipation of the oppressed. Thus she writes in reference to his representation of the masses: "Yet it should be noted that James's poetic and dramatic rendering of Toussaint in *The Black Jacobins* ironically seems to efface that very element: the people."[31] And a little later: "Thus, James's emphasis on the figure of Toussaint in *The Black Jacobins* may obscure the importance of the elements of resistance James himself will later celebrate in *Facing Reality*—the workers (the slaves) themselves and their repeated demonstrations of the capacity for self-government (the maroons, plantation survival, etc.)."[32] In short, Rabbitt's view turns out to be the familiar one that the project of *The Black Jacobins* is, in the last instance, compromised by the unresolved tension between a revolutionary politics and an elitist poetics.

As I hope the reader will very quickly appreciate, I sharply diverge from this preoccupation *as a whole*. My point is not that James in fact resolved this tension between politics and poetics, or that he didn't, after all, betray the subalterns in favor of the elite. Rabbitt and many others are invested in this form of criticism, but I seek neither to impugn James nor to rescue him from himself. My point is that the purchase of this sort of critical appreciation depends on Rabbitt's already knowing what the implications of James's supposed compromise are for the horizon of political action. And while James, writing from within the temporality of anticolonialism's anticipation of sovereignty, had a clearly conceived standpoint from which to make such a judgment (whatever we make of it), Rabbitt, writing from where she is writing, cannot assume this standpoint to be hers. And consequently, the point I want to make (and I make it persistently throughout this book) is that this binary—revolutionary politics versus elite poetics—is not self-evidently relevant to an adequate appreciation of *The Black Jacobins* for a criticism of the postcolonial present.

## IV

My trajectory in the succeeding chapters is as follows: The first chapter, "Futures Past," derives its title from Reinhart Koselleck's fascinating book, *Futures Past*, and is indebted to his suggestive discussion of the relation between the writing of history and the collapse of hitherto existing horizons of possible futures, the historical problem, as he puts it, of "superseded futures" or "futures past." James's preface to the first edition of *The Black Jacobins* is at once a reflection on the problem of historical representation (the relation between the art and science of history writing) in relation to anticolonial revolutionary history, and an explicit evocation of the political present in relation to which he is writing it (the Moscow trials, the Spanish Civil War, the rise in Trotskyism of an alternative revolutionary Marxism). In this opening chapter I suggest that James's acute and self-conscious situation of his history-telling poses the challenge to us of how to write the story of Toussaint Louverture in the wake of the collapse of the futures (specifically the socialist and nationalist futures) that animated his own revolutionary construction of it; it poses, in short, the question of futures past.

The second chapter, "Romanticism and the Longing for Anticolonial Revolution," examines the relation between Romance as a mode of literary figuration and a distinctive mode of historical emplotment and the narrative of anticolonial revolution. I show the complex relation of *The Black Jacobins* to the poetic Romanticism of Jules Michelet and the materialist Romanticism of Leon Trotsky on the one hand and to the vindicationist Romanticism of nineteenth- and early-twentieth-century Black Nationalism on the other (especially that strand of it in which Haiti constituted a watershed and an example of black self-determination). I show how the tropes of Romanticism help to build up and shape the figuring of Toussaint Louverture as revolutionary hero and the story of the slave uprising as a narrative of revolutionary overcoming. My aim here is twofold: one, to carefully explore the tropes, modes, and rhetoric through which an exemplary instance of the narrative of anticolonial revolution is constructed; and two, to show how the efficacy of this narrative depends upon the salience of the horizon in relation to which it is constructed, and to suggest that the collapse of that horizon ought to urge us to rethink the narrative and poetic modes in which we imagine the relation between past, presents, and possible futures.

The third chapter, "Conscripts of Modernity," consists of an inquiry into the question of the modernity of colonial power which I explore in relation to the New World slave plantation. With this chapter I begin an exploration of aspects of the revisions to the second edition of *The Black Jacobins* published in 1963, here the famous appendix, "From Toussaint L'Ouverture to Fidel Castro." I begin by taking issue with the criticism of James for his Eurocentrism and elitism. James, it is often said, committed though he was to a revolutionary story of slave self-emancipation, was insufficiently committed to an Africa-centered or subaltern moral and cultural story. I urge that this criticism is not so much mistaken as misplaced. I argue that although it is easy enough to show in *The Black Jacobins* James's elitist and Eurocentric prejudices, this criticism drives in a direction that assumes the continued critical salience of the demonstration of moral and cultural survival of Africanisms in the New World and, more importantly, obscures attention to Europe as a specific problem about modernity. I develop an argument that modernity was not a choice New World slaves could exercise but was itself one of the fundamental *conditions* of choice. In this sense (and drawing on Stanley Diamond's distinction and Talal Asad's uses of it in particular), I suggest, Toussaint and his colleagues were conscripts — not volunteers — of modernity.

In the fourth chapter, "Toussaint's Tragic Dilemma," I explore the seven fresh paragraphs that James adds to the last chapter of the second edition of *The Black Jacobins*. These seven paragraphs, as I have said, constitute a reflection on Toussaint Louverture's tragic dilemma. My overall concern is to show a different figuring of Toussaint than that of the revolutionary hero of the normative anticolonial reading and to suggest the way this alters the Romantic mode of emplotment of the story of the Haitian Revolution. In my exploration I inquire into some of the conceptual sources of James's understanding of tragedy, in particular his Aristotelian construction of Toussaint's "tragic flaw" and his Hegelian construction of the historical conflict which Toussaint embodies. As I have already suggested, from the end of the 1940s and throughout the 1950s James wrote a good deal about tragedy, both classical and Elizabethan, Aeschylean and Shakespearean. He was impressed by the relation between the rise of Athenian democracy and the origins of tragedy, by the "commonness" of the Dionysian scene of the Athenian tragic drama, and most important of all by tragedy's dramatic ability to contain and represent ambiguous moments of historical transformation, moments when possible futures seem less certain than they once did. This is why Herman Melville's *Moby-Dick* constitutes so significant a novel for James; and, more saliently for thinking about his protagonist, Toussaint Louverture, this is why he takes Shakespeare's *Hamlet* to stand as a paradigm of tragic figuration. If for James that melancholic and obsessively self-regarding Prince of Denmark symbolized the emergence of a new kind of individual, the modern intellectual, I suggest that similarly, for James, Toussaint inaugurates a new kind of individual, the modern colonial intellectual. Toussaint's intellectuality is at once the source of his magnificent successes and of his doom; it is central to the unfolding of his tragic dilemma—one of the most poignant, James says, to be found anywhere.

In chapter 5, "The Tragedy of Colonial Enlightenment," I move to situate *The Black Jacobins* within a wider set of concerns in contemporary social, moral, and political theory. James's insightful argument that Toussaint Louverture's failure was the failure of enlightenment and not of darkness constitutes my point of departure. Specifically I am interested in the ways in which tragedy (perhaps paradigmatically Sophocles's *Oedipus Tyrannus*) complicates the notion of enlightenment and the forms of ethics and politics that can be derived from it. Tragedy, as I will think of it, is about the *paradox* of enlightenment. I get my argument going by suggesting that the either/or of the Enlightenment/anti-Enlightenment binary that has been so central to recent theoretical debates (not least among them the debates about the colonial and the postcolonial) is in need of substantial revision. In urging this I briefly participate in the discussion about Foucault's reading of Kant's response to the question "What Is Enlightenment?" I suggest that there is a defensible view of Enlightenment that does not oblige a simple choice for or against. Following Martha Nussbaum's instructive contrast between tragic and rationalist ethics and Peter Euben's and Christopher Rocco's demonstrations of the uses of Greek tragedy for repositioning a number of concerns in contemporary political debate (about justice, say, or community), I make a claim for tragedy in reorienting our understanding of the politics and ethics of the postcolonial present. And finally, returning via this detour to James, I read *The Black Jacobins* for what it teaches us about the paradoxes of colonial enlightenment. The tragedy of colonial enlightenment, I will argue, is not to be perceived in terms of a flaw to be erased or overcome, but rather in terms of a permanent legacy that has set the conditions in which we make of ourselves what we make and which therefore demands constant renegotiation and readjustment.

Finally, in a short closing epilogue I juxtapose Hannah Arendt's thinking about tragedy, history, and revolution in *On Revolution* with James's in *The Black Jacobins*. Arendt's book was published in 1963, the year the second edition of James's book appeared. It closes with an evocation of Sophocles's last extant work, *Oedipus at Colonus*, and therefore directly links the writing (and memory) of revolutionary history with the poetics of tragedy. Arendt and James, I suggest, are particularly interesting to read with and against each other because of the ways in which they intersect and diverge. But where Arendt (in her famous chapter on memory) can think of the American Revolution as though it were the only New World revolution, James remembers another and perhaps more profound revolution, one that ushered in the beginning of the end of New World slavery. Reflecting on this, my epilogue briefly explores their contrasting uses of tragedy in a politics of memory and forgetting, of setting the past in relation to the present in order to distill from it a politics for a possible future.

IF THE BLACK JACOBINS is a classic work of black and anticolonial history this is not because it provides a definitive study of the great Haitian Revolution, one of the founding events of the modern age, but because it offers in an unparalleled way an endless source of postcolonial reflection on the relation between colonial pasts from which we have come, presents we inhabit, and futures we might hope for. More than teaching us about historical facts or about revolutionary theory (which in any case it also does in an exemplary way), *The Black Jacobins* teaches us about fidelity to a distinctive mode of historical criticism, one in which the nature of the question the past is called upon to answer is self-consciously shaped by the discontent in the present it seeks to change in order to fashion a future without those sources of dissatisfaction. We look back, today, through the remains of a postcolonial present that James looked forward to in *The Black Jacobins* as the far-off horizon of an imagined sovereignty. Of course, that future, when it came, came touched by suffering and ambiguity; it was not exactly the future as James might have envisioned it. But it came, nevertheless, to constitute our present, and now, two generations on since the first publication of that magnificent book in 1938, James's future is rapidly becoming our past. In my view, part of what it will mean to imagine new futures out of the uncertain presents we live in is a fresh encounter with *The Black Jacobins* (and other founding texts of our postcolonial sovereignty). This is not because James's questions continue to be ours (they do not, or not exactly), but because his fidelity to the present out of which those questions arose ought to inspire us to seek out the historical idioms and historical rhythms in which our own present might yield to us a desirable future. As James anticipated, tragedy is useful for this exercise.

ONE

# Futures Past

Tranquillity to-day is either innate (the philistine) or to be acquired only by a deliberate doping of the personality. It was in the stillness of a seaside suburb that could be heard most clearly and insistently the booming of Franco's heavy artillery, the rattle of Stalin's firing squads and the fierce shrill turmoil of the revolutionary movement striving for clarity and influence. Such is our age and this book is of it, with something of the fever and the fret. Nor does the writer regret it. The book is the history of a revolution and written under different circumstances it would have been a different but not necessarily a better book.

I

These, of course, are the memorable closing sentences of the preface to the first edition of C. L. R. James's incomparable work of anticolonial revolutionary history, *The Black Jacobins*, published in 1938. They are unforgettable sentences. But they are unforgettable not only because of the indignation that edges them, or the defiance that surrounds them, or the resolve that breathes through them. They are unforgettable also because they so vividly, so palpably, so proximately, and so self-consciously locate James at the dramatic scene of his history-writing. They situate James in a singular way in relation to the historical experience that makes up his living present and the aspirations that animate his utopian hopes for a possible alternative future. The creative and intellectual labor of political-historical reconstruction that constitutes *The Black Jacobins*—and constitutes it as the kind of narrative that it is—is inseparable from those unfolding dramas he evokes and inscribes into the unnatural stillness of his seaside tableau.

Notice the implicit reference in the quoted passage to Wordsworth's

famous description of the ideal conditions of poetic creation in his preface to the *Lyrical Ballads*.[1] And notice too the allusion to the aesthetic
intensity of Keats's weary melancholy in "Ode to a Nightingale."[2] As we
know especially from his later autobiographical sketches, the English
Romantics and the idea of "poetry as criticism of life" constituted a significant part of James's intellectual self-fashioning in the 1920s in Trinidad.[3] Revolutionary that he had become by the time he wrote *The Black
Jacobins* in London in the 1930s, however, it is understandable that he
should have been impatient with the desire of the English Romantics to
withdraw into an artificial tranquility, to "fade" and "dissolve" into that
seductive silence far away from the cacophony of social and political upheaval that surrounded them in the late eighteenth and early nineteenth
centuries. Like him, after all, Wordsworth and Coleridge and Keats and
Shelley (to name only some of the Romantic poets whose trace one finds
in *The Black Jacobins*) lived and wrote in a time of revolution and reaction.
At the same time, however, and in a way so characteristic of James's
poetics, the passage is not without a finely tuned ambiguity of literary-
critical affiliation and commitment. For in establishing the militantly
disenchanted tone and literary-historical register of his own revolutionary discontent, James is also drawing deeply here on the moral sensibilities, aesthetic ideas, and subversive energies of these very Romantics themselves, on their ideal of redemptive heroism as much as their
republican and antislavery politics. Most important of all though, the
passage shows us James drawing on the Romantics' (almost defining)
preoccupation with the peculiar mimetic powers of the imagination, its
expansive capacity to transcend time and distance and to open itself to a
selfless and sympathetic connection with the suffering and struggles of
others. This relation between imaginative identification and historical
reconstruction is at the heart of the literary-political genius of *The Black
Jacobins*.[4]

THE HISTORICAL SIGNIFIERS James references in the closing sentences of his preface are vividly iconic. The Spanish Civil War had opened
on July 17, 1936, with the generals' coup against the newly elected Popular Front government, the Second Spanish Republic, and, with the help
of Mussolini's Italy and Hitler's Germany, would eventually (in March
1939) see the Nationalists under Francisco Franco come to power. For
a whole generation born around the early years of the twentieth century, the Republican War (as it is sometimes called) was an arousing

and emblematic war, gathering and compressing in the ferocity of the three-year conflict all the ideological confrontations that were beginning to define—and disfigure—the twentieth century: the confrontation between Left and Right, capitalism and communism, fascism and democracy, tradition and progress.[5] Many volunteers risked their lives for Spanish Republicans, and some, like the critic Christopher Caudwell, were killed in battle. As George Orwell (one of the volunteers to fight and return) was to show in his firsthand account, *Homage to Catalonia*, and in the several reviews he wrote during 1937 and 1938, the war simultaneously exposed the political and diplomatic bankruptcy of the liberal democratic West and its Non-Intervention Agreement (sponsored by Britain and France), and the kinds of duplicity, treachery, and murder in which the Communist International (even as it organized and helped to sustain the International Brigades) stood ready and willing to engage to stamp out what was left of the revolution.[6] It was James's war too, if at a somewhat greater distance than for Orwell. In 1937 he wrote a short, insurgent preface to Mary Low's and Juan Breá's *Red Spanish Notebook* in which the revolutionary heroism of the Trotskyist POUM (Unified Marxist Workers' Party) is praised. "They will conquer," James wrote with lyrical determination. "They must. If not to-day then to-morrow, by whatever tortuous and broken roads, despite the stumblings and the falls."[7] It was, if nothing else, more programmatic (and less self-serving) than W. H. Auden's memorable "yes, I am Spain."[8] Reflecting back on this historical moment, Eric Hobsbawm, whose orthodox (communist) political sympathies were never James's (nor, of course, Orwell's), is perhaps nevertheless seeing from a generational perspective roughly shared by his elder when he writes: "What Spain meant to liberals and those on the Left who lived through the 1930s, is now difficult to remember, though for many of us the survivors, now all past the Biblical life-span, it remains the only political cause which, even in retrospect, appears as pure and compelling as it did in 1936."[9]

Not so the legacy of the Russian Revolution of October 1917. Here the ambiguities came early, and remained. The rise of Stalin's dictatorship over the Communist Party of the Soviet Union after Lenin's death in January 1924, his gradual ascendancy over the Communist International, and his declaration of the policy of "Socialism in One Country" represented for many who identified themselves with the emancipatory ideals of Marxism the beginning of the end of the hope in Russia of providing leadership for the anticipated worldwide revolution. Stalin moved rapidly to diminish the space of dissent, moving first against his principal rival, Trotsky, and the so-called Left Opposition. They were effectively defeated between 1927 and 1928, when Trotsky was, in succession, expelled from the party and exiled to Alma-Ata in Kazakhstan. Next came the turn of Stalin's erstwhile associates among the so-called Right Opposition, in particular Nikolai Bukharin and Alexei Rykov. A formidable Bolshevik, Bukharin was not only the theoretician of the New Economic Policy and the architect of "Socialism in One Country," he was also head of the Comintern and chief editor of *Pravda*. Between 1928 and 1929 both Bukharin and Rykov were "exposed" as enemies of the party and removed from their positions. But by the 1930s, Stalin, more secure in power and more determined to eliminate all conditions of opposition, turned his mind from mere denunciation and expulsion to liquidation. The first Moscow trial of the Great Purges was held in August 1936 when Lev Kamenev and Grigorii Zinoviev (heading a group of sixteen defendants) were sentenced to death and executed. The second Moscow trial was held in January 1937 (with Karl Radek heading the seventeen defendants). The last and perhaps the most famous of the trials was held in March 1938 when Rykov and Bukharin (among twenty-one defendants) were tried and put to death.[10] Again, the significance of these events must be difficult to grasp for those of us who grew up in what Hobsbawm calls the moral milieu of the late twentieth century. After all, even as they occurred, many—especially many communists—found the reports of the trials too fantastic to believe. James and his colleagues, however, immediately read a sinister portent into the events unfolding in the Soviet Union. Reflecting on the fates of Zinoviev and Kamenev in what would be the seminal history of the Communist International, *World Revolution* (published in April 1937), James asks with prescient if ominous irony: "What insurance company would risk a penny on Bukharin's life?"[11]

In January 1929, Trotsky was deported from the Soviet Union. Within a few years, however, there had emerged around him (or at least around his name and his work) pockets of an independent Marxist movement—the International Left Opposition, headquartered in Paris—seeking after a vocabulary in which to rethink the revolutionary socialist project.[12] Trotsky's writings (a constant stream of articles and books, first from Turkey, then from Norway, and finally from Mexico) became an important source for an alternative Marxist account and assessment of the situation inside the Soviet Union as well as elsewhere. Especially important, of course, was the publication of his *History of the Russian Revo-*

lution (translated into English by the indefatigable and much maligned American Trotskyist, Max Eastman), the first volume of which appeared in 1932, and the second and third in 1933. James has famously described his encounter with this work soon after his arrival in Britain where the atmosphere of Left politics was rapidly transforming.[13] In the grim years following the 1926 General Strike, political discussion and organization in a Trotskyist direction began to emerge, first inside the almost supinely Stalinist Communist Party of Great Britain (in the Balham Group of Reg Groves, Henry Sara, Harry Wicks, and others), but more importantly around the Independent Labour Party (ILP). Founded in 1893 by the Scottish labor leader Keir Hardie, the ILP maintained an often strained and fragile alliance with the Labour Party for decades, but became more Left-leaning after its break with them (spearheaded by Fenner Brockway and James Maxton) in 1932.[14] By his own account, C. L. R. James had briefly been a member of the Labour Party in Nelson and (subsequently) London, but as he put it, when the Trotskyists decided to go into the ILP he went with them.[15] A number of small Trotskyist groups (each with no more than a handful of adherents) came into being around this time, and James found himself at the center of one of them, the so-called Marxist Group.[16] They were involved in fierce sectarian squabbles with each other over the correct line to take on the world-historical matters of the day: the German question and the role of Stalin in facilitating Hitler's rise to power; the question of whether to enter the Labour Party or build an independent proletarian movement; the question of the formation of a Fourth International; and very importantly for James, Mussolini's invasion of Abyssinia on October 3, 1935.

Indeed, Mussolini's occupation of Abyssinia (a matter of considerable embarrassment to the British government, eager as they were to show colonial rule in a tasteful, benevolent, and progressive light) became a flashpoint for anti-imperialist and anticolonialist agitation and organization. In Britain in the early 1930s, critical discussion of race and Empire (such as it was) was carried on principally by Harold Moody's League of Coloured Peoples (LCP). Founded in 1931 at least partly on the moderate liberal-reformist model of the National Association for the Advancement of Colored People in the United States and involving concerned West Indians in Britain such as the writer Una Marson and the economist W. Arthur Lewis, the LCP campaigned against racial prejudice and lobbied for racial justice. Its magazine, The Keys, carried in its symbolic name Moody's interracial aspirations and his hopes for opening up avenues of opportunity for black people.[17] However, Mussolini's ambition-driven invasion of the ancient African kingdom and the pitiful flight of the emperor, Haile Selassie, altered the character and mood of black and anticolonial sentiment in Britain as well as across the black diaspora, and called into being a more radical response.[18] C. L. R. James, who had spoken at meetings of the LCP and was already an incipient advocate of self-government for the colonies when he left Trinidad with the manuscript of *The Life of Captain Cipriani*, was to be a central part of furnishing that response.[19] He wrote several articles in the ILP's weekly paper, *New Leader*, and in *The Keys*, denouncing the invasion and the spineless response of the League of Nations. "Mussolini, the British Government and the French," James wrote, "have shown the Negro only too plainly that he has got nothing to expect from them but exploitation, either naked or wrapped in bluff. In that important respect this conflict, though unfortunate for Abyssinians, has been of immense benefit to the race as a whole."[20] In 1934, as the crisis in Abyssinia was emerging, James founded the International African Friends of Abyssinia to generate awareness and concern about the imminent threat. In the following year, with his childhood friend and ex-Communist George Padmore in the lead, this was transformed into the International African Service Bureau, an organization with the broader aim of agitating against British imperialism. James served as the editor of its periodical, *International African Opinion*. In these years, the focus of concern among black intellectuals in Britain was the decolonization of Africa. Even though labor riots were erupting across the West Indies as James and his colleagues carried on their opposition, the expectation was that it would be in Africa that the anticolonial struggle would bear the first fruits of victory.[21] As he would later say, he wrote *The Black Jacobins* as part of the preparation for the African revolution that Padmore was calling for.[22]

SUCH THEN, JAMES suggests, was the age of *The Black Jacobins*; such were the events and circumstances, the insurgent and counterinsurgent context of argument, organization, and activism against the background of which in the 1930s he researched and wrote his account of Toussaint Louverture and the San Domingo Revolution.[23] These events and circumstances convey a sense of the intersection of ideological and political terrains—revolution and reaction in Europe, on the one hand, and the incipient black and anticolonial struggles, on the other—in relation to which James was preparing his work. But more than this, they suggest

James's acute sense that he stood in the stream of a historical momentum, his strong faith that he was moving in a certain historical direction, which, even where interrupted or blocked, would work its course toward a better future. This was the view—looking *forward*—from 1938.

But that world-historical moment, with its distinctive fever and fret, belongs to James's historical present in a way that it does not—because it *cannot*—belong to ours. That moment of social, political, and ideological upheaval framed by the Spanish Civil War, the Moscow trials, and the emerging revolutionary anti-Stalinist and anticolonial movements defined for James, in a distinctive cognitive-political vocabulary and through a range of institutional and organizational alternatives, a horizon of possible futures that are not, any longer, ours to imagine, let alone seek after and inhabit. Indeed that horizon of possible futures toward which James looked (now with confident anticipation, now with anxious foreboding, but always with a sense of fervent expectation and hope) defines for us, two generations on, a present that is rapidly receding; a present, one might say, that is rapidly becoming our past. James's erstwhile future, so to put it, is our disappearing present. In a way—the implications of which have yet to be adequately formulated, much less adequately explored—these historical presents are now, as Reinhart Koselleck would call them, former futures. They are "futures past."[24] For who today can hear around them, except as a fading and altogether nostalgic echo, the sounds that reverberated militantly through those interwar years, fashioning the revolutionary utopian spaces of nation and socialism in which James researched and composed his historical narrative about slave emancipation in San Domingo? Today nation and socialism do not name visionary horizons of new beginnings any of us can look toward as though they were fresh thresholds of aspiration and achievement to be fought for and progressively arrived at; to the contrary, they name forms of existing social and political reality whose normative limits we now live as the tangible ruins of our present, the congealing context of our postcolonial time.

Yet at the same time, in the poignant closing phrases of that deliberately worded preface to *The Black Jacobins*, James seems to offer us a provocative challenge, one that we, from where we are today, would do well to consider with care and focus. Having told us what made his historical moment what it was for him and that the book we hold is intimately connected to it, even driven by it, he further says that "under different circumstances" he would have written "a different but not necessarily a better book." How are we to understand the nature of this historicizing gesture? What are its normative implications for writing a history of the postcolonial present today? To my mind, what James is offering us here is nothing less than a provocation: to think the difference between the problem-space out of which he wrote—the questions he felt obliged to answer, the arguments he undertook to intervene in, the positions he sought to advance and defend—and the problem-space that constitutes the predicament and the demand of our own present. What might that difference consist of? More than half a century of eventful history has passed between James's writing in the late 1930s and our reading at the beginning of the twenty-first century. Significant aspects of the global political landscape have changed, and with these changes have come significant alterations in what we might perhaps call our conditions of worldly expectation and hope. If, as James suggests, there is a fundamental way in which the story he tells about Toussaint Louverture and his role in the making of the San Domingo Revolution is connected to the present he evokes for us in that unsurpassable preface, what is the story about Toussaint that we ought to tell out of the present we ourselves inhabit?

This is what interests me. And it interests me, as I have already indicated (and as I will continue to underline throughout), because my overall preoccupation here is with expanding, so far as this is conceivable, the cognitive possibility of thinking critically through our postcolonial political present. C. L. R. James's The Black Jacobins is doubtlessly a classic work of early-twentieth-century anticolonialism. But this is not only because of the complexity and sympathy with which it treats the events that comprise what is now known as the Haitian Revolution. It is a classic work, also, because it gives to these events the shape of an allegory of emancipationist redemption that embodies in a compelling and inspiring way the great longing for black and anticolonial revolution. The doubt that inspires my own preoccupations and that sustains the investigation I seek to carry out in this book, however, is that the critical purchase of this particular allegory is less than it formerly was—indeed, considerably less. My suspicion, in fact, is that, faced as we are with the virtual closure of the nationalist Bandung project that grew out of the anticolonial revolution, this story is an enfeebled and exhausted one. It can no longer enable us—as it once enabled James and the generation of anticolonials that succeeded his—to give utopian point to the project of social and political change. Part of the astonishing brilliance and enduring value of *The Black Jacobins*, as we will see however, is that James provides us with significant clues about the kind of story we might usefully tell—through Toussaint Louverture—about the relation between our past, our presents, and our possible futures.

MY LIMITED AIM in this chapter is to reflect on some of the problems posed by the idea of a history of the present that seem to me especially pertinent for approaching the challenge I have derived from C. L. R. James's preface in *The Black Jacobins*. First, I want to consider the preface in a bit more detail, inquiring into the range of questions about the representation of the past it raises and seeks to address. The preface, I will argue, is a self-conscious rhetorical device employed by James to signal to the reader the mode and ethos of his enterprise, and a complex if unresolved statement about his commitment to thinking about the nature of a properly historical discourse. James was alive to questions of historical representation—the problem of the role of the "literary" as opposed to the "scientific," the problem of the role of authorial voice and authorial intervention, and the problem of the identification of causality in explaining historical change—that continue to be argued over in contemporary debates about the past in the present.

What are the conceptual tools needed for the elaboration of the provocation embodied in this preface? Second, then, in pursuit of this question, I turn to some problems raised by so-called histories of the present. I want to suggest that alleged histories of the present (postcolonial or otherwise) tend to elide the problem of "futures" in historical temporality. I do not mean by this that they are non- (or anti-) utopian in formulation (though they typically are this too). I mean, rather, that these histories tend *not* to inquire systematically into the ways in which the expectation of—or longing for—particular futures helps to shape the kind of problem the past is constructed as for the present. In reflecting on this problem I shall make use of Reinhart Koselleck's very instructive discussion of the relation (and therefore distinction) between what he calls "the space of experience" and "the horizon of expectation" in the generation and representation of historical time. I am not going to follow Koselleck's purposes exactly, however (his concern with the contrast between modern and nonmodern temporalities). Rather, pursuing my own ends regarding the history of the present, I am going to suggest that this relation between "experience" and "expectation" is of especial importance for an interrogation of the postcolonial present because anticolonial histories of the colonial past (such as *The Black Jacobins* is) tend to organize a distinctive connection between the pasts they are seeking to overcome, the presents they inhabit, and the futures they are anticipating. And it is part of my argument that unless we make this relation visible to critical inquiry we will not be able to adequately discern the extent to which this expectation (or longing) is continuing to exercise a shaping effect on the analysis of our own present, nor, consequently, will we be able to judge whether or in what measure this is warranted or not.

The historiographical relation between past, present, and future is, if nothing else, a problem about narrative. Third, therefore, I want to consider an aspect of the familiar understanding of historical reconstruction as a kind of narrative. Of course, the idea that a historical text—especially one as self-consciously crafted as *The Black Jacobins*—contains literary features, a figurative constructedness, an attention to form, a style of representation, is perhaps neither controversial nor itself any longer productive of novel insights. But one aspect of this idea seems to me worth exploring further than it typically is, or at least worth connecting up with other related ideas. This is the idea that certain of the formal features of a historical narrative—plot, for instance—contain within them determinate story potentials derived from the myth-model or mythos (as Northrop Frye might have it) that underlies it. These formal features help to give the written history, irrespective of its other semantic or thematic content, the recognizable shape of a story of one kind (say, Romance) rather than another (say, tragedy). This is what Hayden White memorably called the "content of the form" of historical narrative, and his scholarly concern has been to argue the significance of paying attention to the effects of these formal features on the composition, uses, and understandings of history. I shall make considerable use of this idea in the reading I want to perform on *The Black Jacobins*. In a word, I am interested in the myth-model, the mythos, of *The Black Jacobins*; or rather, as we will see, I am interested in its mythoi, for I shall want to suggest that James's book contains not one story-form but two story-forms that are in some tension with each other.

And finally, fourth, I want to inquire into the problem of how one chooses between kinds of story-forms, or how one decides that a particular story-form, a particular mode of emplotment, say, no longer yields the critical insight it once accomplished, and how one decides whether it might be usefully displaced by another. In other words, how does one judge the critical purchase of the literary form of a historical narrative? I am interested, remember, in suggesting that we ought no longer to cast the relation of the colonial past to the postcolonial present in the way that James did in *The Black Jacobins*. How then do we make the argument for altering his story of Toussaint Louverture? Hayden White very deliberately provides no guidance here, famously disavowing that this is an answerable question. I disagree. Or at any rate I should like to qualify this judgment of White's somewhat. I do not think that so far as critical purchase is concerned the relation between literary form and historical representation should be thought of as entirely arbitrary. I am interested in pursuing the intimation that at any given historical conjuncture the story generated by the literary form of a historical narrative may be perceived to no longer perform the oppositional tasks the present demands of criticism; in other words, that its critical edge, given the new conjuncture, may have become blunted. And in seeking an approach to this question I will turn (as I have done in previous work) to R. G. Collingwood's profoundly insightful idea that a proposition has always to be understood as an answer to a question, and to Quentin Skinner's Wittgensteinian refurbishing of it.[25] I can hardly overemphasize the importance of this work because what I believe it enables is an approach to understanding both the colonial question to which *The Black Jacobins* was formulated as an anticolonial answer, and the extent to which that question which it sought to answer continues to be a salient question for us to pursue an answer to in our postcolonial present.

NEEDLESS TO SAY, the point of this exercise is not to construct a new model of historical inquiry, much less a new protocol for writing histories of the present. Far from it; indeed it is not even clear—it may even be very doubtful—that it is possible to synthesize Koselleck, White, and Skinner into a seamless historical methodology. My enterprise is much more partial and exploratory. From Koselleck's attention to the relation between experience and expectation (the historicity of given futures), White's attention to the formal modes of emplotment of historical narrative (their mythoi, or the content of their form), and Collingwood's and Skinner's attention to the linguistic action performed by a historical text (the question for which it is an answer; the move it makes in an argument), I want only to assemble some strategic tools with which to try to approach and elaborate James's provocation in that immortal preface to *The Black Jacobins*. I want them to help me to think the difference between the politicodiscursive problem-space out of which he emplotted his story about Toussaint Louverture and the San Domingo Revolution and our own problem-space. I want them to help me to grasp something of the difference between the distinctive problems about colonialism and anticolonialism in relation to which James's narrative unfolds for his colonial present and what the problems about colonialism and anticolonialism might be for our postcolonial present. I want them, in short, to help me clarify the kind of story—different, but not necessarily better— we might tell about the relation between our pasts, our presents, and our possible futures.

II

The preface to The Black Jacobins is nothing if not a profound reflection on the idea of the writing of history: the problem of the representation of the past in the present and the problem of the historian's relation to that practice of historical representation. From beginning to end of this short, densely organized text, James leaves the reader in little doubt as to the deliberate self-consciousness of his historical undertaking, the authorial will of which the writing is possessed and to which it gives an intensely engaged and richly commanding expression. It is, by itself, a matchless rhetorical performance. James's preface does not operate through any simple assertion of a Rankean or Actonian fetishism of objectivity. Whatever the internal shape of the narrative, history is not going to write itself in a fastidious act of self-generation. To the contrary, the self-conscious "narrative presence" of the authorial subject establishes itself and makes itself visible to the reader in a deliberate if not intimate way.[26] James's autobiographical subject, his sense of voice, of tone, his anticipation of audience and reception are inseparable from the historical knowledge being constructed.

Not surprisingly, the reader is reminded immediately of two other famous prefaces: Jules Michelet's 1847 preface to his History of the French Revolution and Leon Trotsky's 1932 preface to his History of the Russian Revolution. Indeed, if the mood and atmosphere are obviously different, James's preface is no doubt indebted to them both, or to speak more correctly, James's preface may be read as an attempt to resolve the one-sidedness of each. I return to James's relation to Michelet and Trotsky in the following chapter, but here I want to recognize something of the rhetorical performativity with which his preface is invested: it opens vividly and uncompromisingly with the curt statement of a set of seemingly irrefutable and quantifiable historical facts.

> In 1789 the French West Indian colony of San Domingo supplied two-thirds of the overseas trade of France and was the greatest individual market for the European slave-trade. It was an integral part of the economic life of the age, the greatest colony in the world, the pride of France, and the envy of every other imperialist nation. The whole structure rested on the labour of half-a-million slaves.[27]

Here, so to speak, are the bare economic facts. Nothing in the way of argument or discussion is necessary to establish their significance or their warrant. But notice how their deliberately causal arrangement serves to enable James a small but rhetorically transgressive act of historiographical displacement. Against the dominant Eurocentric view that the eighteenth-century bourgeoisie were the generative economic agents of the dawning age of capital and markets, and the slaves merely dumb inputs into the process, James reverses the relation and says that, to the contrary, the "economic life of the age" rested, in the end, "on the labour of half-a-million" of these slaves. It is, noticeably, a point regarding the weight of world-historical priority and the identification of world-historical agency, but it is also, and perhaps more importantly for James, a point about the fragility of the structure, its fundamental dependence on, and vulnerability to, the action (however coerced) of the "half-a-million slaves." James is quite self-consciously undermining the consoling European fantasy of self-possession.

And this is exactly the direction of the paragraph that follows. In 1791, in the wake of the French Revolution, these "half-a-million slaves" revolted and threw that entire structure into chaos, disorganization, and collapse. Each of James's sentences here is carefully constructed to maintain the perspective of the action of the slaves defeating "in turn the local whites and the soldiers of the French monarchy, a Spanish invasion, a British expedition of some 60,000 men, and a French expedition of similar size under Bonaparte's brother-in-law."[28] It is to their action that James principally attends. Again, these are the bald facts of the historical case. They are, James suggests, of incontrovertible importance. But they are, even so, only the essential scaffolding for the real story he has to tell. For of course the world-historical significance of the revolt of the San Domingo slaves is, as James writes, that it is the only successful slave revolt in New World history. "The transformation of slaves, trembling in hundreds before a single white man, into a people able to organise themselves and defeat the most powerful European nations of their day, is one of the great epics of revolutionary struggle and achievement."[29] How to tell the story of this "struggle and achievement" is James's meta-historical preoccupation.

The preface to The Black Jacobins is framed by two interconnected but not identical problems about historical discourse. One is the problem of how to account for historical causality. Are historical events to be understood as principally the outcome of the action of individuals imposing their sovereign wills upon the world, or the result of external and impersonal forces determining the direction of individual action? The other is the problem of whether to consider historical discourse an art of representation or a science of demonstration. Is history a matter of literary evocation and aesthetic rendering or a matter of the discovery and presentation of underlying laws of motion? Neither of these, needless to say, is a small problem of historiographical criticism, and both of them continue to be matters of contemporary contention and unresolved debate. James's treatment of them is by no means exhaustive, but it is suggestive enough to indicate the complex way in which his historiographical imagination sought to grapple with the representation of the past in the present. It is no doubt part of the brilliance of The Black Jacobins that James achieves, over the course of his long and involved (and sometimes uneven) historical narrative, an irreducible tension between "agency" and "structure" on the one hand and "art" and "science" on the other.

As we will see in more detail in chapter 2, James had a Romantic inclination to privilege the historic role of the heroic personality. History was to be read not as the collective agency of "the people" transforming their world, nor as the consequence of impersonal forces determining the course of events, but as a catalogue of the actions of great men. And in The Black Jacobins it is, above all, the heroic actions of his protagonist Toussaint Louverture that moves and fascinates James. The Black Jacobins is the story of this extraordinary man and the way he changed the course of history. But not quite; or, at least, not entirely. James doubtlessly means us to focus our attention firmly on what Toussaint does, but his understanding of his historical role is deftly, complexly, constructed.

The writer believes, and is confident the narrative will prove that between 1789 and 1815, with the single exception of Bonaparte himself no single figure appeared on the historical stage more greatly gifted than this Negro, a slave till he was 45. Yet Toussaint did not make the revolution. It was the revolution that made Toussaint. And even that is not the whole truth.[30]

Notice the dramaturgical image: history is a "stage" on which actors appear to more or less dramatic effect. But notice also that James is not merely cautious in identifying and formulating Toussaint's role in making the San Domingo Revolution; he is deliberately paradoxical. James's sentences have the effect of doubling back upon themselves recursively, qualifying without disavowing, conditioning without erasing the mutual yet uneven co-construction of agency and structure. Toussaint, the indisputable eminence of the revolution, is neither reducible to himself as the sovereign subject of a historical event, though he is, nevertheless, fully an actor; nor is he reducible to being a passive object of external forces, though these forces, nevertheless, shaped the conditions in which he acted. Toussaint Louverture neither simply made nor simply did not make the great revolution. The tension in this formulation is all the more important to appreciate because as the action in his own narrative gets going James will often lean more in one direction than in the other.

The relationship between agency and structure, between actors and their conditions, tends to map onto another relationship, namely, the relationship between history understood as an art and history understood as a science. Or at any rate, those who argue for history as a matter of identifying structural conditions have tended to agree with J. B. Bury that history is a scientific discourse; those who, on the contrary, hold up the privilege of the role of the actor have tended to agree with G. M. Trevelyan that history is a literary representation that waits upon the inspiration of Clio, its Muse.[31] In his preface, James (who is almost certain to have been conversant with Bury and Trevelyan) sought to get out of the impasse created by these binary positions.

The writing of history becomes ever more difficult. The power of God or the weakness of man, Christianity or the divine right of kings to govern wrong, can easily be made responsible for the downfall of states or the birth of new societies. Such elementary conceptions lend themselves willingly to narrative treatment and from Herodotus to Michelet, and from Thucydides to Green, the traditionally famous historians have been more artist than scientist: they wrote so well because they saw so little. To-day by a natural reaction we tend to a personification of the social forces, great men being merely or nearly instruments in the hands of economic destiny. As so often the truth does not lie in between. Great men make history, but only such history as it is possible for them to make. Their freedom of achievement is limited by the necessities of their environment. To portray the limits of those necessities and the realisation, complete or partial, of all possibilities, that is the true business of the historian.[32]

Where once the idealist historian-as-artist wrote as though history were a mere outcome of human frailty or genius or Christian charity, now the materialist historian-as-scientist tends in the opposite direction and reduces everything to an effect of social or economic forces. James very deftly urges a mode of historical representation that is neither simply an either/or choice of one or the other of these options nor a mere clean path between them ("the truth does not lie in between"). Evading these simple alternatives, James mobilizes a gloss on Marx's famous formulation that opens the second paragraph of The Eighteenth Brumaire of Louis Bonaparte ("Men make their own history") as a way of holding a paradoxical tension between personality and its circumstances.[33]

It is a striking fact that while Marx is evoked, his name is omitted from the passage I have quoted. Indeed, it is curious that Marx's name occurs nowhere at all in James's preface since this formulation of the problem of the relation between great men and history is one consuming preoccupation throughout The Black Jacobins. Clearly, however, in his own mind what separates "artists" like himself from admired "artists" like Herodotus and Michelet is the Marxism that gives him the "science" with which to see beneath the surface of things and grasp the essentials.

In a revolution, when the ceaseless slow accumulation of centuries bursts into volcanic eruption, the meteoric flares and flights above are a meaningless chaos and lend themselves to infinite caprice and romanticism unless the observer sees them always as projections of the sub-soil from which they came. The writer has sought not only to analyse, but to demonstrate in their movement, the economic forces of the age; their moulding of society and politics, of men in the mass and individual men; the powerful reaction of these on their environment at one of those rare moments when society is at boiling point and therefore fluid.³⁴

James's preoccupation throughout is with the relation between the personality and history, between agency and structure, between individual creativity and moments of fundamental change in human society. He was concerned to take issue as much with those historiographical practices in which transcendental forces drive events as with those in which the action of individuals appears as the mere epiphenomena of underlying causes. Neither of these could adequately grasp those unstable moments of upheaval in which an individual seems to embody the historical will and shapes decisively the course of events (Robespierre and subsequently Bonaparte in the French Revolution; Lenin in the Russian Revolution). James's genius lies perhaps in his attempt to keep the tension alive, in his refusal to slide reductively in either direction.

QUITE EVIDENTLY, THEN, James was alert to the fact that there is no single way in which the history of an event—any event, let alone one as momentous and epoch-making as the one with which he was concerned—can be told. That the history of an event such as the San Domingo Revolution gets written in one way rather than another, that the sequence of recorded actions gets cast in this way rather than that, cannot be simply read off from the historical facts by themselves. This is because the constitution of a historical discourse and the composition of a historical narrative are interpretive exercises and, therefore, partly at least aesthetic, moral, and political choices—or commitments—made by the historian writing. James is consequently alive to the positivist fallacy that the role of facts is that of arbiter and adjudicator of historical meaning. And he is alive to the error in the idea (again a positivist one) that it is possible—indeed necessary—to dissociate factual content from literary form as a condition of maintaining the historian's fidelity to truth. For James the language in which his story is cast is no mere neutral container for the facts of the San Domingo Revolution to be poured into. For him, history is not merely the provision of useful information about "what really happened," but the endowment of events with significance and meaning. James, I am going to suggest, is a storyteller—a mythmaker.

Therefore, there is no simple transparency between the realities of the past and the modes of historical representation. There is, rather, a contingent relationship. Or to put it another way, the sense that a work of history has captured the past about which it speaks is a realist effect produced in the writing itself. And as a corollary of this, the critical judgment as to the adequacy of an account—an account like *The Black Jacobins*, for example—cannot be reduced to a correspondence with the facts: for, as James says, at another conjuncture, looking back at the same past from a somewhat different angle, responding to a different set of imperatives and prerogatives in the present, the historian might have written a "different but not necessarily a better book." In fact, as we will see later (in chapter 3), James himself does precisely this when he looks back to the writing of the story of Toussaint Louverture from the conjuncture of the early 1970s.

### III

"The world upon which I open my eyes," wrote Michael Oakeshott in a memorable essay, "is unmistakably present." [35] What is at stake in writing a history of this "unmistakably present" world? What are the protocols of reading and critical assessment upon which it depends? What, if anything, has the future to do with the present out of which we write and the past about which we compose our stories? It may be useful to remember another remark of Oakeshott's: "Both future and past . . . emerge only in a reading of present; and a particular future or past is one eligible to be evoked from a particular present and is contingently related to the particular present from which it may be evoked." [36] This proposition about the future's contingent relation to the present is one that seems to me to bear considerably more reflection than it has so far received.

It has certainly become a commonplace of contemporary criticism—or anyway, historically minded criticism—that historical discourse is, whatever else it is, a form of linguistic representation, a structure of language. It has followed epistemologically from this that far from flowing transparently out of the "facts" of the past themselves (as empiricists and correspondentialists of one sort or another might be given to believe), historical knowledge is constructed, which is to say *made* rather than simply given or found. And consequently it has come to be widely held as an accepted truth that historical discourse is irreducibly contemporary, perspectival, partial, and connected in inextricable ways to the present in which its production and circulation is being carried on.

The "historical past" (to invoke the irrepressible Michael Oakeshott yet again) is never anachronistic. It is of course this ensemble of ideas that has made it possible to talk, as Michel Foucault began to do in the 1970s, not merely of a "history of the past in terms of the present" but more significantly of a "history of the present."[37] I take the import of Foucault's point here to be that it is not merely that, epistemologically, the past is only available through the present (in any case, a fairly uncontroversial idea among intellectual and social historians), but that morally and politically what ought to be at stake in historical inquiry is a critical appraisal of the present itself, not the mere reconstruction of the past. The present, then, not the past, is what histories of the present are supposed to be about.

However, it has seemed to me a curious and largely underreflected-upon feature of histories of the present that they take for granted precisely the "present" in relation to which the critical force of their recharacterization of the "past" is supposed to operate. Or else the present is described in such large cognitive-political terms—as "modernity," for instance, or "postcolonial"—that it is often difficult to specify what aspect of it is being illuminated or why illuminating this particular aspect of it is of immediate (or more than academic) significance. At any rate, quite often a certain stability of duration is tacitly attributed to the present—so that even as the past now has about it a usable contingency, the present appears to have congealed into an immobile structure of implicit and unchanging determinations. In relation to past and future, the present appears atemporal. It is as though we always-already know the salient shape of the present to be called into question by the intervention of our criticism.

But what if the present in relation to which the recharacterization of the past has been constructed loses its critical salience? What, in other words, if this present loses the features that had compelled that particular reexamination of the past in the first place? And what if the present's demand on the past has altered in part *because* it is no longer clear what its relation to the future might be? In other words, what if the imagined futures that had given point and direction to the intervention in the present and the rehistoricization of the past suddenly evaporated as a possible horizon of hope and longing? How would this affect the kind of "effective history" histories of the present purport to be? It seems to me that these questions about history are especially difficult to address but also especially important ones to make visible, because they attune us to features of the question of the history of the present that are otherwise often obscured. If our sense is (difficult as it may be to establish with verifiable empirical certainty) that our present constitutes something of a new conjuncture, and that consequently the old story about the past's relation to the present and to possible futures is no longer adequate, no longer provides or sustains critical leverage, how do we go about altering that story?

THE QUESTION OF the contingent relation the present has to both the past and the future has been taken up and elaborated in a most instructive way by that remarkable historian of social and political concepts, Reinhart Koselleck. In the inspiring work from which I derive the title of this chapter, Futures Past, Koselleck seeks to consider the relation between what he calls a "given past" and a "given future" in historical discourse. "How, in a given present," he asks, "are the temporal dimensions of past and future related?"[38] What we call "historical time," he urges, grows out of the disjuncture and the (consequent) tension between these temporal dimensions, past and future. Part of his project is to distill a vocabulary that will enable him to explore and articulate something about the nature of this temporality. This is one of the aims of Begriffsgeschichte (conceptual history).[39] For Koselleck, the relation a given present has to a given past and a given future is constituted, on the one hand, by "experience," and on the other, by "expectation." These two categories, central to all his work, constitute what he calls a conceptual couple: there is no expectation without experience and, conversely, no experience without expectation.[40] They are, Koselleck further says, a "metahistorical" or "anthropological" conceptual couple inasmuch as concrete histories are inconceivable without them: the experience/expectation couple is the metaconceptual condition of any possible history. Concrete histories, he writes, are always produced "within the medium of particular experiences and particular expectations."[41]

The terms "experience" and "expectation" are used by Koselleck in specific ways. By "experience" he means the "present-past," that part of the past that, as he says, has been incorporated, reworked, preserved, distilled, and remembered in the present. Consequently he will speak of a "space" of experience, that layered simultaneity in which the past is, as he puts it, "assembled into a totality." By contrast, "expectation" comprehends the "future-made-present," the hopes, fears, curiosities, desires, and so on that give point to the "not-yet" of time. And in this regard, Koselleck speaks of a "horizon" of expectation, "that line behind which a new space of experience will open, but which cannot yet be seen."[42] In this view, therefore, both experience and expectation are fundamentally "present-centered," even though, as Koselleck is quick to point out, they do not constitute the same kind of presentness.[43]

For Koselleck, it is true, the problematization of the relation between the space of experience and the horizon of expectation is meant to help theorize the distinctiveness of modern (as opposed to nonmodern) temporality. *Futures Past* as a whole is one long meditation on the nature of the distinctiveness of the temporal structures built into modern concepts. His argument is that the modern age constitutes a break in which the gap between experience and expectation has considerably expanded, in which, in other words, expectations have increasingly distanced themselves from prior experience. (Koselleck's work has focused on the period he calls the *Sattelzeit*, the transition period, roughly 1750 to 1850, in which he discerns an acceleration of transformations in German social and political concepts.) In the nonmodern age, Koselleck suggests (and he is being deliberately schematic in his formulations here), expectations "subsisted entirely on the experiences of their predecessors, experiences which in turn became those of their successors."[44] He does not mean, naively, that this was a world without change, but that such change as there was occurred "so slowly and in such a long-term fashion that the rent between previous experience and an expectation to be newly disclosed did not undermine the traditional world."[45] Nor does he mean to suggest that this "seamless transference" of experience into expectation was uniform across social strata. He means rather to mark the discontinuity between the modern and the nonmodern in terms of their relation to historical temporality and to underline the categories — first among them being the category of "progress" ("the first specifically modern category of historical time")[46] — that have helped to shape the reorganization of our experience and expectation of time.

This idea of historical discontinuity between the modern and non-modern is not entirely immaterial to my own later considerations of the modernity of the New World slave plantation (see chapter 3). Nor is it irrelevant to my concern (in chapter 2) with the distinctive modernity of revolutionary temporality (a matter to which Koselleck has devoted considerable attention). But for my immediate purposes here — that is, for the temporal question of futurity in the history of the present — I want to press Koselleck's conception of the relation between the "space of experience" and the "horizon of expectation" in a somewhat different direction. I want it to do a different—and perhaps more preliminary and prosaic—job of work. This is because on my reading of it what Koselleck is drawing our attention to—the relation between the "space of experience" and "horizon of expectation" as the relation of a kind of temporality—is not only a feature of the historical process writ large, namely the transformation from nonmodern to modern dimensions of time. I want to suggest that it is also a potential feature of any historical shift in which the prospect of old futures has faded from view and unsettled, as a consequence, our prior notions about what to do with the pasts in the present. In other words, it seems to me useful and justifiable to mobilize Koselleck's relational couple for a discussion of a transformation *within* the modern, from one rhythm of modern time to another: from a moment, for example, when the future appears guaranteed by the present to one in which it seems undermined by it. Here what is crucial is less the proximate distance between the "space of experience" and "horizon of expectation" than the *reorganization* of the relation between their ideological contents.

Following from this, I want to take Koselleck's terms as suggesting possible effects at the level of the reception, or rather appreciation, of specific historical texts inasmuch as these texts both embody reconstructions of past events (the solidified relations between an already past "space of experience" and "horizon of expectation") and are themselves, as textual constructions written in a particular historical present, ideological effects of a distinctive relation between a certain "space of experience" and "horizon of expectation." Each work of history, in other words, contains two relations of experience and expectation, the one *about* which it writes and the one *in* which it writes. Indeed, I suggest that the way a historical text figures the former relation is directly connected to the way it figures the latter. This seems to me one way of articulating what we ought to mean by a history of the present. Consequently, I take Koselleck's distinction between "experience" and "expectation" as implying that in the appreciation of a historical text it cannot be assumed that there is a constant durable relation between presents, pasts, and futures. That is to say, if any given historical text may be thought of as embodying not only the reconstruction of a given past, but also the interrogation of a given present, and the projection of expectations about a hoped-for future, it needs also to be considered that an alteration in the present may induce an alteration in the relation between the space of experience of pasts and the horizon of expectation about the future.

And this, in a very elementary way, is what I would like to say about C. L. R. James's The Black Jacobins for our postcolonial present: not only does it embody a story about the past, but we cannot read it today as though we inhabited the same relation between the "space of experience" and "horizon of expectation" as James inhabited when he researched, wrote, and published it in the 1930s. The Black Jacobins is an anticolonial history (perhaps in many ways a paradigmatic one) written out of and in response to a particular colonial present and projected toward a particular postcolonial future. "Such is our age and this book is of it." That future which constituted James's horizon of expectation (the emergence of nation-state sovereignty, the revolutionary transition to socialism) and which The Black Jacobins anticipated, we live today as the bleak ruins of our postcolonial present. Our generation looks back, so to put it, through the remains of a present that James and his generation looked forward to (however contentiously) as the open horizon of a possible future; James's erstwhile future has elapsed in our disappearing present. But if this is so, if the longing for anticolonial revolution, the longing for the overcoming of the colonial past that shaped James's horizon of expectation in The Black Jacobins is not one that we can inhabit today, then it may be part of our task to set it aside and begin another work of reimagining other futures for us to long for, for us to anticipate.

IV

The relation between pasts, presents, and futures is a relation constituted in narrative. Koselleck's focus in the theoretical practice of Begriffsgeschichte, while linguistic and textual, is directed more toward concepts and their mutations than toward stories and their narrative forms. But one historian (or philosopher of history) who has given a distinctive formulation to our understanding of the constituent problems associated with this narrative relation—history as art as opposed to history as science; the relation between events, facts, and interpretation or between factual and fictional narrative; the problem of the politics of historical representation; and so on—is Hayden White.[47] For a number of years White has sharpened our focus on the formal literary dimensions of historical texts in part by emphasizing and demonstrating the relevance of contemporary literary theory's conceptions of literariness for the understanding of historical writing. Literary theory, he urges, permits "a finer discrimination of the relation between the form and the content of the historical discourse than was formally possible on the basis of the idea that facts constituted the body of the historical discourse and style its more or less attractive, but by no means essential, clothing. It is now possible to recognize that in realistic, no less than in imaginary, discourse, language is both a form and a content and that this linguistic content must be counted among the other kinds of content (factual, conceptual, and generic) that make up the total content of the discourse as a whole."[48] The content of a historical discourse, in short, cannot be extracted from its linguistic form, for this is to "ignore the one 'content' without which a historical discourse could never come into existence at all: language."[49]

The focus of White's attention, then, has been on the literariness of the historical text, on the "fictive elements" it necessarily contains. Because the past has no inherent form, no inherent significance or meaning—because, as White puts it, the past does not itself possess the shape of stories—these are necessarily imposed upon it in the course of the construction of the historical narrative. In this sense, a certain "style of representation" is part of every work of history (as well as every work in the philosophy of history). This style of representation is composed of the interpretive strategies the historian brings to bear on transforming what White calls the "primitive elements" of history (data and chronicle, for instance) into an intelligible narrative.

For my purposes here I am chiefly interested in White's theorization of the relation between the formal features of plot and historical representation. The theorization of what White calls the mode of emplotment, that is, the way the meaning or significance of a story is carried in the kind of story that is being told, is of course part of a larger and more complex (and now much commented upon and criticized) theory of the poetics of historiography first spelled out in his opus, *Metahistory*, and subsequently elaborated and amended in later work.[50] Every history, White argues, is emplotted, that is, is rendered into a story of a particular kind. Emplotment comprehends the way a number of temporally connected events are constituted into a narrative such that readers recognize it to be a particular kind of story. White writes: "Providing the 'meaning' of a story by identifying the kind of story that has been told is called explanation by emplotment. If in the course of narrating his story, the historian provides it with the plot structure of a Tragedy, he has 'explained' it in one way; if he has structured it as a Comedy, he has 'explained' it in another way. Emplotment is the way by which a sequence of events fashioned into a story is gradually revealed to be a story of a particular kind."[51]

Northrop Frye is White's inspiration here.[52] Following his suggestions for the classification of plot structures, White identifies four different elementary modes of emplotment in Western literary history: Romance, tragedy, comedy, and satire. He acknowledges that there may be others, epic for instance, or pastoral. Further, he says that any given historical account is likely to contain stories cast in one mode as aspects or phases of the whole set of stories emplotted in another mode. However, he argues, "a given historian is forced to emplot the whole set of stories making up his narrative in one comprehensive or archetypal story form." And doing so, one of the archetypal plot structures comes to the fore. Romance, he says, is "fundamentally a drama of self-identification symbolized by the hero's transcendence of the world of experience, his victory over it, and his final liberation from it. . . . It is a drama of the triumph of good over evil, of virtue over vice, of light over darkness, and of the ultimate transcendence of man over the world in which he was imprisoned by the Fall."[53] Romance, in short, is a drama of redemption. By contrast, satire is a drama of "diremption." It is, White says, "dominated by the apprehension that man is ultimately a captive of the world rather than its master, and by the recognition that, in the final analysis, human consciousness and will are always inadequate to the task of overcoming definitively the dark forces of death, which is man's unremitting enemy."[54] Comedy and tragedy are different again from these. "In Comedy, hope is held out for the temporary triumph of man over his world by the prospect of occasional reconciliations of the forces at play in the social and natural worlds. Such reconciliations are symbolized in the festive occasions which the Comic writer traditionally uses to terminate his dramatic accounts of change and transformation."[55] In tragedy, by contrast, "there are no festive occasions, except false or illusory ones; rather, there are intimations of states of division among men more terrible than that which incited the tragic agon at the beginning of the drama. Still, the fall of the protagonist and the shaking of the world he inhabits which occur at the end of the Tragic play are not regarded as totally threatening to those who survive the agonic test. There has been a gain in consciousness for the spectators of the contest. And this gain is thought to consist in the epiphany of the law governing human existence which the protagonist's exertions against the world have brought to pass." [56]

It is central to White's argument in *Metahistory* that there is no epistemological privilege among the interpretive strategies he identifies. There is no a priori decision-procedure by which they can be ranked as being more or less "realistic," more or less "true." In approaching the historical record, therefore, we are, as he says, "indentured to a choice." And consequently, "the best grounds for choosing one perspective on history rather than another are ultimately aesthetic or moral rather than epistemological." [57] A number of critics have attacked the relativism they see in this sort of argument. If one perspective on history is just as valid as any other, they maintain, then historical truth has been supplanted by the vagaries of political will, and the way is open for history to be at the service of reprehensible and mendacious political regimes. [58] Other critics have suggested that there is an ahistoricity at work in White's argument. His formalism and textual self-referentiality (some might say, solipsism) obscure the relation between the narrative form chosen and the larger context that gives point to its use. [59]

In some of his later work, however, White has sought to amend his view somewhat. In a discussion, for example, of the problem of historical emplotments of Nazism and the "Final Solution," White raises the question whether there are "any limits on the kind of story that can responsibly be told about these phenomena? Can these events be responsibly emplotted in any of the modes, symbols, plot types, and genres with which our culture provides us for making sense of such extreme events in our past?" [60] While reasserting the general contention that there is no necessary relation between the factual record and the mode of narrativization, he nevertheless wants to insist that there are some modes of emplotment that may be illegitimate for responsible histories of the Third Reich. "In the case of the emplotment of the events of the Third Reich in a comic or pastoral mode," he says, "we would be eminently justified in appealing to the facts in order to dismiss it from the lists of competing narratives of the Third Reich." [61] He goes on to suggest that as itself a "modernist event"—indeed, "the paradigmatic modernist event"—the Holocaust requires a modernist style of representation to do justice to it. Modernist modes of representation, he says, "may offer possibilities of representing the reality of both the Holocaust and the experience of it that no other version of realism could do." [62]

Whatever else this may mean (and it is by no means clear that the Holocaust is any more *paradigmatically* modern than other barbarisms that have besmirched the modern age), it certainly looks as though a concession is now being made to the idea of a connection of some sort between preferred modes of historical representation and the historical moment being represented.[63] The historian, in this late formulation, is not—or is not entirely—"indentured to a choice," as White had insisted earlier. Now there is at least the determinate modernity of the event to be considered. It is not hard to see why even some of his more sympathetic critics should feel a certain frustration that the cohesion of his argument (agree with it or not) is coming apart at the seams. This is especially so in the light of the significant use of the phrase "responsibly emplotted" in the above formulation. White doesn't bother to clarify this phrase or justify its use (responsibility to whom? to what?), so that it sounds very much like a careful hedge against the moral dangers that writing about the Holocaust carries in the contemporary West. The lapse is not an insignificant one.

At the same time, and reading, as one might say, for the best White, it is hard not to be sympathetic to—and inspired by—the profoundly utopian impulse that animates his arguments, namely, the desire to release us from the seeming "burden of history" and to open up historical discourse to the possibility of alternative futures. The challenge of the historian, for White, is less the resurrection of the past than the redirection of the future. This is what he had long ago discerned in the "realistic historicism" of Hegel, Balzac, and Tocqueville.

> The exponents of realistic historicism—Hegel, Balzac, and Tocqueville, to take representatives from philosophy, the novel, and historiography, respectively—agreed that the task of the historian was less to remind men of their obligation to the past than to force upon them an awareness of how the past could be used to effect an ethically responsible transition from present to future. All three saw history as educating men to the fact that their own present world had once existed in the minds of men as an unknown and frightening future, but how, as a consequence of specific human decisions, this future had been transformed into a present, that familiar world in which the historian himself lived and worked. . . . Thus, for all three, history was less an end in itself than a preparation for a more perfect understanding and ac-

ceptance of the individual's responsibility in the fashioning of the common humanity of the future.[64]

I wish to endorse this purpose. But I wonder whether it is best achieved in exactly the manner urged by White. Just as White seems to want to do in some of his later writing, I too want a way of connecting (without reducing) the narrative strategy employed in historical representation to the historical conjuncture or historical moment. I agree with White that this is a connection that turns not on cognitive or epistemological adequacy but rather on moral-political usefulness. Where White asks about "responsible" emplotments, however, I want to ask about *critical* ones, ones that attempt to open up conceptual space, to make it possible to see what has hitherto been obscured. What mode of emplotment of the past might best enable a critical rethinking of the present we inhabit such as to open up new ways of thinking about possible futures? In other words, I want to be able to ask whether a story-form that may have become prominent (say, Romance) in certain kinds of arguments (oppositional ones, for example) continues to have the same usefulness, the same salience, the same critical purchase, when the historical conjuncture that originally gave that argument point and purchase has passed, has been displaced by another. Perhaps this is not a question about their absolute truth so much as a question about the *best* truth for our time.

And this is what I want to understand about *The Black Jacobins*. My concern is to inquire into some of the features of the mode of emplotment that organizes the story James tells about Toussaint Louverture and the San Domingo Revolution. It will not be hard to recognize the plot structure as that of Romance, even if (as we shall see in the following chapter) Romance of a particular kind. What interests me, however, are the implications of this mode of emplotment for an understanding of the colonial past or, rather, for an understanding of the way the story-form of Romance produces a distinctive rhythm of historical connection between colonial pasts and postcolonial futures. To fold Koselleck and White into a single formulation here, my aim is to understand the way in which James's Romance in *The Black Jacobins* constructs a distinctive connection between the space of experience of colonial pasts and the horizon of expectation of postcolonial futures. But in fact I am interested in understanding more than this. As I have already indicated, *The Black Jacobins* contains elements of another plot structure besides Romance, namely, tragedy; indeed, I have said that this doubling of plot structures is partly what makes The Black Jacobins so compelling a work to think the problem of the narrativization of colonial pasts with. If, as White argues, tragedy organizes the relation between pasts, presents, and futures differently than Romance does, the question in which I am interested is what the implications are of this difference for the narrativization of the relation between colonial pasts and postcolonial futures in our postcolonial present.

V

The problem, of course, is how to gauge whether the sort of story about a particular past conceived and told in the context of a particular present as part of the project of aiming at a particular alternative future continues to be the sort of story worth telling in the context of a new present. And if not, why not?

Neither Koselleck nor White provides us with much guidance here. In approaching this question, however, I have found it helpful to think with some of R. G. Collingwood's ideas and especially with Quentin Skinner's restatement of them.[65] Collingwood, of course, is best remembered for the doctrine, famously expressed in The Idea of History, that history should be understood as the "re-enactment" or "re-thinking" of past thought or past experience in the mind of the historian. ("The history of thought, and therefore all history, is the re-enactment of past thought in the historian's own mind.")[66] This idea has been the subject of a good deal of fascinating discussion in recent years as Collingwood's work in the philosophy of history has started to receive more—and more considered—attention.[67] But there is another idea, also to be found in The Idea of History but perhaps most plainly stated in An Autobiography, which seems to me of more crucial—perhaps, even prior—significance than the justly celebrated doctrine of reenactment. This is the "logic," as he called it, of "question and answer." Simply stated, Collingwood maintained that a proposition is only properly understood if the question to which it forms an answer is identified and articulated. The meaning of a proposition, in other words, is relative to the question it answers and cannot, as a consequence, be discovered by lifting it out of the discursive process or milieu of which it is a constitutive part. Question and answer form a single "correlative" unit, and you will not have understood the latter until you have reconstructed (since it is never simply given, never simply self-evident) the former.[68] This logic, as Mink has helpfully pointed out (in drawing our attention to the affinities between Collingwood's thought and that of pragmatists like Dewey), is not a "formal" logic in the traditional sense; it is not a key to the possession of a timeless body of truths but rather something like a "theory of inquiry."[69]

It is hard to overemphasize the profound import of this insight. Indeed, many of Collingwood's now numerous commentators and interpreters have of course acknowledged the centrality of this principle of question and answer, the "primordial role" (the phrase is Dray's) it plays in Collingwood's views on the nature of historical inquiry.[70] But few, to my knowledge, have given it the sort of attention accorded to the idea of history as reenactment. One historian, however, who has built this Collingwoodian idea into the undergirding of his own conception of intellectual history, and in particular the history of political thought, is Quentin Skinner.[71] It is well known that Skinner, since his early methodological writings on meaning, intention, and so on, has been much concerned to alter the ways in which we think about historical texts, historical contexts, and the relations between them.[72] In this endeavor he has drawn on the linguistic pragmatics of J. L. Austin, especially his distinction between the "locutionary" and "illocutionary" dimensions of linguistic action.[73] Austin maintained that in the performance of any linguistic action the author of that action not only is saying something that can be analyzed for its sense and reference (the locutionary dimension) but also is *doing* something that can be analyzed for its intended point or force (the illocutionary dimension). These latter forms of linguistic action are "speech acts."

Like Koselleck, Skinner is a historian of the language of social and political understanding and action. Indeed, there is a growing interest in the points of contact between their respective theoretical approaches to history.[74] But Skinner's explicit interest has been on discourses and ideologies rather than concepts per se; he has in fact explicitly denied the very possibility of a history of concepts.[75] More precisely, Skinner has been concerned to focus his attention on the performative dimensions of language in order to elaborate an interpretative approach to the analysis of historical texts as instances of linguistic action. To understand Locke's *Two Treatises on Government*, for example, it is not sufficient to grasp the sense and reference of the words Locke used in his discussion of sovereignty; it is necessary to reconstruct what he was doing in "putting forward" the particular argument he advanced about liberty and the state. Locke is performing a piece of linguistic action in a determinate linguistic or discursive context. Or, as he has put it in more general terms, to understand any proposition we need to see it as "a move in an argument," and we need therefore to "grasp why it seemed worth making that precise move" and not some other at that particular moment. "I am claiming," Skinner goes on to maintain, "that any act of communication always constitutes the taking up of some determinate position in relation to some pre-existing conversation or argument. It follows that, if we wish to understand what has been said, we shall have to be able to identify what exact position has been taken up."[76] Similarly, in his remarkable study of Hobbes's rhetoric, he again distinguishes between approaches to the interpretation of historical texts that are largely concerned with "the dimension of meaning" and those concerned with "the dimension of linguistic action." This latter dimension, seeking to identify what authors are "doing" in writing their books, is one that takes seriously Wittgenstein's well-known injunction that "words are also deeds."[77]

This approach to the study of historical texts will be of especial importance to me in the operations I would like to perform on *The Black Jacobins*. It will enable me, first of all, to treat James's text as a piece of linguistic action, as an ideological maneuver that takes up a position and puts forward a move in a particular historicodiscursive context of argument. What are the conventions (I am following Tully's useful schematization here), the assumptions, the concepts, and so on that define the larger language of politics in relation to which James's work makes its move?[78] It will enable me, secondly, to think the particular political location of this ideological move. What are the relevant features of this historicopolitical problem-space in which *The Black Jacobins* was written? And finally, it will enable me to focus attention on the normative dimension of the political vocabulary the text deploys, the uses of those terms that are simultaneously descriptive and evaluative; this is especially important where terms like "revolution" (terms that have become a part of the normative vocabulary of the Left) are concerned.[79]

At the same time, however, Skinner seems to me to draw back from what I take to be the full implications of his own reformulation of Collingwood's question and answer logic for a critical history of the present. It is not that Skinner is unconcerned with the role historical inquiry might play in better understanding the present in which we live and write (though it is interesting that he does not link Collingwood's question and answer logic to this problem explicitly).[80] To the contrary, Skinner is very much alive to the demand the present might make on history and is attuned, moreover, to the emancipationist commitments that historical inquiry might itself serve to enhance. In the concluding chapter of one of his recent books, *Liberty before Liberalism*, significantly titled "Freedom and the Historian," Skinner reflects on precisely this issue of the uses of historical inquiry. Troubled "deeply" by the "accusation of antiquarianism," as he rightly insists every historian should be, Skinner is nevertheless cautious about making too large or too general a claim for "the point of it all" of intellectual history. Where his own practice is concerned, however, his suggestion is that an understanding of the extent to which the present and the values it embodies "reflect a series of choices made at different times" might "help to liberate us from the grip of any one hegemonal account of those values and how they should be interpreted and understood. Equipped with a broader sense of possibility, we can stand back from the intellectual commitments we have inherited and ask ourselves in a new spirit of enquiry what we should think of them."[81] In short, a practice of history ought to enable us to "stand back" from our beliefs and assumptions and perhaps subject them to reappraisal. Like Hayden White (from whom he differs in several respects, but with whom he shares the view that historians have something to learn from literary critics), Skinner seeks to use history to get us from "under the spell of our own intellectual heritage."[82]

Needless to say, I agree with much of this. But when Skinner goes on to suggest, as he does, that the upshot of this reconstructive exercise is that the reader can now "like a cow" go and "ruminate" on the "neglected riches of our intellectual heritage" put on "display" for them I confess to feeling a twinge of disappointment.[83] Skinner seems to me at this point, if not to abdicate the very line of argument he himself is pursuing, then at least to suddenly take refuge in a curiously ironic complacency. The image is not altogether unfamiliar: the historian, having discharged her or his duty of reconstructing the past, bows and exits just at the point at which the question arises of determining and judging the stakes in the present of the rehistoricizing intervention. Indeed this is underlined when he admits that his "admiration is reserved for those historians who consciously hold themselves aloof from enthusiasm and indignation alike when surveying the crimes, follies and misfortunes of mankind."[84] Perhaps I don't share this negative view of "enthusiasm" and don't consider "indignation" as, necessarily, a lapse in the etiquette of criticism. In this, as with much else, I should like to follow the example of C. L. R. James's preface and worry about the supposed advantages—or privileges—of tranquility for the kind of historical reflection motivated by a critical concern with the present.

More importantly, though, the view that I have been commending is that the logic of question and answer—and Skinner's own restatement of it, especially—can, and should, be pressed in a more self-consciously critical and actively interventionist direction than Skinner himself is prepared to go. In my view Collingwood's principle can be reoriented, so to speak, on its axis, so that it faces less the historian's past than the critic's present, and so that its purchase has less to do with the ironist's desire to unmask the pretense of the present than the utopian's desire to make the present yield more attractive possibilities for alternative futures. Where Skinner's conceptualization of Collingwood's principle of question and answer is to be applied to the inquiry into the historical past with a view perhaps to historicizing the present, to disclosing its contingency and its constructedness,[85] the direction I want to lead the investigation is into testing ongoing practices of criticism to determine whether to continue with them or else abandon them.[86] Consequently, I am interested in more than reconstructing the move in the argument that constitutes James's *The Black Jacobins*; I am interested in determining whether in the current conjuncture this move continues to be a move worth making. In significant ways (as we will see in chapter 2) the move *The Black Jacobins* makes is a recognizably anticolonial vindicationist one, one seeking to stake a claim against the racist colonial historiography that denied that African peoples—and peoples of African descent in the New World—were capable of heroic leadership and self-government. In the construction of this vindicationist narrative James was writing not only within a revolutionary socialist tradition but also within an important tradition of black Romanticism in which Haiti, the first black state, stood out as an inspiring and exonerating achievement. But what ought we, today, to do with this story? Does this discursive move of vindicationist Romanticism continue to be as salient a move in our postcolonial present as it was for James in his colonial one? Does it continue to answer a warrantable question? I have a doubt about this, and this is what this book is concerned to explore.

MANY CONTEMPORARY READERS of C. L. R. James read *The Black Jacobins* as though it might provide them with answers to present problems, as though, for instance, it might tell them how to conduct oppositional politics today. There are two sorts of such readers. On one side, there are those who feel that James's analysis was incorrect or at least woefully inadequate and, consequently, that it would fail to give good guidance in the present (these are often the critics of Eurocentrism who find in James an unconscionable infatuation with the West). And on the other side there are those who would urge that James was largely right but that he needs supplementation or revision or both in the direction of a deeper subaltern appreciation (these are often the critics who deplore the tendency in James to slide in an elitist direction). Both sorts of readers, though coming away with different evaluations of it, are alike in looking to see how far James was right or wrong in his analysis. I think that readings of this sort—on the one side as much as on the other—are mistaken (and I come back to them in chapter 3). In both there is a misconception of the role that historical texts can play in the present, a misconception based on their assumption that the questions to which James sought answers continue to be questions for us. At the same time it should be clear that this view will not lead me to abandon *The Black Jacobins* as having no bearing whatsoever on how we think about acting morally and politically in the circumstances in which we find ourselves. Connecting up Skinner and Koselleck and White I am going to suggest that the critical purchase of this Romantic mode of emplotment—this vindicationist move—depended on a certain space of experience and horizon of expectation, and I am going to urge that, insofar as our postcolonial present is characterized by the collapse or enfeebling of that problem-space, that mode (and move) stand in need of revision. Ours, in other words, is not James's context of argument, and thus the task before us is not one of merely finding better answers than he did to existing questions—as though his anticolonial questions were timeless ones—but of pursuing the possibility that the questions he posed and challenged might themselves have altered. At any rate this is the story I aim to tell.

TO SUM UP: I am suggesting that C. L. R. James's magnificent work of anticolonial history, *The Black Jacobins*, offers a distinctive vantage from which to think about the problem of an oppositional criticism of the postcolonial present. It offers, more specifically, a vantage from which to reconceive the story we tell about the ways in which colonial pasts are connected to postcolonial presents and through these presents to possible postcolonial futures. *The Black Jacobins* is a classic work of early twentieth-century anticolonialism not merely because of the complexity and sympathy with which it treats the events that make up what is now known as the Haitian Revolution. It is a classic work, rather, because it gives to these events the shape of an allegory of emancipationist redemption that embodies in a compelling way the great longing for black and anticolonial revolution. The doubt that inspires my own preoccupations and that sustains the investigation I seek to carry out here, however, is that the critical purchase of this particular allegory is less than it formerly was. Much less. In fact my suspicion is that, faced as we are with the virtual deadend of the Bandung project that grew out of the anticolonial revolution (the nationalist and liberationist visions of sovereignty as self-determination), this story is an exhausted one. It cannot enable us—as it enabled James and the generation of anticolonials that succeeded his—to give point to the project of social and political change. But the singular brilliance of The Black Jacobins is that it is more than this allegory of redemption. It is also explicitly an exercise in writing a history of the present. In this chapter I have sought to raise some questions about this by-now-familiar idea, and I have drawn upon the work of Reinhart Koselleck (his idea of the relation between given pasts and given futures), Hayden White (his idea that the forms of historical narrative themselves have determinate contents), and Quentin Skinner (his idea that historical texts are best understood as moves within an argument) to help me do so. In the preface to The Black Jacobins James states concisely his concern with the connection between the nature of his own politico-historical present and the appropriate literary form in which to cast the story of his great protagonist, Toussaint Louverture. And in doing so he at once invites us to see his work—the factual and conceptual content of it as well as the content of its form—in relation to the cognitive-political problem-space out of which it was conceived and written, and, much more importantly, he directly challenges us to ask ourselves what kind of story might be best for the politicohistorical presents within which we now live and write. It is this that makes The Black Jacobins a work of unending critical value.

# TWO

# Romanticism and the Longing
# for Anticolonial Revolution

The [San Domingo Revolution] is the only successful slave revolt in history, and
the odds it had to overcome is evidence of the magnitude of the interests that
were involved. The transformation of slaves, trembling in hundreds before a
single white man, into a people able to organise themselves and defeat the most
powerful European nations of their day, is one of the great epics of revolutionary
struggle and achievement. Why and how this happened is the theme of this book.

I

Succinctly expressed, this is the central aspiration of C. L. R. James's
*The Black Jacobins*. This is its animating impulse, its shaping ambition.
*The Black Jacobins* is the history of one of the most remarkable—perhaps,
indeed, one of the defining—social and political events of the modern world, the Haitian Revolution. It sets before us with prodigious
scholarship and sublime eloquence the world-historical drama of black
slaves rising up en masse against their white enslavers and with courage and fierce resolve breaking their chains and laying claim to their
freedom. But, of course, as this passage already makes evident, James
does not mean *The Black Jacobins* to be merely the history of a remarkable
revolution; he means it to be much more than this. With pointed self-
consciousness and deliberate motivation, James means *The Black Jacobins*
to be a *revolutionary* history of that remarkable revolution. As a consequence, *The Black Jacobins* is not an uninterested description of what happened in San Domingo between Boukman's antislavery insurrection in
the summer of 1791 and Dessalines's unprecedented declaration of independence thirteen years later in January 1804; it is James's very distinctive
interpretation and appraisal of the political meaning and moral signifi-

cance of those events for his own time. I am going to argue here that *The Black Jacobins* is, above all, a literary-historical exercise in revolutionary Romanticism. This is what it is, though this (as we will later see) is not all that it is: a modernist allegory of anticolonial revolution written in the mode of a historical Romance.

WE HAVE ALREADY seen, in a preliminary way, how in the preface C. L. R. James sets the stage for his history of Toussaint Louverture and the San Domingo Revolution through an oblique (or perhaps, not-so-oblique) reference to English Romanticism. "The violent conflicts of our age," James wrote in the penultimate paragraph of the preface, "enable our practised vision to see into the very bones of previous revolutions more easily than heretofore. Yet for that very reason it is impossible to recollect historical emotions in that tranquillity which a great English writer, too narrowly, associated with poetry alone."[1] By evoking English Romanticism in this way, James situates *The Black Jacobins* in a genealogical relation to a profoundly resonant complex of sources and influences.[2]

In the past two decades or so, Anglo-American scholarship on English Romanticism has undergone a considerable mutation, urged as it has been in the direction of a greater ideological and historical self-consciousness.[3] This has contributed to a more explicit theoretical attention to hitherto unasked questions about the ways in which gender, sexuality, race, and empire have shaped Romanticism's sensibilities and preoccupations. So that, for example, if the poetic imagination of this period was once thought largely in relation to the upheavals in America and France, it is now increasingly being argued that mapping Romanticism in this way presents and preserves too Eurocentric a view of its constituent voices and discursive traces. Romanticism, in other words, has been undergoing its own post-Orientalist revolution. Long associated with the tropes of the exotic and the primitive embodied in the pastoral figure of the Noble Savage, it is argued that Romanticism has to be understood in relation to the "discursive presence of Empire in the seemingly autonomous literary work" of the period.[4] As Mary Louise Pratt has put it, in an often-quoted phrase, "one might be tempted to argue that Romanticism originated in the contact zones of America, North Africa and the South Seas."[5]

In the late eighteenth century the "contact zones" uppermost in the English imagination were the slave plantations of the West Indian "sugar islands." If for most of its history the institution of New World slavery had appeared to the English both geographically and morally distant from their everyday concerns, during the last three decades of the eighteenth century this began to change substantially. Two dramatic events are often cited as helping to stimulate this change. One of them was the 1771–72 court case involving James Somerset, a slave brought to England who was being forced to return to the colonies, and the landmark decision of Chief Justice Lord William Mansfield establishing his freedom in Britain.[6] The case, around which the famous abolitionist Granville Sharp agitated, brought into the open the troubling question of the compatibility of slavery with the understood traditions of English liberty. Another, and perhaps more riveting and disturbing event, was the publication of the horrible details surrounding the Liverpool slave ship *Zong*. Again Granville Sharpe was centrally involved, the court case having been brought to his attention by the black abolitionist Olaudah Equiano. In 1781, on the way from the west coast of Africa to Jamaica with a cargo of slaves, among whom the mortality rate was growing at an alarming rate, the captain, Luke Collingwood, made the extraordinary decision of throwing more than a hundred and thirty sickly but still living slaves overboard to their deaths in order to ensure compensation through the insurance provision for slaves lost at sea.[7] This incident made stunningly clear just how callous and depraved — how calculatedly instrumental and inhumane — the whole enterprise of slave trading was, and the lengths to which Englishmen were willing to go to secure their profits. Such events shaped the moral and political climate of the age and gave an impetus to the growing momentum of antislavery activity. It contributed importantly, for example, to the Quaker-led founding of the Committee for the Purpose of Effecting the Abolition of the Slave Trade in 1787. And the pronounced sentiments of pity, mercy, and compassion, the yearning for the amelioration of the condition of the powerless and the oppressed that distinguished the Romantic temper (however defensively, anxiously, or ambivalently) was inseparable from it.

Given James's background and colonial education, it is not surprising that English Romanticism is signaled in the preface to *The Black Jacobins* by reference to that "great English writer," William Wordsworth, the commanding and even paradigmatic poet of the period. But we have also noticed the ambiguity of James's reference, the affiliation hedged about by dismissal. This is understandable given Wordsworth's own powerfully ambivalent relation to the central issues of *The Black Jacobins*, namely, revolution and black slave emancipation. When Wordsworth wrote the preface to his and Samuel Taylor Coleridge's *Lyrical Ballads* he was no longer the enthusiast of the French Revolution he had been in the early 1790s.[8] Nor was he the enchanted reader of William Godwin's radical democratic tract, *An Enquiry Concerning Political Justice*, the two volumes of which were published in 1793[9]; by the late 1790s Wordsworth had turned away both from Godwin and from political associations altogether.[10]

Moreover, and perhaps more directly telling from the point of view of *The Black Jacobins*, Wordsworth's relation to the cause of slavery abolition was disappointingly lukewarm, sometimes even antagonistic.[11] Unlike his poet friends, Coleridge and Robert Southey, and his abolitionist friend, the very eminent Thomas Clarkson, Wordsworth never subscribed to the cause of antislavery.[12] Not, of course, that the issue was avoidable. This, after all, was the same Wordsworth who, in late 1802, two years after the preface to the *Lyrical Ballads*, would write the memorable sonnet "To Toussaint L'Ouverture." This poem could hardly have been far from James's mind when he invoked the dissonant presence of Wordsworth in his own preface. Composed shortly after Toussaint's deportation to France and his imprisonment by Napoleon in the Fortress of Joux in the Jura Mountains, it was first published in February 1803, a few months before he fatally succumbed to the bitter cold and the calculated ill-treatment of his captors.

> Toussaint, the most unhappy man of men!
> Whether the whistling Rustic tend his plough
> Within thy hearing, or thy head be now
> Pillowed in some deep dungeon's earless den;—
> O miserable Chieftain, where and when
> Wilt thou find patience! Yet die not; do thou
> Wear rather in thy bonds a cheerful brow:
> Though fallen thyself, never to rise again,
> Live, and take comfort. Thou hast left behind
> Powers that will work for thee; air, earth, and skies;
> There's not a breathing of the common wind
> That will forget thee; thou hast great allies;
> Thy friends are exaltations, agonies,
> And love, man's unconquerable mind.[13]

The dignity and noble feeling in the elegy's tribute to the fallen black Jacobin are undeniable. But at the same time James could not have but noticed the transcendental complacency of the poet's regard. While

Wordsworth appears to offer a salute and an outraged sympathy for the liberator captured and imprisoned without either trial or hearing ("Pillowed in some deep dungeon's earless den"), and while he seems to commiserate with him languishing in the fierce cold and desolation ("Toussaint, the most unhappy man of men!"), what is nevertheless striking is the superior air and patronizing condescension with which he admonishes Toussaint for seeking too much too fast ("O miserable Chieftain! where and when / Wilt thou find patience!). And even if we are assured that Toussaint will not be forgotten ("There's not a breathing of the common wind / That will forget thee"), it is only nature's elements ("air, earth, and skies"), not abolitionist or libertarian political solidarities, that are the "powers" that will work in his favor—these and the ubiquitous imagination that ever lifts "man's unconquerable mind" beyond the merely mundane agonies of wrongful captivity.

Shedding (for the most part, at least) the aloof and slightly sententious air of the Wordsworthian voice and its pastoral tone and conservative politics, James's later anticolonial figuration will share something of this English Romantic's evocation of Toussaint's ineliminable dignity, his heroic courage, and his undaunted belief in liberty. But whatever The Black Jacobins owes to this sonnet there is another—submerged—line of connection between James and Romanticism, one that aggressively disrupts and challenges some of its cherished assumptions about Englishness and Empire. I am thinking of the genealogical line connecting him to late eighteenth-century black abolitionists such as Olaudah Equiano and black radical activists like Robert Wedderburn. Both were displaced and dispossessed "blackbirds" living in London at the end of the eighteenth century, conscripts of modernity who were decentering and recasting the redemptive discourse of radical dissenting Protestantism and using it to intervene in the contemporary problem of slavery. Equiano's Interesting Narrative of the Life of Olaudah Equiano, or Gustavus Vassa, the African, Written by Himself, published in 1789, is one of the founding texts of that eighteenth- and nineteenth-century literary genre, the slave narrative.[14] The confessional frame of the autobiography served as a vehicle for a gripping moral account in which the sufferings, humiliations, and miseries of the slave were a background to his or her attainment of physical liberty and spiritual emancipation. The autobiographical narrative, in other words, offered the unique possibility of dramatically staging the black self in a way that vindicated both its essential humanity and its potential for worthy achievement.

Wedderburn, by contrast with the genteel Equiano, was a rough, disreputable, and notorious character, given more to blasphemous and subversive oratory than to elegant literary prose and pious supplication.[15] A member of the revolutionary Jacobin underground in London in the early years of the nineteenth century, he invoked the dreaded image of the San Domingo Revolution (in his periodical *Axe Laid to the Root*) as a model of opposition to tyranny.[16] So that while his 1824 tract *The Horrors of Slavery* resembled in many respects the genre of spiritual autobiography employed by predecessors like Equiano (in its narrative of redemptive deliverance, for instance), Wedderburn had a very different agenda of political reform—for both England and the slave colonies—than did any other black abolitionist. Together, however, both map the space of black Romantic antislave discourse in the late eighteenth and early nineteenth centuries. The Romantic vindication of the humanity of blacks and the purpose of slavery abolition they embodied and gave expression to stood in rebuke of those apologist Romantic formulations (such as Wordsworth's) that denied to Africans and peoples of African descent an equal emancipation. *The Black Jacobins* is their descendant.[17]

MY AIM IN this chapter is to do a number of things with the anticolonial Romanticism of *The Black Jacobins*. I want, first of all (in the spirit of Hayden White's historical poetics), to elucidate its mode of emplotment, or at least its dominant mode of emplotment, the one that has stood out most prominently for successive generations of James's readers. This is the mode of Romance, indeed of *epic* Romance. James more or less tells us this is what he is doing in the opening pages of his book. My concern in drawing out this narrative strategy and sketching in its contours, therefore, is less to reveal something that was hitherto obscured or hidden than to observe the way in which that strategy of realist dramatic composition promotes the emergence of a certain kind of story about the relations among colonial past, anticolonial present, and postcolonial future. And my concern with inquiring into this story in this way, in the final analysis, is to learn something about the ways in which the content of a distinctive political desire and political expectation has been given narrative shape and form. This is the first move.

Second, I want to be able to say what the *point* is of this strategy of Romance, or anyway what the point *has been*. By this I am not referring to the meaning of this strategy in some semiotic sense. Rather, I am interested here in what James is *doing* (in the sense that Skinner derives from

Austin) in mobilizing the strategy he mobilizes in his text, what the move is that he is making by so composing his Romantic drama of anticolonial revolution. This will entail an inquiry into something of the ideological problem-space in relation to which The Black Jacobins may be thought of as an intervention, or in Collingwood's sense, an answer to a question. My concern here is with the ideological discourses—the conventional or stereotypical ideas, images, assumptions, and so on—which constitute James's arena of challenge or provocation, and to which his text can be read as a response. In particular I will be concerned with the ideological context and character of mid- and late-Victorian colonialist racism and the ways in which The Black Jacobins constitutes an indignant vindication of the negated achievements of blacks and of the justice of their anti-colonial claims to self-determination and political sovereignty. This is the second move.

Finally, I think that if we want to understand how the purchase of the narrative strategy employed by The Black Jacobins is constructed and sustained, we need to inquire into some of the conceptual underpinnings of its argument, in particular the assumptions that govern the concept of "revolution" on which the radical literary-modernist labor of its criticism so crucially depends. This will be my third move. In particular, I am interested in two related kinds of investigation into the idea of revolution, both concerned with the historicity of the concept. One kind of investigation will focus on the distinctive modernity of the idea of revolution, and, consequently, on its dependence upon distinctive ways of conceiving political change, and distinctive assumptions about temporalities and history. (I shall take some guidance here from Reinhart Koselleck and Hannah Arendt who are concerned with the modern concept's relation to the Enlightenment.) The other kind of investigation is inspired by the work of Bernard Yack and is concerned with the way in which the modern longing for revolution is connected to distinctive ways of defining the problem to be overcome (the problem with the modern world) so as to achieve satisfaction. Interestingly, he shows this longing to have distinctively Romantic sources. Specifically I am interested in the way the problem about New World colonial slavery is defined in The Black Jacobins in such a manner as to generate a distinctive form of this Romantic longing, a longing for anticolonial revolution.

The direction of my argument in this chapter is, to a large extent, a skeptical one. My aim is to raise some questions about the continued efficacy of a mode of emplotment shaped by the mythos of Romance, and to cast some doubt on the continued usefulness of a discursive strategy in which political change is thought in terms of a vindicationist narrative of liberation or a concept of revolution. Indeed, for some years now I have been raising this doubt, and this exercise is in large part an attempt to clarify, elaborate, and develop the gist of that argument.[18] I have wanted to suggest that perhaps we have to face up to the implications of the historical and conceptual shifts that have fundamentally altered the conditions in which social and political change can be critically thought. Certainly these shifts have altered what our attitude can be to the problem of revolution. It needs to be emphasized, however, that my doubt here is not the existence or the possibility or the desirability of social upheavals of greater or lesser intensity; I do not doubt the historical possibility of, say, the violent overthrow of a government by some organization of oppositional power. What I doubt is the normative usefulness of continuing to understand these upheavals in terms of the modern concept of revolution. It is obvious that it was once possible to do so. Indeed, in a certain sense, revolution once defined the very horizon of radical oppositional politics and haunted the imagination of modern intellectuals. I think that the enfeebling (to call it that for the moment) of revolution as a salient category in our oppositional political vocabulary and oppositional political calculations has to have profound implications for how we think about the possibilities and limits that lie within our political present, how we think and think *against* the historicity of our present.

II

There are two Romantic historians of revolution who, more than any others, hover around the pages of *The Black Jacobins*, watching over its passages, inspiring its language, its formulations, its idiom, its rhythms, and who, in many ways, help to shape its longing for anticolonial revolution. One is Jules Michelet, the first great historian of the French Revolution; and the other is Leon Trotsky, the first great historian of the Russian Revolution. It is hard to avoid the impression that when in his preface James invokes that much traversed distinction between the art and science of history—in which, as he says, the "analysis is the science and the demonstration the art"—he has in mind these two historians of modern Europe's defining revolutions.[19]

Michelet and Trotsky may be said to exemplify the tension between history as art and demonstration on the one hand and history as science and analysis on the other. Neither, it is true, was completely oblivious to either one or the other, art or science. Michelet, writing with the hand and heart of a Romantic poet, was at the same time an archivist (under Louis-Philippe in the 1830s, he was appointed Conservateur des Archives) with a passion for the documentary record;[20] and Trotsky, guided though he was by the strictures of the science of Dialectical Materialism, nevertheless wrote with a profound sensitivity to the literary craft of historical narrative. But at the same time, it is equally true that each looked more in one direction than in the other, Michelet toward the art of the story and Trotsky toward the analytical discovery of history's governing laws. In this regard, it may be argued that a significant part of the task James set himself in The Black Jacobins is to explicitly join these two seemingly incommensurable approaches to historical writing, to bring the literary art of Michelet and the Marxist science of Trotsky into a single (if not seamlessly unitary) narrative strategy. Whether or not he succeeds in doing so is not a matter I seek to judge or argue. All that interests me here is the way Michelet and Trotsky participate in the genealogy of the mythos of Romance that constitutes The Black Jacobins as the particular story that it is.

MICHELET WAS ONE of the masters of nineteenth-century history writing. A disciple of Giambattista Vico (whose New Science he translated), an admirer of Victor Hugo, he was in Hayden White's words, "the presiding genius of the Romantic School of historiography," and in Arthur Mitzman's, the "apostle of the revolutionary tradition."[21] Michelet's History of the French Revolution (1847–53), written in the years of European upheaval when the republican meaning of the Revolution of 1789 seemed to have been obscured and to stand in need of rescuing, is explicitly cast in the language of resurrection, renewal, and redemption.[22] Concerned less with recording the details than with identifying the animating principle of the revolution (though, of course, as is well known, he was one of the first historians to make use of the archival record of the events), the History captures the movement and drama of its actors, great and small. For Michelet, the revolution was, first and foremost, the result of a contest or conflict between two opposing principles or spirits: liberty against despotism, reason against dogma, justice against tyranny, and the rule of law against the rule of arbitrary authority. The revolution represented the triumph of one over the other, as he says, "the triumph of right, the resurrection of justice, the tardy reaction of thought against brute force" (HFR, 5). The two adversarial principles were exemplified in the opposition between Christianity and the revolution and between the old monarchy and the new republic: they were as Darkness and Light, Evil and Good, and they confronted one another in an irreversible mortal combat.

In Michelet's anticlerical account, during the Middle Ages an arbitrary power had become "fixed, armed and inflexible" and "for a thousand years veiled the face of eternal justice" (HFR, 26, 27). However, justice, if "banished" and "proscribed," was not extinguished. With difficulty she ventured to raise her head "beneath the weight of woes and oppression" in order to "resume the consciousness of right." And this consciousness, says Michelet, "slowly endeavouring to awake throughout a period of six centuries of religious efforts, burst forth in the year 1789 in the political and social world" (HFR, 27). In short: "The Revolution is nothing but the tardy reaction of justice against the government of favour and the religion of grace" (HFR, 27). Or in tones more apocalyptic, he says to the weary justice: "Be not alarmed with thy doubt. That doubt is already faith. Believe, hope! Right, though postponed, shall have its advent; it will come to sit in judgment, on the dogma and on the world. And that day of Judgment will be called the Revolution" (HFR, 30).[23] Thus for Michelet, the events of the first year of the revolution, from the storming of the Bastille on July 14, 1789, to the abolition of the hereditary nobility on June 19, 1790, mark a New Day. The new principle had vanquished the old, France itself was born, and a new unity and a new sociability were abroad in the world. All the old barriers to fraternity had been broken down. "Where are the old distinctions of provinces and races of men?" Michelet asks. "Where those powerful and geographical contrasts? All have disappeared: geography itself is annihilated. There are no longer any mountains, rivers, or barriers between men. Their language is still dissimilar, but their words agree so well that they all seem to spring from the same place,—from the same bosom. Everything has gravitated towards one point, and that point now speaks forth; it is a unanimous prayer from the heart of France" (HFR, 444). It was such an immense and glorious transformation, such a dramatic reconciliation of spirit and nature, of love and politics, said Michelet, that even Immanuel Kant, that "perfectly abstract being," that granite rock "on which every religion, every system of philosophy had struck and been shipwrecked" was moved—so moved in fact that he could be seen in Koenigsberg "going forth on the road, like a woman, to inquire the news" of the revolution (HFR, 455). This is the sense of historical drama, the cataclysmic clashing of counterposed forces, that propels *The Black Jacobins*. For James too the story of revolution will be the story of a great moral contest between incommensurable principles, slavery and freedom; and these will be mapped onto a temporal contrast between the Old and the New and harnessed to a momentum of eventual victory of Right over Wrong.

TROTSKY'S *History of the Russian Revolution* (1932–33), also written in a time of European upheaval, belongs in many ways to a quite different revolutionary age than Michelet's *History of the French Revolution*.[24] Or at any rate, there are both lines of continuity as well as discontinuity between the ages they belong to. The Revolution of 1848, on which Marx and Engels had pinned such hope, and which so shaped the world of Michelet's Paris, was for Trotsky's generation a fading memory. Between the 1840s and 1930s there lies, among much else, the rise of the organized working class movement, the emergence of the Marxist science of history (and the method of the materialistic dialectic in particular), and most importantly, the Bolshevik idea of the professional proletarian party which led to the Russian Revolution of October 1917. Lenin, to invoke Edmund Wilson's splendid and semiotically saturated image, had made it to the Finland station. Trotsky's *History* belongs, moreover, to an age in which, in the wake of the Great War and what H. Stuart Hughes referred to as the "reorientation of European social thought" in the interwar years, there is a new confidence in the prospect of social transformation.[25] So that the old dream of revolution came to be keyed to a new idea of the rhythm of history, a new conception of historical agency, and a new idea of how to self-consciously wrest the future from the past. At the same time, if the tone of Trotsky's narrative is less oracular and the composition less lyrical, less given to rhapsodic flights of poetic flourish than Michelet's, the dominant mode of emplotment nevertheless remains that of Romance.

Trotsky's story of the Russian Revolution, again like Michelet's of the French, is less concerned with the details of events (though, of course, Trotsky's *History* is nothing if not a closely followed record of some of the minutiae of the unfolding day-to-day events) than with the underlying principles of the revolution. Or rather, the details of events really serve to illustrate the constitutive laws of their motion. "The history of a revolution, like every other history," Trotsky says, "ought first of all to tell what happened and how. That, however, is little enough. From the very telling it ought to become clear why it happened thus and not otherwise. Events can neither be regarded as a series of adventures, nor strung on the thread of some preconceived moral. They must obey their own laws. The discovery of these laws is the author's task" (HRR, 1:xvii). However, if history writing was about identifying such laws, it was also about the agency of the oppressed. As Trotsky writes, the central point or the "most indubitable feature" of the revolution (indeed, of a revolution) is "the direct interference of the masses in historic events" (HRR, 1:xvii). In "ordinary times," Trotsky says, whatever the character of the political order, history is made by specialists, politicians, and technocrats. "But at those crucial moments when the old order becomes no longer endurable to the masses, they break over the barriers excluding them from the political arena, sweep aside their traditional representatives, and create by their own interference the initial groundwork for a new régime" (HRR, 1:xvii). The history of the revolution has necessarily to be the history of classes in conflict. This conflict, after all, is the motor of history, as Marx and Engels famously declared in The Communist Manifesto (a book which perhaps bridges the ages of Michelet and Trotsky). But the character of the conflict of classes and thus "the course of the revolution itself" cannot be simply read off from the economic base or social structure. There is also an important subjective factor at work which cannot be dismissed. "The dynamic of revolutionary events is directly determined by swift, intense and passionate changes in the psychology of classes which have already formed themselves before the revolution" (HRR, 1:xvii). Or again, he writes:

> The swift changes of mass views and moods in an epoch of revolution thus derive, not from the flexibility and mobility of man's mind, but just the opposite, from its deep conservatism. The chronic lag of ideas and relations behind new objective conditions, right up to the moment when the latter crash over people in the form of a catastrophe, is what creates in a period of revolution that leaping movement of ideas and passions which seems to the police mind a mere result of the activities of "demagogues" (HRR, 1:xvii).

James too will inscribe his account of revolution in relation to this idea of the objective laws of the movement of history. For as he put it in The

*Black Jacobins*: "Men make their own history, and the black Jacobins of San Domingo were to make history which would alter the fate of millions of men and shift the economic currents of three continents. But if they could seize opportunity they could not create it" (BJ, 17 [25]). Change is brought about by the passionate action of men and women. But such action is always constrained by the conditions in which it takes place and which make it possible in the first place.

In characterizing Michelet's histories as emplotted in the mode of Romance, Hayden White has said of them that they were emplotted "as dramas of disclosure, of the liberation of a spiritual power fighting to free itself from the forces of darkness, a redemption. And his conception of his task as a historian was to serve as the preserver of what is redeemed." [26] Making allowances for the obvious—for the displacement of Providence by the Dialectic—much the same could be said of Trotsky's *History*. In both you can see what Northrop Frye means when he says that the Romance is "nearest of all literary forms to the wish-fulfillment dream." [27] Their narratives move in sequential and processional form, moving steadily and rhythmically (one might even say, teleologically) in the direction of an end already in some sense known in advance. It has the shape of "a quest": the protagonists (invariably associated with the new, with Light, with order) undertake a perilous journey; there are encounters with antagonists or enemies (invariably associated with the old, with Darkness, with disorder); the inevitable conflict ensues between these irreconcilable principles; there are heightened moments when Darkness seems poised to vanquish Light; and finally the victorious deliverance or overcoming from bondage, from evil, comes: what Frye calls "the point of epiphany."

THE BLACK JACOBINS, I shall argue, shares deeply (if distinctly) this mythos of Romance: the rhythms of redemption, the epic momentum of successive historical events, the metaphysical movement from Darkness to Light, Bondage to Freedom, and so on. Like Michelet's revolutionary history, and Trotsky's, James's is a Great Story, a Romantic fable of great deeds and masterful accomplishments. Like them, James is not looking to write a mere secular historical account that faithfully records the facts (in each of their histories, indeed, the details are far less memorable than the narrative sweep of the story), but to fashion a myth, a legend, an emblem. He is looking to write something in the tradition of what Matthew Arnold would have called the "grand style," something, that is, in which the local, even remote, events of a particular place and time are raised to a universal moral significance.

At the same time, if *The Black Jacobins* is a revolutionary account of a seminal revolution, it is nevertheless told in a distinctive way: as the quasi-biographical myth of the hero. James writes in the preface:

> By a phenomenon often observed, the individual leadership responsible for this unique achievement was almost entirely the work of a single man—Toussaint L'Ouverture. Beauchamp in the *Biographie Universelle* calls Toussaint L'Ouverture one of the most remarkable men of a period rich in remarkable men. He dominated from his entry until circumstances removed him from the scene. The history of the San Domingo revolution will therefore largely be a record of his achievements and his political personality (BJ, vii [x]).

Time and time again, as is well known, James was drawn to the form of the biography.[28] This is not surprising, because for the Romantics (or at least for Victorian Romantics), the biography was of special significance as a literary form. It allowed the figuring of a certain kind of individuality: a man of action and achievement, of wisdom, courage, endurance, compassion, self-sacrifice, a man of both genius and virtue whose life could be thought of as exemplary and which in consequence could be deployed for didactic and inspirational purposes.[29] For Victorians, like Thomas Carlyle, for example, biography and history were interconnected modes of inquiry; indeed, biography was understood to be a privileged form of historical discourse.[30] In Toussaint Louverture James can imagine for us such a mythical hero; the individuality of a man born in the most unpropitious of circumstances and who rises up from the crowd of ordinary and mediocre mortals to provide guidance and salvation in a Time of Troubles. Moreover, he can, in so casting his story, not merely affirm the humanity of the black slave, but enable the indomitable spirit of that slave to stand, emblematically, for the best hope of humanity.

In the biohistorical frame of *The Black Jacobins*, then, the most prominent figuring of Toussaint Louverture is that of the admired revolutionary leader whose heroism opens the way for a victory over adversity. This is the great narrative of Toussaint's rise and subsequent fall and of the strengths and weaknesses of his political personality. In outline, this is the story of an ex-slave of exceptional gifts and significant learning (BJ, 12 [19–20]) who late in his years rises from comparative obscurity to become a leader of world-historical stature. In it Toussaint is figured as a man of consummate deliberation, strategic calculation, and immense—almost unbelievable—compassion and restraint. He hesitates to join the slave uprising when it begins on the night of August 21, 1791, under the inspiration of Boukman. More than this, he even undertakes to safeguard his former master and mistress (BJ, 70 [90]). But when he does, finally, join the insurrection he is fully master of himself, and of the moment. He rises swiftly and without serious rival: from one of the handful of leaders of the insurrectionary forces fighting for the Spanish up to 1794, he becomes a commander of forces for republican France sometime between Sonthanax's emancipation of the San Domingo slaves in August 1793 and the French Convention's general emancipation decree of February 4, 1794; and from his appointment by Laveaux as Governor of the colony in April 1796 and his brilliant diplomatic negotiation of the British withdrawal and his dismissal of the French representative, Hédouville, in 1798, to his assumption of complete rule over the entire island by the end of 1800. These are the signposts of his magnificent career.

Up until this point James's Toussaint fully embodies the hopes and the will of the ex-slaves. He is at once a leader of immeasurable diplomatic skill and a popular leader of tremendous energy and vision. He is at one with the masses, leading but not from afar. In James's words: "He lived with the men and charged at their head. If cannon needed to be moved, he himself helped, once getting a hand badly crushed in the process. All knew him from the months before when he was merely old Toussaint. He shared all their toils and dangers" (BJ, 118–19 [147]). In short, James portrays Toussaint as a man of the people, totally devoted to their interests, who gains their confidence and absolute loyalty by working tirelessly on their behalf. At the same time, however, there is another side to Toussaint's personality: a certain taciturnity, a slightly superior aloofness, and most of all, an autocratic unwillingness to communicate what he was thinking to his subordinates. As James says: "His extraordinary abilities, his silence, the sharpness of his tongue when he spoke, kept even his most trusted officers at a distance. They worshipped him, but feared rather than loved him" (BJ, 119 [148]). This attitude of reserve and distance was the one flaw in an otherwise unimpeachable political personality. In James's story, however, it remains enabling only in the early days of the struggle when extraordinary levels of discipline are called for.

As the revolution begins to consolidate itself after 1800 and Toussaint turns his attention to cementing his position and rebuilding the ravaged economy—this is when his stern and impenetrable manner and his incipient authoritarianism become counterproductive. Not only does he explain nothing of his purposes and his plans to his subordinates (not to mention the ordinary people), not only does he become progressively alienated from the masses from among whom he himself had so recently come, but he implements and polices a Draconian regime of plantation labor that is only a few degrees removed from slavery. At the same time, and as though to rub salt into the wounds of the ex-slaves, he inexplicably appears to be granting favors to the former white plantocracy, and to be, moreover, excessively loyal to the colonizing French republic. "But, too confident in his own powers," James writes, "he was making one dreadful mistake. Not with Bonaparte nor with the French Government. In nothing does his genius stand out so much as in refusing to trust the liberties of the blacks to the promises of the French or British Imperialism. His error was his neglect of his own people. They did not understand what he was doing or where he was going. He took no trouble to explain. It was dangerous to explain, but still more dangerous not to explain. His temperament, close and self-contained, was one that kept its own counsel" (BJ, 200 [240]).

It is in this context that he reaches his nadir. Popular desperation turns to open revolt against Toussaint. His adopted nephew and trusted commander for the Northern Province, Moïse, is implicated, tried for treason, and hurriedly executed. In nothing so much as this does Toussaint betray the trust and confidence of the people whose liberty he has so valiantly and selflessly fought for. It is a fatal error. Drawing once again on the analogy with the Russian Revolution, James writes: "It was almost as if Lenin had had Trotsky shot for taking the side of the proletariat against the bourgeoisie" (BJ, 238 [284]). And it is in this context of "revolutionary degeneration" (as James calls it) that some months later—in February 1802—Bonaparte's brother-in-law General Leclerc arrives at the head of the initial 16,000-man-strong expedition of reconquest. It is the beginning of the end for Toussaint Louverture. In June, with several of the commanding officers (including Henri Christophe) agreeing to make peace with Leclerc, Dessalines cooperates in having Toussaint arrested. He is ignominiously and with great haste transported into exile in France where, alone in his dungeon at the infamous medieval Fortress of Joux in the Jura Mountains, he dies on April 17, 1803.

The drama is impeccable. In many ways this is James's story of Toussaint Louverture, the most memorable story, the portrait he draws with the most profound subtlety and adoring compassion, with the devoted concern that the reader reads with the same empathy and understanding with which the writer writes. It is at once a moral and political story: the story on the one hand of the kind of heroic agency that can inspire the masses to overcome great odds in their quest for self-determination; and on the other hand, an exploration of the great danger to any revolutionary process, of elitism and high-handedness, and of the bureaucratization and sclerosis that can overtake and undermine revolutionary energies.

IT IS OF course well known that in his location of Toussaint Louverture as the kind of historical actor that he is, James is engaged in a debate internal to Marxism, one of particular importance in the 1930s (and indeed since) to the critique of Stalinism. And it is well known that in this he is indebted to Marx's attempts to rehistoricize the aftermath of the February Revolution in France (1848–51) in *The Eighteenth Brumaire of Louis Bonaparte*. The now famous aphorism at the beginning of this book—"Men make their own history, but they do not make it just as they please; they do not make it under circumstances chosen by themselves, but under circumstances, given and transmitted from the past"[31]—is a source of considerable leverage for James's endeavor to hold the tension between the claims of agency and the claims of structure.[32] This is why James turns the aphorism first one way—"Great men make history, but only such history as it is possible for them to make" (BJ, viii [x])—and then another—"Great men make history and Toussaint made the history he did because he was the man he was" (BJ, 70 [91]). But what interests me here is less this dialectic of agency and structure per se (that is, the question of the metaphysics of causal determinations) and more the moral implications of the figuration of the heroic. In *The Black Jacobins* Toussaint is not merely an agent; he is a *hero*. And in this figuration of Toussaint I want to suggest that James has sources other than Marxism, sources that are to be found in the Romantic Victorian admiration—indeed reverential admiration—for the hero as an inspiring man of action and exemplary achievement who stands out against the crowd.

Hero worship, as Houghton describes it, was a nineteenth-century preoccupation. In drawing the contrast between the Victorian attitude toward the hero and that of the previous century, he writes:

When Hume and Gibbon submitted the heroic to the cold glance of reason, they tended to see it as a mask to hide selfish ambition or else a patent form of madness and delusion (that is, of enthusiasm in the derogatory sense). But when enthusiasm became a virtue second only to earnestness, the Romantic-Victorian eye brought with it the power to see man as a hero and the heart to respond with the appropriate worship.[33]

This moral attitude toward the hero animated a wide swathe of mid-Victorian intellectuals, from Tory luminaries such as Thomas Carlyle and John Ruskin to Whig liberals like John Stuart Mill and Charles Kingsley. Or to put the matter somewhat differently: since, arguably, Marxism is itself a child of German Romanticism (at least as much as of the German and Scottish Enlightenments), both Marx and James are indebted to a larger nineteenth-century moral-aesthetic of the man-of-action in which Hegel's idea of the hero as a "World-Historical Individual" plays a significant part. For Hegel, in his 1830–31 lectures on *The Philosophy of History*, "great historical men" (Alexander, Caesar, and Napoleon are the ones he names) are men in whose aims the historical Idea or Truth strives toward self-consciousness. "They may be called Heroes," Hegel writes, "inasmuch as they have derived their purposes and their vocation, not from the calm, regular course of things, sanctioned by the existing order; but from a concealed fount—one which has not attained to phenomenal, present existence—from that inner Spirit, still hidden beneath the surface. . . . They are men, therefore, who appear to draw the impulse of their life from themselves; and whose deeds have produced a condition of things and a complex of historical relations which appear to be only their interest, and their work."[34]

James, it is true, is not likely to have read Hegel's lectures on history before (or while) writing *The Black Jacobins* (his study of Hegel comes later, in the United States in the 1940s). But one link between the German Romantic sources of Hegel's hero worship and Victorian Romanticism is, of course, to be found in Thomas Carlyle, whose work James most certainly knew, in all likelihood thoroughly. In his ideas on history, and in particular on the function of the hero in history, Carlyle was influenced in a profound but complicated way by Goethe, Fichte, and Novalis.[35] It is through them, at least in part, that his reverence for the man of genius takes the messianic shape that it does. Clearly James would not have shared Carlyle's infamously racist estimate of the worth of blacks[36] or his ridiculing contempt for democracy,[37] but he would, I think, have found much to embrace in his portraits of Cromwell and Napoleon and, in general, in his idea of the role of great men in history. It may therefore be useful to consider briefly Carlyle's well-known lectures on heroes and the heroic in history to gain an appreciation of the Victorian Romanticist conventions of heroic figuration in which, I argue, James's representation of Toussaint Louverture as an indomitable revolutionary hero participates.[38]

Carlyle says in the first paragraph of the first lecture:

> Universal History, the history of what man has accomplished in this world, is at bottom the history of the Great Men who have worked here. They were the leaders of men, these great ones; the modellers, patterns, and in a wide sense creators, of whatsoever the general mass of men contrived to do or to attain; all things that we see standing accomplished in the world are properly the outer material result, the practical realisation and embodiment, of Thoughts that dwelt in the Great Men sent into the world: the soul of the whole world's history, it may justly be considered, were the history of these (H, 1).

Carlyle has no truck with the (as he calls it) "melancholy" view of history, as much Whig as Utilitarian, according to which men are to be understood as products of their time. "He was the 'creature of the Time,' they say; the Time called him forth, the Time did everything, he nothing" (H, 12). As Carlyle says, there have been occasions when time seems to call loudly, and no one appears. "The great man, with his free force direct out of God's own hand, is the lightening" that kindles the "dry dead fuel" of time (H, 13).

The chief characteristic of the hero is sincerity. More sublime than grace, more authentic than reason, sincerity is a moral force that connects the actor to his action or belief or idea (the gendered assumption here is Carlyle's, though it was also James's). It is what redeems the heretical doctrines of Muhammad: earnestness, faith, fearlessness, honesty—these are the virtues that make up sincerity (H, 67). Sincerity is the very measure of all worth, as Carlyle repeats. And it is sincerity, not novelty, which makes for originality (H, 125–26). But sincerity also makes for the quality of "great-hearted simplicity" which all heroes have. It is this that allows them that sympathy or pity with which they connect to the world around them. The hero is also an embattled soul. He is, like Dante descending into hell to discover the truth, "a captive struggling to free himself" (H, 92). His immanent perfection is born of suffering and travail. And yet he knows that the burden he carries is a burden of truth, straight from the "Infinite Unknown," the "bosom of Nature," the "heart of the world." The word of the hero, Carlyle says, comes "Direct from the Inner Fact of things" (H, 45). The great man, therefore, is a very force of nature, springing up from some inarticulate deep to give inspiration and leadership to those less blessed. What he sees no one else can, because he sees beyond the superficial semblance of things into their inner reality. The hero, says Carlyle, sees "through the shows of things," into the soul of the truth (H, 55). He has a depth of vision. This was the greatness of Shakespeare, his "calm perspicacity" (H, 104). As a consequence, the hero is an isolated man. Like Cromwell, the hero is unable entirely to share himself with others. He is a man of silences, reticence, a man who withdraws into himself and keeps his own counsel without "wearing his heart upon his sleeve for daws to peck at" (H, 220). As Carlyle waxes lyrical about them: "The great silent men! Looking round on the noisy inanity of the world, words with little meaning, actions with little worth, one loves to reflect on the great Empire of Silence. The noble silent men, scattered here and there, each in his department; silently thinking, silently working; whom no Morning Newspaper makes mention of! They are the salt of the Earth" (H, 224).

James's Toussaint is one of these original men, a classic Romantic hero from a late Victorian age. Singular and single-minded, more "world-deep" than "world-wide" (a phrase Carlyle uses in his description of Dante), alone and inward, grave and taciturn, reading his Raynal late into the night, endlessly repeating to himself the memorized phrases: "A courageous chief only is wanted. Where is he, that great man whom Nature owes to her vexed, oppressed and tormented children? Where is he? He will appear, doubt it not; he will come forth and raise the sacred standard of liberty" (BJ, 17 [25]). In James's account, Toussaint lives the terrible struggle within his soul to give birth to his vision of a new society. He resists its formation. At the outset he is unsure. And yet, finally, he is driven, despite himself, overcoming a powerful counter-inclination, to heed the voice of truth that he and he alone carries for his people, the insight with which he is blessed and which is his to give to the world. To be sure, James's vision of the hero is a much more secular one than Carlyle's; he does not share Carlyle's apocalyptic sense of the divine will shaping the hero's mastery of the elemental chaos. And for James, moreover, history consists of a progressive movement, not, as it is in Carlyle, an endless cycle.[39] But, nevertheless, his Toussaint is very much infused with a Carlylean idea of the heroic.

It is interesting to note that the idea of the heroic functions in *The Black Jacobins* in a way that it does not, for example, function in either Michelet's *History of the French Revolution* or Trotsky's *History of the Russian Revolution*, those two classic histories of revolution on which, I have suggested, James leaned in the emplotment of his own story. For Michelet there are no individual heroes, strictly speaking. There is in his *History*, to be sure, a warm admiration for the abbé Sieyes, from whose speech in the assembly on June 10, 1789, Michelet marks the moment when "the vessel of the Revolution, in spite of storms and calms, delayed, but never stopped, sails onwards to the future" and whose "simple formula," the "title of National Assembly," "contained the Revolution" (HFR, 108, 236).[40] But the abbé Sieyes is not figured in the historical narrative as a hero in the way that Toussaint is. Indeed, Michelet is quite explicit and deliberate about this subordination of the hero. He has a suspicion, as he says cynically, of "the party leaders, those heroes of the prepared scene" (HFR, 13). For him: "The chief actor is the people."[41] And in order to "restore," he says, "the latter to its proper position," he has had to "reduce to their proportions those ambitious puppets . . . in whom, till now, people fancied they saw, and have sought for, the secret transactions of history" (HFR, 12). For the metaphysical Michelet, in short, it is the "spirit of the Revolution" itself that is the only real hero of his story.

Similarly, in Trotsky's *History*, the hero-function is muted (it is not completely absent). For Trotsky, the history of the revolution is not about great men so much as about the "forcible entrance of the masses in the realm of rulership over their own destiny" (HRR, 1:vii). And although there is no question that Lenin is the most revered personage and in some sense towers head and shoulders over everyone else, he is not really a hero in the sense of embodying the whole spirit of the historical moment. Lenin is figured much as the classical Marxist midwife of history: "As air currents carry seeds, the whirlwinds of the revolution scattered the ideas of Lenin" (HRR, 3:24).[42] He, better than anyone, understands its drift, the changing shapes of the opportunities it provides, and thus knows when to seize the time. Trotsky's story is partially the story of the gradual elevation and spread of "the name of Lenin," but he is not, like

Cromwell in Carlyle's story or Toussaint in James's, identified with the course of history itself.[43]

III

I have been sketching the mode of emplotment of *The Black Jacobins* and the distinctive use it makes of the figure of the hero. To grasp what it is that has given compelling force to this mode of emplotment, however, and especially to the place of the heroic in its dramatic narrative, it is necessary to inquire into the ideological problem-space into which that work inserted itself in the 1930s, the context of argument—to recall Quentin Skinner's terms—in relation to which it constituted itself a distinctive move. Two interconnected aspects of this ideological context, in particular, will interest me. One is the context of raced—and racist—discourse that shaped the ideological construction of the black in the first decades of the twentieth century. The central question at the heart of the problem of race was the question of the humanity and achievement of blacks. The other is the context of colonialist discourse that shaped the ideological construction of the colonized in the interwar years. And the crucial question animating this context of argument concerned the capacity of non-European people for self-government, for sovereignty. These contexts of argument, while they overlapped in significant ways, while they often drew from each other a common set of terms, themes, and images, were by no means synonymous. Not all blacks (using the term here to mean Africans and people of African descent) were members of the colonized, strictly speaking; and not all the colonized were black. My aim in what follows, I should underline, is designed less to provide an exhaustive historical account of these contexts than to identify the conditions that make intelligible the aspects of James's text with which I am chiefly interested.

THE SPECIFIC FEATURE of *The Black Jacobins* that I want to attend to here is the operation in the story it tells of a particular theme, namely, "vindicationism." This is a theme, of course, that has been central to Black Nationalist and Pan-Africanist writing in North America, Africa, and the Caribbean since at least the latter half of the nineteenth century.[44] Robert Hill has alerted us to the way in which *The Black Jacobins* participates in this discourse of vindicationism.[45] He reminds us, moreover, that vindicationism is indeed the theme of one of James's earliest known essays, "The Intelligence of the Negro," published in *The Beacon* in August 1931, the year before he left Trinidad for England.[46] The essay was a rebuttal of the claims made by Sidney Harland in an article entitled "Race Admixture," published in the previous issue—July 1931—of the same journal.[47]

Harland, a senior teacher at the Imperial College of Tropical Agriculture in Trinidad, had set out a case for the inferiority of blacks to whites and, among other racist imputations, had cast doubt on the intelligence of Toussaint Louverture. Beginning with the assertion that, "hitherto opinions about races and their hybrids have been arrived at by mental processes which are entirely irrational," Harland offered to present an argument about racial hierarchy from a strictly "biological point of view."[48] Essentially Harland wanted to establish the salience of the relationship between race and intelligence. Scanning the "results" of various experiments he concluded that "while it is not apparent to what extent the negro is inferior in intelligence to the white man, there is little doubt that on average he is inferior."[49] He then went on to invoke Francis Galton's 1869 book, *Hereditary Genius: An Inquiry into Its Laws and Consequences*, in which the author had set out a classificatory scale for grading intelligence and linking it to such features as race.[50] Comparing the "Negro with the Anglo-Saxon for qualities capable of producing judges, statesmen, scientists, artists and divines," said Harland, we "are met by the fact of great social disabilities in the negro."[51] Even Toussaint Louverture found himself placed in Class F, "the lowest of the superior classes." "I think," intoned Dr. Harland, "that all those who have had very much to do with the negro, and I think I am fortunate because I have actually taught them in schools, will not be inclined to dispute the validity of Galton's conclusions."[52]

Needless to say, Harland's self-confidence was quite misplaced. The intellectuals around *The Beacon*—Albert Gomes, Alfred Mendes, Ralph de Boissiere, C. L. R. James—were men of an antiestablishment cast of mind. The journal's purpose, after all, was social criticism. And James's intervention, not surprisingly, was swift and incisive. It is particularly important, moreover, because in his defense of the insulted Toussaint Louverture we see him prefigure some of the essential elements of his argument in *The Black Jacobins*. Tacking between high irony and outrage, and disclaiming that he will make "excessive claims for West Indian negroes,"[53] the strategy James deploys against Harland is twofold. First, he criticizes him for scientific incompetence and ignorance ("The kind of proof he offers is a measure of the kind of proof he accepts").[54] Calling upon successive editions of that august bastion of scientific authority, the *Encyclopaedia Britannica*, James shows that between 1884 (the ninth edition) and 1911 (the fourteenth) there is in fact a shift away from the idea that blacks are inferior in "mental capacity." Second, in Harland's use of Galton's scheme of classifying types of ability, he finds not merely ignorance but "raw dishonesty."[55] James dismisses the assessment of Toussaint Louverture's intelligence as an "absurdity" and, relying in particular on the recently published work of Percy Waxman, *The Black Napoleon* (a book he will later declare "superficial"),[56] rehearses the familiar virtues that animate the episodes in Toussaint's "marvellous career" — the passionate faithfulness to the cause of liberty, the singular courage, the diplomatic skill, the elegant and enlightened statesmanship, the administrative dexterity, indeed all the qualities that enabled him to rise from ex-slave coachman to commander-in-chief in the space of a mere decade.[57]

It is easy to see in this that James is interpellated in the problem-space of vindicationism. While he professes personal disinterest in the matter of race ("I am not 'touchous' on the race question"),[58] he is nevertheless certainly touched by the demand to confront and repudiate the affront of racism's slander and to defend the integrity and equality of his race through what Hill felicitously refers to as the "work of vindication."[59] What is the character of this discourse of black vindicationism? What is the ideological problem-space that best illuminates its appeal to people like James? Or if you like, what is the ideological question about race to which vindicationism may be understood to constitute an answer? My aim in this, however, is to do more than identify this context of raced and racist questions. My aim is to link vindicationism to the wider formal features of the mythos of Romance and, in particular, to the figuration of the hero. And, of course, my longer-range hope in this, as the reader may now well anticipate, is to offer a doubt as to whether the problem-space of questions that gave compelling force to this trope of vindicationism is one we, in the postcolonial present, continue to inhabit.

IT IS NOW a commonplace that in the second half of the nineteenth century, the mid- to late-Victorian age, the character of raced discourse — or more properly, the debate on the "Negro Question" — underwent a significant alteration.[60] From the optimism and humanitarianism of the abolitionists and philanthropists of the early decades of the nineteenth century, there was a shift in the 1850s and 1860s to an aggressive and openly derogatory racialism undergirded by the new science of anthropology and espoused by travel writers, scholars, missionaries, and politicians.[61] Among an increasing (and increasingly influential) number of mid-Victorians there was a frustrated and agitated sense that the great project of slave emancipation had failed to live up to their expectations. The West Indian plantation economies were continuing their long decline, and the black ex-slave population had not, by and large, cultivated the habits and moral virtues that the philanthropic liberals had hoped they would. The "outbreak" of the "Jamaica Insurrection" in October 1865 only sharpened their sense of resentment at black ingratitude and confirmed the emerging opinion that blacks were, if not completely uneducable in the superior ways of white Englishmen, then at least so far from that prospect as to require a prolonged period of coercive paternalism to set—and keep—them upon the path. Thomas Carlyle's 1853 pamphlet "Discourse on the Nigger Question" was only the most deliberately provocative version of a view of "Quashee" gaining considerable prominence among mid-Victorians. This view was given a scientific patina by the appearance in the work of people like James Hunt and Robert Knox— and in authoritative places like the Encyclopaedia Britannica—of a view of race as fixed, inscribed in the very anatomy of the body.[62]

This transformation in racial attitudes, it is important to understand, is not really a shift in the content of the stereotype of the black. As much in the early period as in the late, the standard and pervasive view of Africans and their descendants in the West Indies is as inferior savages, either childlike in their grinning simplicity or fearfully barbaric, insatiably lustful, and irrationally prone to violence. Africa is assumed to be a dark and debased place in need of civilization. Thus, no sensible nineteenth-century intellectual—not even the great paragon of liberal tolerance and open-mindedness, John Stuart Mill, whose On Liberty (1859) is a product of this age of doubt—believed in the inherent moral and intellectual equality of blacks. But whereas among the philanthropic liberals of the 1830s and 1840s such as William Wilberforce and Thomas Buxton there was a lively sense that a sturdy regime of graduated reforms would help break down the differences between blacks and whites, people like Anthony Trollope, Charles Kingsley, and James Anthony Froude, toward the end of the century, wrote as though these differences were immutable—or at least very nearly so.[63] For them, no black could ever be quite the equal of any white.

Victorian discourse on the "Negro Question," therefore, was itself cast in the language of vindication. This was because the worthiness of the black could not be assumed. It had to be demonstrated. But where the abolitionist Whigs of the first third of the nineteenth century were prepared to believe that emancipated West Indian blacks could prove themselves worthy of inclusion in the fellowship of civilized humanity, and indeed urged them to vindicate themselves and their race, late Victorians were more apt to believe that such proof was impossible and to ridicule as absurd efforts to provide it. It is this *conceit* of Victorian racism, the *arrogance* of this exclusion or denial that, in my view, the element of vindicationism in Black Nationalist writing is a response to. Black vindicationism, in other words, is not merely a response to a sense of oppression or exploitation, but a response to a sense—indeed an *aggrieved* sense— of being wronged, or worse, slandered. (It is notable, then, that vindicationism is largely an *intellectual*'s response to wrong; it is one intellectual demanding the recognition withheld by another who not only has the political power to withhold it, but also the social authority to make the withholding matter.) Vindicationism is a response not only to subjection but to subjection in which something vital to the integrity of one's sense of being—honor, dignity, pride, for example—has been impugned or traduced or wounded or besmirched. Vindicationism is therefore at once a practice of providing evidence to refute a disagreeable or incorrect claim and a practice of *reclamation*, and, indeed, of *redemption* of what has been denied. This is why moral indignation—indeed, outrage—is most often the tone of black vindicationist discourse.

IN THIS DISCOURSE of vindicationism, Haiti has very often played a prominent role.[64] For New World Black Nationalists, as Wilson Moses has suggested, the Haitian people have always been revered as "the heroic vanguard of the spirit of black pride and independence."[65] For some, like the Reverend James Theodore Holly, an advocate of Haitian emigrationism in the middle of the nineteenth century, Haiti was figured as a place of racial promise. In the 1850s he delivered and subsequently published an extraordinary lecture on Haiti entitled, "A Vindication of the Capacity of the Negro Race for Self-Government, and Civilized Progress."[66] In this lecture Holly proposed to earnestly "defend the inherent capabilities of the negro race, for self-government and civilized progress" ("VNR," 21). His view was that Haitian history, from the revolution to his present, would arm him with the materials to "prove and defend" his points concerning the capacities and the achievements of blacks. I want to spend some time with the language of Holly's argument because I think that in it one can see clearly the connection between Romanticism and vindicationism that animates *The Black Jacobins*. My purpose of course is not to suggest that James is merely repeating Holly but to show something of the ideological conventions that they both depend on in performing the work of vindication.

In setting out his reasons for undertaking his defense of the capabilities of blacks, Holly explained: "Notwithstanding the remarkable progress of philanthropic ideas and humanitarian feelings, during the last half century, among almost every nation and people throughout the habitable globe; yet the great mass of the Caucasian race still deem the negro as entirely destitute of those qualities, on which they selfishly predicate their own superiority" ("VNR," 21). At the same time, Holly continued, he was directing his discourse not solely at those who "openly traduce the negro," but as well at the "noisy agitators of the present day" (presumably he has in mind the white abolitionists) "who would persuade themselves and the world, that they are really christian philanthropists" but who have "lurking in their heart of hearts, a secret infidelity in regard to the real equality of the black man, which is ever ready to manifest its concealed sting, when the full and unequivocal recognition of the negro, in all respects, is pressed home upon their hearts" ("VNR," 21). Indeed so "overpowering" is the influence of the vilification and debasement of the black that "many of the race themselves, are almost persuaded that they are a brood of inferior beings" ("VNR," 22). Against these "vile aspersions and foul calumnies" heaped upon his race, Holly sets out a "fearless but truthful vindication" ("VNR," 22).

But Holly's vindicationism is more than refutation or truth telling. He has, in fact, another—and inspirational—project in mind.

> I wish hereby to contribute my influence—however small that influence—to effect a grandeur and dearer object to our race than even this truthful vindication of them before the world. I wish to do all in my power to inflame the latent embers of self-respect, that the cruelty and injustice of our oppressors, have nearly extinguished in our bosoms, during the midnight chill of centuries, that we have clanked the galling chains of slavery. To this end, I wish to remind my oppressed brethren, that dark and dismal as this horrid night has been, and sorrowful as the general reflections

are, in regard to our race; yet, notwithstanding these discouraging considerations, there are still some proud historic recollections, linked indissolubly with the most important events of the past and present century, which break the general monotony, and remove some of the gloom that hang[s] over the dark historic period of African slavery, and the accursed traffic in which it was cradled ("VNR," 23).

For Holly, the Haitian Revolution was one of the "noblest, grandest, and most justifiable outbursts against tyrannical oppression that is recorded on the pages of the world's history" ("VNR," 23). For here, a "race of almost dehumanized men" oppressed by centuries of slavery "arose from their slumber of ages, and redressed their own unparalleled wrongs with a terrible hand in the name of God and humanity" ("VNR," 23). In this, he maintains, the Haitian Revolution far surpassed the American Revolution in significance. Where the latter was a revolution of "people already comparatively free, independent, and highly enlightened," the Haitian revolution "was a revolt of an uneducated and menial class of slaves" against oppressors who not only demanded a tax on their labor but "also usurped their very bodies" ("VNR," 24). There was no comparison, therefore, between them. "Never before," Holly contended, "in all the annals of the world's history, did a nation of abject and chattel slaves arise in the terrific might of their resuscitated manhood, and regenerate, redeem, and disenthrall themselves: by taking their station at one gigantic bound, as an independent nation, among the sovereignties of the world" ("VNR," 25).

The story that Holly then goes on to narrate is concerned not only to refute the imputations of black ignorance, barbarism, and cowardice but to demonstrate the calculated foresight and calm intelligence of the Haitian blacks. When news of the French Revolution arrives in San Domingo it precipitates a "furious excitement" among the whites. In contrast, the blacks demonstrated a "stern self-possession" and continue to "toil and delve on, in the monotonous round of plantation labor" because they knew that "the hour of destiny, appointed by the Almighty, had not yet tolled its summons for him to arise, and avenge the wrong of ages" ("VNR," 27, 28).

Under the leadership of the courageous but narrowly self-interested Vincent Ogé the "freed men of color" make their move and bring back from revolutionary France the decree (of March 8, 1790) granting them equal political rights with the whites. Their case is met with violence from the "infatuated colonists," and Ogé is captured, tortured, and hanged. As hope of liberty seems about to fade completely from view, the blacks themselves take matters into their own hands. This, Holly says, is "the ominous moment reserved for the chained bondman to strike; and he rises now from his slumber of degradation in the terrific power of brute force" ("VNR," 41). Beginning with Boukman, the "Spartacus of his race," there is a quick succession of leaders before Toussaint Louverture makes his way to center stage. From here until he is removed the drama belongs completely to him:

> No man was more competent to sway the civil destinies of these enfranchised bondmen than he who had preserved such an unbounded control over them as their military chieftain, and led them on to glorious deeds amid the fortunes of warfare recently waged in that island. And no one else could hold that responsible position of an official mediator between them and the government of France, with so great a surety and pledge of their continued freedom, as Toussaint L'Ouverture. And there was no other man, in fine, that these rightfully jealous freemen would have permitted to carry out such stringent measures in the island, so nearly verging to serfdom, which were so necessary at that time in order to restore industry, but one of their own caste whose unreserved devotion to the cause of their freedom, placed him beyond the suspicion of any treacherous design to re-enslave them.
>
> Hence by these eminent characteristics possessed by Toussaint in a super excellent degree, he was the very man for the hour; and the only one fitted for the governorship of the colony calculated to preserve the interests of all concerned ("VNR," 44).

Even in his capture and hasty dispatch in a "vessel already held in readiness for the consummation of the vile deed," Toussaint shows himself superior in every way to the scheming and dishonorable French ("VNR," 51). For "the negro's heart had not yet descended to that infamous depth of subtle depravity, that could justify him in solemnly and publicly taking an oath, with the concealed and jesuitical purpose, of thereby gaining an opportunity to deliberately violate the same" ("VNR," 50–51). It is only in being capable of a "double-dyed act of villainy" that they are able to gain the confidence of Toussaint, a man so untouched by corruption that he would never have suspected the plot against him. Yet even as Toussaint is taken away, other leaders "fill up the gap now left open," especially that "heroic but sanguinary black chief, Dessalines" who leads his people to independence on January 1, 1804 ("VNR," 52). "That freedom and independence are written in the world's history in the ineffaceable characters of blood; and its crimsoned letters will ever testify of the determination and of the ability of the negro to be free, throughout the everlasting succession of ages" ("VNR," 54).

THE BLACK JACOBINS is a direct heir to this vindicationism that operates through the Romance of Haiti and the figuration of a heroic Toussaint Louverture. Like the Reverend Holly's lecture, it too is a repudiation of the "unjust aspersions of our unprincipled oppressors" and a vindication of "the capacity of the negro race for self-government and civilized progress" ("VNR," 63). Like Holly, James "summoned the sable heroes and statesmen of that independent isle of the Caribbean Sea, and tried them by the high standard of modern civilization, fearlessly comparing them with the most illustrious men of the most enlightened nations of the earth" ("VNR," 63). Undeniably, there is as much that separates the revolutionary Marxist James from the Christian emigrationist Holly as joins them. Indeed, James was not offering a solution to a "race" problem as such. James was antagonistic to the kind of race determinism espoused by nationalists like Marcus Garvey and even to some extent by his friend George Padmore after his break with Moscow. As he declared in a well-known passage in The Black Jacobins: "The race question is subsidiary to the class question in politics, and to think of imperialism in terms of race is disastrous. But to neglect the racial factor as merely incidental is an error only less grave than to make it fundamental."[67] At the same time The Black Jacobins does participate in the doctrine of Romantic racialism and African civilizationism. Of course, Holly's Christian Providentialism is replaced in James by a Marxist secular hidden hand guiding and securing the future redemption of black people. In both, however, the progressivist assertion of the vindication of the right of blacks to dignity and intellectual regard is the central plank of the scaffolding on which the ideological claim to self-determination stands.

IV

Finally, in order to properly appreciate the cultural-political purchase of The Black Jacobins, its ability—and for so long—to make a persuasive claim on oppositional modes of political conduct, we have one more investigation to make, namely, an inquiry, however brief, into the conceptual context that sustains the argument it makes about historical change. Here what interests me is the salience — or rather the *continued* salience — of one of the concepts that enables *The Black Jacobins* to perform the labor of criticism it has been widely — and justly — understood to perform: the modern idea of revolution. *The Black Jacobins*, as I have repeatedly said, is not only the study of a revolution. It is a *revolutionary* study of a revolution. In it, therefore, the concept of revolution does both descriptive as well as appraisive work; indeed, revolution defines the *normative* horizon of its political desire.

How might we usefully historicize the concept of revolution? In my view, the stakes are crucial in the sense that if you are persuaded by the exercise of historicization undertaken here, there is no way back to the sociological functionalism that reads books like *The Black Jacobins* through normative questions about the true causes of revolution (how much economic crisis, how much state and how much intellectual will and how much ideology go into making them) or what causes them to go bad and what might induce them not to do so, and so on. These questions play themselves out in a game of political discourse and theoretical discourse about politics that unreflexively presupposes that revolution is a concept that can and ought to continue to make a claim on our political calculations and our political hopes. In my view, it is precisely this assumption that has to be brought into question. In other words, it seems to me that what is crucial is whether the cognitive-political world in which we live continues to make revolution plausible to think — and think *with* — as criticism.

As a number of scholars (among them Reinhart Koselleck and Hannah Arendt) have reminded us, the concept of revolution, as we understand it today, is a distinctively modern one.[68] Prior to the modern age, and the French Revolution most particularly, "revolution" had a rather different signification. It connoted a closed cycle of perpetual returns. As Arendt put it, the successive changes that occurred did not appear to introduce something entirely new, they "did not interrupt the course of what the modern age has called history, which, far from starting with a new beginning, was seen as falling back into a different stage of its cycle, prescribing a course which was preordained by the very nature of human affairs and which therefore itself was unchangeable."[69] Koselleck and Arendt suggest that this whole conceptual framework altered with the Enlightenment. For the thinkers of the Enlightenment, everything was seen and described in terms of change and upheaval. Every facet of life—law, morals, religion, economy, state—had now to be comprehended through change, and change moreover in a *progressive* direction. Revolution understood as a repetition of political orders already known in advance was displaced by a concept of revolution as a form of change that looked forward into an unknown and novel future. It is, of course, in this sense that Arendt (to whom I return at the end of this book) speaks so memorably of revolutions as "the only political events which confront us directly and inevitably with the problem of beginning."[70] Revolution now depended—among other things—upon an idea of historical time that was moving upward and onward in a rhythmic series of successive stages. In this way, revolution "congealed into a collective singular," as Koselleck puts it. It became an abstract meta-historical concept; it assumed transcendental significance; it became a regulative principle of knowledge whose place could be formulated within a speculative Philosophy of History.[71] And this metahistoricity now formed the cognitive background against which all other features of the modern concept of revolution—as well as the concept of modernity itself—would have to be understood.

The argument I wish to advance here is that the narrative of revolution is inseparable from the larger narrative of modernity and inseparable, therefore, from those other cognitive and ethical-political categories that constitute and give point to that narrative—categories such as "nation," "sovereignty," "progress," "reason," and so on. It is undeniable that in the past two decades or so there has been a profound challenge—both a philosophical and a political challenge—to these hitherto familiar categories. And my question is this: what happens to our appreciation of anticolonial texts like *The Black Jacobins* when both the cognitive and the political space for that narrative of revolution alters in such a way that these categories are no longer available for—perhaps no longer even intelligible within—the labor of criticism that once defined them? At least part of the answer is that our appreciation of *The Black Jacobins* has to be revised in such a way as to make visible the distinctive conceptual labor that "revolution" has performed in its anticolonial narrative.

One way of making this labor visible is through a form of analysis suggested some years ago by Bernard Yack in *The Longing for Total Revolution*.[72] As I have already suggested (in the prologue), Yack elaborates a form of inquiry that bears some resemblance to Collingwood's logic of question and answer and Quentin Skinner's adaptation of it. In his book, Yack is less interested in the vicissitudes of a concept's history as such and more interested in the way the emergence of new concepts, by altering the cognitive conditions for apprehending the world, alters how we think about what ought to be done to improve it.[73] "The awareness of our present inability to satisfy desires," he says, "tends to refocus our uneasiness on the obstacles to achieving this satisfaction. We tend to wonder about what prevents the satisfaction of our desires; and our present uneasiness increases the urgency of such reflections. When we discover the obstacle to our satisfaction we generate a new object of desire: a world without that obstacle to our satisfaction."[74] For Yack, in other words, there is a direct relation between how we perceive the obstacles to our satisfaction and our formulation of the path to overcoming them. Discontent and desire for social transformation may be universal, he argues, but the distinctive character of our longing is shaped by the specific ways in which our dissatisfactions are perceived and described.

> The way the obstacle to such a world is defined shapes the character of new desires and longings. The Platonist who sees the impermanence of the world as the major obstacle to satisfaction will not share the indignation against individuals and institutions of those who long for a world without sin or exploitation. The Marxist who sees a particular form of social interaction as the obstacle to satisfaction will not reject the world in the same way as the Christian or Platonist who sees the ontological condition of man as the source of our dissatisfaction. Uncovering new definitions of the obstacle to a world without sources of dissatisfaction is thus one way to identify new forms of social discontent.[75]

In short, the discovery of new obstacles to the satisfaction of our desires tends to generate a new object of desire, namely, a world in which that obstacle has been overcome. I think that this approach to conceptual inquiry can usefully be understood as a version of the logic of question and answer. Like Collingwood and Skinner, Yack thinks that understanding a proposition is less a matter of elaborating the solution it provides than grasping the problem it purports to resolve. Like them, he is interested in identifying the shape that must have been given to a question for the answer to come out the way it has.

Specifically, Yack argues that many studies of revolutionary discontent have failed to adequately understand the role of new concepts in generating social discontent. This is because they have mistakenly focused on the way these concepts define alternatives to the present social limitations rather than on the way they shape our understanding of these limitations themselves; they have been more concerned with the discovery of new ideals than with the discovery of new objects of discontent. What Yack wants to show, then, is how the development in the last half of the eighteenth century of a new set of concepts makes possible the form of social discontent that issues in the modern longing for total revolution. He shows that this longing for total revolution grows out of the redefinition of that obstacle first suggested in the second half of the eighteenth century, namely, the "dehumanizing" spirit of modern society. Since the eighteenth century, Yack argues, the greatest source of indignation among European intellectuals (especially those educated in the German philosophical tradition) has been the "spirit" of modern social relations. The conditions of modern social life, so it is argued, deform and dehumanize individuals. Yack's concern is to identify and account for the concepts that make possible the designation of the dehumanizing spirit of modern society as the obstacle to a world without social sources of dissatisfaction and to show how this redefinition of the obstacle to our satisfaction generates a new and more intense form of social discontent, a longing for total revolution. In the story he tells—and instructively, it is by and large a story about European Romanticism's argument with the Enlightenment—seeing the dehumanizing spirit of modern society as the obstacle to our satisfaction entails believing at least two things about human life. First, one must think of the "human" as a term of distinction among individual human beings, not just as what distinguishes "man" from "animal." In other words, one must understand the humanity of the human as an achievement, not a species-specific characteristic. Second, one must believe that there is a general spirit of interaction that informs all social phenomena in a given epoch. New ways of thinking about freedom and history, Yack argues, spread these two beliefs especially among German intellectuals at the end of the eighteenth century. In the first place, the use of "human" as a term of distinction developed out of the new understanding of freedom introduced by Rousseau and Kant. For both of them, freedom gives us our distinctively human character in that it allows us to oppose our own ends to those imposed on us by nature and society. In the second place, that strand of historicism associated with Montesquieu began to use the historical comparison of epochs to identify the specific character or spirit of social interaction that informs individual phenomena. Employing in particular ancient to modern comparisons, the peculiar character of contemporary society—and specifically the failure of modern society—was identified and represented. These new attitudes toward human freedom and historical context made possible the new interpretation of the obstacles to a world without sources of dissatisfaction. The Rousseauian-Kantian understanding of human freedom introduced a new way of viewing the failings of social institutions, and the Montesquieuian understanding of history suggested that the sources of fundamental problems were historical and, therefore, changeable.

TO RETURN, THEN, to *The Black Jacobins*, I want to grasp the distinctive way in which James's work participates in the longing for total revolution, and the longing in particular for anticolonial revolution. How does James identify the particular problem with colonial slavery, and what is the connection between this and the anticolonial story he tells? What is the nature of the discontent embodied in *The Black Jacobins*? How does his conception of the obstacles to satisfaction shape his longing for anticolonial revolution? More specifically, what is the relation between the picture of colonial slavery he elaborates and the story of anticolonial revolution he endorses?

The point in posing these questions, needless to say, is not to disarm James's great work. Nor is the issue to criticize the project of anticolonialism of which it was a part. They are, it goes without saying, the conditions of my own postcolonial possibility and I should like to honor that. I am not interested in where, it might be said, *The Black Jacobins* (or anticolonialism more generally) went wrong. My point is to understand how the internal connection between question and answer, between discontent and solution, were constructed in a paradigmatic anticolonial discourse. The important issue, therefore, is not whether *The Black Jacobins* (or again, the anticolonial project more generally) was misconceived, but how it conceived the problem of colonialism it did in fact conceive out of the colonial present it inhabited, and what the implications might be for how we might *reconceive* the problem of the legacy of colonialism from within our own postcolonial present.

In *The Black Jacobins*, the problem of colonial plantation slavery in the Caribbean is pictured in a particular way, namely, as a system of degradation and dehumanization, indeed an all but totally overwhelming system of degradation and dehumanization. The first chapter, "The Property," is devoted to a description of this system. In typical Romantic fashion, James begins by describing how the slave trade destroyed the idyll of precolonial Africa, breaking up traditional tribal life and setting African warring with African. "The stockades of grinning skulls, the human sacrifices, the selling of their own children as slaves, these horrors were the product of an intolerable pressure on the African peoples, which became fiercer through the centuries as the demands of industry increased and the methods of coercion were perfected" (BJ, 1–2 [7]). This, however, was only the beginning of an escalating process of oppression and misery. The Middle Passage followed capture in Africa. And here, as James says with unparalleled poignancy, amidst the festering flesh and the fetid air, the slaves "died not only from the regime but from grief and rage and despair" (BJ, 3 [9]). For those who survived the horrors of the transatlantic passage, next came the auction block where physical brutality was combined with systematic humiliation: "The purchasers examined them for defects, looked at the teeth, pinched the skin, sometimes tasted the perspiration to see if the slave's blood was pure and his health as good as his appearance. Some of the women affected a curiosity, the indulgence of which, with a horse, would have caused them to be kicked 20 yards across the deck. But the slaves had to stand it. Then in order to restore the dignity which might have been lost by too intimate an examination, the purchaser spat in the face of the slave" (BJ, 3 [9]). Finally, despite those who, "ashamed of the behaviour of their ancestors, try to prove that slavery was not so bad after all, that its evils and its cruelty were the exaggerations of propagandists and not the habitual lot of the slaves" (BJ, 7 [13]), James lays bare the barbarisms that constituted the everyday life on the plantations. Not only was the slave subjected to severe and inhumane conditions of work and life, but in order to inspire docility and obedience they were subjected to torture and mutilation. The difficulty, however, as James writes, "was that though one could trap them like animals, transport them in pens, work them alongside an ass or a horse and beat both with the same stick, stable them and starve them, they remained, despite their black skins and curly hair, quite invincibly human beings; with the intelligence and resentments of human beings. To cow them into the necessary docility and acceptance necessitated a regime of calculated brutality and terrorism, and it is this that explains the unusual spectacle of property-owners apparently careless of preserving their property: they had first to ensure their own safety" (BJ, 5 [11–12]). This was the system. And it not only maimed the body of the slaves but it stunted their minds and warped their character. "The majority of the slaves accommodated themselves to this unceasing brutality by a profound fatalism and a wooden stupidity before their masters. 'Why do you ill-treat your mule in that way?' asked a colonist of a carter. 'But when I do not work, I am beaten, when he does not work, I beat him — he is my Negro' " (BJ, 8 [15]).

This description, like all descriptions, has a *point*. Its moral point, obviously, is to show in compelling detail the violence, degradation, squalor, terror, and humiliating subjection that characterized the whole regime of slavery, from the capture on the African continent, through the Middle Passage and the sale on the auction block, to the daily round of life on the Caribbean slave plantation, *so as* to inspire in the reader a shocking disgust. Partly of course the justification for the description is, as James says, that propagandists past and present have sought to give the impression that Africans were happier and better off under slavery in the Americas than they were in their villages in Africa, and this is an image he is especially concerned to refute. But this explicitly moral point is supported by a less visible *conceptual* operation in which colonial slavery (and colonialism more generally) is constructed as a problem or obstacle of a particular kind. And it is the shape given to this description of the problem that will condition the specific solution *sought* and sustain the narrative drive toward it. For James, colonial slavery is defined essentially by what it *denied*: its debasements, its burdens, its repressions, its cruelties, its degradations, its inhumanities, and so on. It is *this* picture of the ill effects of colonial slavery, I argue, that inspires and gives point to the longing for anticolonial revolution. If what is crucial to an understanding of slavery is what it negated, then there is hardly another critical stance to adopt to it than the demand for its immediate overthrow. If what is at stake in a description of slavery is that it maimed and stunted those it subjected to its brutalizing power, then clearly the objective will be an intense longing for the removal of the sources of this brutalization. If you identify the problem of colonialism as essentially one of degradation, then it is hard to offer any other kind of solution than that of anticolonial overcoming. The longing for anticolonial revolution in *The Black Jacobins* is, in my view, inseparable from this image of colonialism as a regime of negative—or rather, negating—power.

This idea—that colonialism was constituted by an essence, namely, a totalizing principle of degradation and dehumanization—became, of course, central to the construction of anticolonial criticism. Perhaps the most schematic and programmatic articulation of it is to be found in Frantz Fanon's *The Wretched of the Earth*. This strategy enabled the formulation and sharp expression of the anticolonial demand—the unequivocal demand for immediate sovereignty. The anticolonial demand operated through the construction of a picture of colonialism as denial, terror, and violence. (I return to this problem of picturing colonialism in chapter 3.)

Now again, it should be clear that I do not mean by this to suggest that colonialism, let alone colonial slavery, was not—in reality—degrading or dehumanizing. That would be absurd. My point is not in any way to diminish the enormity of the colonial past and of the colonial slave plantation past especially, with its unspeakable brutalities and indignities, its everyday practices of racial and sexual violence and humiliation. Nor do I mean to diminish the heroism of those who challenged and confronted their oppressors. My point rather is to demonstrate that in books like *The Black Jacobins* a certain kind of politics has hitherto been derived (and I mean, fruitfully derived) from the construction of a determinate characterization of what the problem to be confronted is. And my point in indicating this is not to censure that work but to enable us to ask whether this is a politics that we want to continue to endorse. In other words, I am not concerned to argue one way or another about what exactly colonialism (or colonial slavery specifically) essentially was—or wasn't. I should like to set that preoccupation aside. Again, not because I think there is nothing to be gained by arguing over the colonial past. To the contrary, in my view there is much to be gained. But I want to keep that argument about the colonial past alert to the present into which it is being drafted as evidence of a world to be overcome in the politics of an imagined future. And therefore my concern is to suggest how picturing colonialism in one way—as a system of totalizing degradation—enables (indeed obliges) the critical response to it to take the form of the longing for anticolonial overcoming or revolution. The question and the answer constitute one integral language-game. Consequently, my argument is that insofar as we formulate our historical discontent around the picture of colonial slavery as degradation and dehumanization there is no way out of that Romantic (and vindicationist) language-game of revolutionary overcoming and rehumanization that supports and sustains it. Or to put the argument the other way round, if we are to set aside the longing for total revolution that has so vitally animated the anticolonial politics of *The Black Jacobins* and that continues to haunt our postcolonial imagination, we shall have to give up the idea that the crucial thing to demonstrate about the (slave) colonial past is its essential degradation and dehumanization.

TO SUM UP my argument so far: I have been concerned in this chapter to link The Black Jacobins to the literary forms and ideological themes and motifs of Romanticism, calling attention to its Romantic mode of emplotment and its heroic figuration. And I have suggested (pace Hayden White, to whose poetics I am, nevertheless, deeply and profoundly indebted) that the choice of this dramatic strategy is not—or not entirely— arbitrary. Rather, it has to be understood as a move (in the sense Quentin Skinner adapts from R. G. Collingwood's logic of question and answer) that C. L. R. James is making in a determinate ideological problem-space, one defined by a certain (racist and colonialist) conception of blacks and their capacity for political sovereignty. This is why the indignantly affirmative vocabulary of vindicationism is the distinctive narrative idiom of its revolutionary Romanticism. But more than this, taking a leaf from Bernard Yack's very subtle exercise, I have wanted to argue that The Black Jacobins depends upon the conceptual salience of the formulation of the question of colonial slavery as essentially a question about totalizing dehumanization; and this formulation, I have argued, obliges one to construe criticism of it in terms of a longing for anticolonial revolution.

But suppose that the question to which the vindicationist story of black anticolonial revolution forms an answer loses its persuasive force? Suppose the questions of slave resistance and anticolonial overcoming are no longer as compelling as they once used to be? Suppose, in other words, our present does not oblige us, as it did James (and a whole generation after him), to fashion a narrative of resistance and liberation? Not, obviously, because forms of domination or racism or asymmetry no longer exist or have been resolved, but rather because the story of liberation presupposed a direction, a teleology, an end toward which we were inevitably moving, and it is no longer as clear today at the beginning of the twenty-first century as it was in 1938 (or 1971, when, as we will see, James returned again to the problem of history in The Black Jacobins) what our options are and where that anti-imperialist emancipation is supposed to lead.

This is my doubt: that the figuring of Toussaint Louverture as the martyred revolutionary hero of a Romantic anticolonial drama is compelling only insofar as the explicit or implicit problem-space into which it is read is one in which the animating demand is the demand to meet and displace a racist and colonial claim about the possibility of black political agency. Without this ideological problem-space, without this demand, the story—while no less brilliant—has less purchase as a strategy for criticizing the present. And this is why I want to focus my attention (in chapters 4 and 5) on another figuring of Toussaint Louverture in *The Black Jacobins*, one not as prominent, it might be true, as the Romantic portrait of the revolutionary hero, but one which may be more important because it is more illuminating for the postcolonial present we inhabit. This is because our present, unlike Toussaint's and unlike James's, does not ring with the strong cadences of revolutionary anticipation. To the contrary, our present is characterized much more by a profound skepticism about the teleologies of nationalist and socialist liberation in which those cadences rang. And therefore if we wish neither to simply lament the passing of that heroic past nor to merely valorize the self-congratulatory present, we may wish to press *The Black Jacobins* in directions it itself signals but, understandably, does not develop.

# THREE

# Conscripts of Modernity

The history of the West Indies is governed by two factors, the sugar plantation

and Negro slavery. That the majority of the population in Cuba was never slave

does not affect the underlying social identity. Wherever the sugar plantation and

slavery existed, they imposed a pattern. It is an original pattern, not European,

not African, not part of the American main, not native in any conceivable sense

of that word, but West Indian, *sui generis*, with no parallel anywhere else.


I

One of the most touching—and at the same time most significant—moments in C. L. R. James's biographical construction of Toussaint Louverture as the kind of man and leader he is imagined to have been is the description of his hero's encounter with the work of the remarkable antislavery philosophe, the abbé Guillaume-Thomas-François Raynal (1713–96). The abbé Raynal was the author of (among many other books) a massive, multivolume treatise on the colonial enterprise, *Philosophical and Political History of the Settlements and Trade of the Europeans in the Two Indies*. First published in 1770, it went through dozens of reprintings over the succeeding decades and quickly established itself on both sides of the Channel as the most incisive antislavery work of the prerevolutionary period. "It was a book famous in its time," James writes, "and it came into the hands of the slave most gifted to make use of it, Toussaint Louverture."[1] Indeed, the encounter between Toussaint and Raynal's *Philosophical and Political History* is one of the most decisive moments in the overall architecture and narrative economy of *The Black Jacobins* because it helps James to establish Toussaint as a figure of enlightened sensibility and modern—indeed, modernist—political desire. If Toussaint Louverture's modernism, and especially his political modernism, is constituted by the radical natural rights tradition of the French Enlightenment (as clearly in James's view it is), it is his fundamental encounter with the abbé Raynal that announces and symbolizes this inaugural intellectual formation.

The abbé Raynal was one of the most eloquent and outspoken critics of slavery in a period in which abolitionism was still inchoately formulated and as yet unaccompanied by serious organization and political agitation.[2] (The *Societé des Amis des Noirs*, remember, was founded in 1788, more than a decade after Raynal's *Philosophical and Political History* was first published and only one year before the outbreak of the French Revolution.) As James notes, at the time of the publication of Raynal's book, French liberalism was in its infancy, and while the Encyclopaedists attacked slavery with spiky satire and lavish deprecations, these attacks were of little weight and were in fact often counterproductive.[3] Raynal's *Philosophical and Political History* was different altogether. It was distinguished first by the fact that it was a systematic and comprehensive analysis of slavery in the Americas, and second (and more important) by the fact that it was not merely fueled by a tone of unmitigated indignation and outrage, but underwritten by an openly revolutionary objective: Raynal stood willing to sanction the insurrectionary violence of the black slaves against the white aristocracy in their bid for freedom. "Whoever justifies so odious a system [as slavery]," he wrote, "deserves the utmost contempt from a philosopher, and from the negro a stab with his dagger."[4] For Raynal, slavery was contrary to humanity, reason, and justice. It was not merely an abomination; it was against nature. So much his philosophe colleagues would have agreed with. But Raynal, who was aware of the 1760 Tacky revolt and the great Maroon war of liberation in Jamaica (1730–39) as well as the diverse practices of slave resistance, was prepared to go further than most (perhaps all) of his contemporaries.

Will it be said, that he who wants to make me a slave does me no injury, but that he only makes use of his rights? Where are those rights? Who hath stamped upon them so sacred a character as to silence mine? From Nature I hold the right of self-defence; Nature, therefore, has not given to another the right of attacking me. If thou thinkest thyself authorised to oppress me, because thou art stronger and more ingenious than I am; do not complain if my vigorous arm shall plunge a dagger into thy breast; do not complain when in thy tortured entrails thou shalt feel the pangs of

death conveyed by poison into thy food: I am stronger and more ingenious than thou; fall a victim, therefore, in thy turn, and expiate
the crime of having been an oppressor.[5]

Though slavery was contrary to reason, Raynal did not believe that right
reason or the reason of right—of any right, however universal in the
scope of its claim—was enough to convince the slave traders and slave
owners of their cruelty. Some other force—one more spontaneous and
elemental—was necessary to accomplish the "revolution"; some upheaval in which nature itself revolted against the suffering to which it
was wrongly subjected. From hence came Raynal's astonishing image of
the rise of a Black Spartacus through whom natural reason would speak
with righteous indignation to reverse the old wrongs and in a torrential
wave carry the enslaved into their deserved freedom.

It was this revolutionary, almost apocalyptic vision of the righteous
self-emancipation of the slaves that distinguished Raynal from his contemporaries. His language was an incitement. And it is through this
incendiary vision that James stages the inception of his hero's education into the vocabulary of political modernity. He allows us to imagine
a classic pedagogical scene of modernist self-fashioning drawn almost
straight out of Rousseau's *Émile*. In the dim flickering light of a slave hut
we can just make out the silhouette of a solitary but determinedly reflective Toussaint, inwardly focused on the project of his self-development.
Shutting out the dejection and squalor of his surroundings, he pores
with diligence and solemn animation over the pages of the *Philosophical
and Political History* which he has found in his master's library. There is
at once surprise and gladness at the new and exhilarating language he
is acquiring and through which he is learning to envision a new future,
and trembling at the implications of responsibility to which he is slowly
being drawn. And in it, James says, he reads over and over again the
rousing passage:

> If self-interest alone prevails with nations and their masters, there
> is another power. Nature speaks in louder tones than philoso-
> phy or self-interest. Already are there established two colonies of
> fugitive negroes, whom treaties and power protect from assault.
> Those lightnings announce the thunder. A courageous chief only
> is wanted. Where is he, that great man whom Nature owes to her
> vexed, oppressed and tormented children? Where is he? He will

appear, doubt it not; he will come forth and raise the sacred standard of liberty. This venerable signal will gather around him the companions of his misfortune. More impetuous than the torrents, they will everywhere leave the indelible traces of their just resentment. Everywhere people will bless the name of the hero who shall have reestablished the rights of the human race; everywhere will they raise trophies in his honour.[6]

In short, in *The Black Jacobins* James's Toussaint Louverture is imagined as a slave who in an act of radical will and self-determination transforms himself into the prefigured image of Raynal's modernist Spartacus.[7] Admittedly, Toussaint will never be merely Raynal's hero, but for James, this will be the Enlightenment idiom that gives conceptual and ideological voice to his emancipationist ambitions.[8]

THERE IS AN important reading of *The Black Jacobins* in which such constructions of Toussaint Louverture are seen as evidence of two very considerable shortcomings in James's approach to the study of the San Domingo Revolution, namely, elitism and Eurocentrism.[9] These criticisms are of course not identical: where one—elitism—principally points to social relational concerns (the internal structuring of the slave population and the relative roles of mass and elite in resistance and rebellion), the other—Eurocentrism—has a more emphatically cultural focus (the relative place of African cultural retentions and continuities in shaping the consciousness of such resistance and rebellion). But they are, nevertheless, interconnected criticisms inasmuch as, arguably, the subaltern perspective of the slave masses is precisely one that affirms and accords primacy to their relative cultural autonomy.

James, so these critics suggest, had a certain inclination to overvalorize Europe (and Western civilization more generally) and the elites who assimilated its ethos and values. He displayed, they find, an insufficient (anthropological and/or philosophical) appreciation of African—or African-derived—cultural practice and, in consequence, tended to diminish the space for its generative role in shaping the insurgent black agency at the base of the social order that made the San Domingo Revolution and made it, moreover, what it was.[10] Needless to say, these are not trivial criticisms of James; they suggest shortcomings that are at once lapses of aesthetic-political taste, moral judgment, and historical understanding. At the same time it is important to recognize and acknowledge that these are not—or anyway not necessarily—deliberately unfriendly criticisms. Quite the contrary, they are often offered by sympathetic readers seeking only to go beyond James, by supplementing him, correcting him, or with late-twentieth-century hindsight, enlarging the ethnographic canvas on which his great story of black resistance and anticolonial revolution is told. This, we will see, is not my view.

Undoubtedly, however, this criticism of *The Black Jacobins* is not easily discounted or ignored. While unambiguously written against the racist historiographical assumptions of its time (in particular the assumption that New World slaves were incapable of self-emancipation and required the intercession of humanitarians and politicians of goodwill),[11] James tells his story largely through the career of the revolution's most famous leader, Toussaint Louverture. Moreover, it is certainly true that there are a large number of passages in *The Black Jacobins* in which James appears to be an unthinking advocate of the virtues of European civilization (as when, for example, he warmly appraises Toussaint Louverture's aspiration to acquire the trappings of European cultivation and learning).[12] And there are a correspondingly small number of passages in which he demonstrates even the remotest knowledge of, let alone sympathy for, retentions of African culture among the San Domingo slaves (one thinks of the dramatic opening of chapter 4 in which James perfunctorily acknowledges the role of *vodoun*).[13] What is more, there are a significant number of passages in which James's characterization of San Domingo blacks (regarding their supposed ignorance, barbarism, and so on) seems shockingly insensitive, even condescending, or worse.[14] So that whereas there are, to be sure, other passages in which James deliberately ironizes the idea of European moral superiority[15] and others again in which he pointedly and contemptuously dismisses the prejudice,[16] on balance the weight of the evidence for Eurocentrism and elitism is hard to disavow. It has to be admitted then that James, that self-described "British intellectual," subscribed to a rather Victorian idea of civilization and the hierarchies and progressivist teleologies this idea depended upon.[17]

James, it is true, offered his own auto-criticism of some aspects of his book's elitism and Eurocentrism. In one of a series of three remarkable lectures on the writing of *The Black Jacobins* given at the (now defunct) Institute of the Black World in Atlanta, Georgia, in the summer of 1971—a lecture significantly entitled "How I Would Rewrite *The Black Jacobins*"— James declared, with that arresting sensitivity to his historical present that we first encounter in the 1938 preface, that were he writing now he would completely recast the perspective from which the story is told.[18] In the first place, he said, he would not depend so heavily on the writings of European observers for his representation of the attitudes of the African slaves. Referring, for example, to the vivid and not unsympathetic late-eighteenth-century description of a gang of slaves at work by the Swiss writer, Justin Girod-Chantrans, James says:

> It's a very famous description and I used it. Today I would not do that. I would write descriptions in which the black slaves themselves, or people very close to them, describe what they were doing and how they felt about the work that they were forced to carry on. I don't blame myself for doing this in 1938; it is a famous description. It is accurate enough, but I wouldn't do that today. I don't want today to be writing and say that's what they said about how we were treated, and I know that information exists in all the material. But it was easy enough in those days to go ahead.[19]

Notice the subtle politics and poetics of identification ("how *we* were treated") through which the voice of James's authorial subject is constructed in this passage. We can almost hear in it the contemporary (late 1960s, early 1970s) cultural-nationalist challenge of Black Power to the historiography of New World slavery specifically and the study of Africans in the Americas in general.[20]

In the second place, following more closely the old example of Michelet's model of the people-as-hero as much as the later work of Georges Lefebvre, the great Marxist historian of the French Revolution, James says that he would now shift the perspective away from Toussaint Louverture himself and tell the story from the point of view of the many lesser-known leaders thrown up by the revolutionary process but overlooked by historians. In 1938 James already had an inchoate sense of this, but in an extraordinary footnote added to the 1963 edition James writes: "Michelet had shown that such was also his view of the French Revolution [that as James quotes Pamphile de Lacroix as saying of San Domingo, it is typically not "avowed chiefs" but "obscure creatures" who give the "signal for revolt"]. But it is in Georges Lefebvre, the great contemporary historian of the French Revolution, who on occasion after occasion exhaustively examines all the available evidence and repeats that we do not know and will never know who were the real leaders of the French Revolution, nameless, obscure men, far removed from the legislators and the public orators."[21] However James, who already had it on Leclerc's account that after Toussaint had been removed from the scene there were still "two thousand leaders to be taken away," now felt that the "real leaders" of the San Domingo Revolution could indeed be identified by the historian.

> You see, in 1971, what I have to say about Lefebvre is that he is concerned with the obscure leader—*I am not.* I am concerned with the two thousand leaders who were there. That is the book I would write. There are two thousand leaders to be taken away. If I were writing this book again, I would have something to say about those two thousand leaders.[22]

These auto-critical gestures, however, are not likely to entirely mollify all of James's admiring readers. Some will insist that James has still not paid sufficient attention to the African cultural logic of the subaltern insurgents in the revolution.[23]

STILL, IN MY view, this kind of criticism of *The Black Jacobins* is beside the point. Or to put it another way (and in terms of the critical language I am commending in this book), my view is that this kind of criticism of Eurocentrism, for instance, only has a point in the context of a particular ideological dispute or problem-space, one in which something is at stake in our own present in the move in the argument that demonstrates that African culture (however that is identified and characterized, a not-insubstantial conceptual problem in itself) was an animating force in the San Domingo Revolution. There is, of course, an important archive of historical scholarship that has sought precisely to demonstrate that African slaves in the New World did not lose their natal culture, that, to the contrary, Africa survived in the "folk" culture or the "little" community of the slaves, and that, moreover, it constituted a fundamental underground resource out of which resistance was possible. When, for example, the remarkable works of Kamau Brathwaite and Monica Schuler on Jamaica and John Blassingame, Lawrence Levine, and Albert Raboteau on the U.S. antebellum South appeared in the early and middle 1970s, they constituted not only work of considerable scholarly excellence but an incisive historiographical intervention, because *in that conjuncture* there was real conceptual and ideological work to be done in demonstrating against the prevailing assumptions that Europe's values did not entirely supplant Africa's in the New World, and consequently that African slaves—and their descendants—always had an alternative moral or cultural ground on which to think and act.[24] I have been offering a doubt, however, as to the continuing critical purchase of this cultural-nationalist history in the conjuncture that constitutes our own postcolonial (and postnationalist) present.[25] I do not mean to suggest that in retrospect it is now apparent, three decades on, that these historians of the African Americas (all of them profoundly distinguished in their own right) got something wrong about the past and stand, as a consequence, in need of correction or revision. That would be the sort of presentist hubris this book is meant to criticize. I mean to suggest, rather, that their reconstructive conceptual moves were made in response to a distinctive (ideological-historiographical) demand, the demand for an answer to a certain kind of question (a decidedly hostile question about the autonomous moral value of Africa in the New World), and my doubt is whether this question continues to be a salient question for us to respond to.

IN THIS CHAPTER, I pursue this doubt in relation to our reading and understanding of The Black Jacobins for our postcolonial present. What is the relevant framework of historiographical questions to be put to this classic book? How best might we think about The Black Jacobins in relation to the problems that have so—and so fruitfully—preoccupied students of the New World African diaspora? A large part of my purpose here will be to lift The Black Jacobins out of the conventional field of concerns about Africa and resistance that have framed its reading and criticism, and to relocate it in a domain of problems in which neither of these—Africa nor resistance—are, properly speaking, at stake, or anyway at stake in the old way. I am going to urge that for our postcolonial present, the relevant problem for The Black Jacobins is not "Europe" understood as a moral space, and therefore the relevant questions are not those formulated with a view to unmasking or correcting its alleged Eurocentrism. Or again, I shall argue that for our postcolonial present the problem for The Black Jacobins is not the "subaltern" one of the resistance or self-emancipation of the enslaved, and consequently the relevant questions are not those concerned with criticizing its tacit or explicit elitism, its devotion to and elevation of Toussaint Louverture, and its elision or nonrepresentation of the dynamic role of the majority of the insurgent slaves. Rather, my contention is that the relevant questions are those posed in terms of the problem of modernity, where modernity is understood in the Foucauldian sense of a positive structure of power, a historical formation of certain constitutive and productively shaping material and epistemological conditions of life and thought. Consequently, the relevant questions are those posed in terms of the new conditions in which the possibility and the idiom of resistance took shape and was articulated. And on this account, the questions that come to the fore are those that recognize Toussaint Louverture as a conscript and not merely as an agent (however resisting an agent) of modernity.

If the previous chapter constituted an exploration of the understanding of *The Black Jacobins* that has so far predominated among its readers and some of the conceptual and ideological sources and assumptions that govern that understanding, this chapter opens a preoccupation with how we might otherwise understand James's text, and why. My plan of work is threefold. First, I discuss two contrasting approaches to the study of the making of the African Americas (taking this term in its hemispheric sense): one tending in the direction of a neo-Herskovitsian concern with the retention of African culture among New World slaves and the significance of that culture in the making of their lives in the Americas, and the other tending in the direction of an emphasis on the slaves' creation of new institutions and practices in the new conditions in which they found themselves in the New World. What interests me is that quite apart from their contrasting preoccupations there is a good deal that these two approaches share, especially the conceptual dependence upon the same image of slavery as essentially a structure of *negative* power, power that represses and restricts, and both are animated by the same ideological demand to decipher the resisting agency that overcomes that limiting or blocking power. My view is that this whole way of "questioning slavery" ought to be set aside and a different complex of questions put in its place[26] — again less because it is wrong than because it sets up a story line of resistant overcoming, a Romantic mode of emplotment that depends for its critical salience on a discernible direction in which (and horizon toward which) overcoming is taking place. I think that our postcolonial present demands a story more attuned to the productive ways in which power has shaped the conditions of possible action, more specifically, shaped the cognitive and institutional conditions in which the New World slave acted. Because New World plantation slavery was a constitutive part of the making of the modern world (something of which *The Black Jacobins* was acutely aware), crucial to this story will be the role of modern power in destroying the old and constructing the new conditions in which the lives of African slaves were lived.

Second, therefore, and following out this line of argument, I will sketch a conception of history and historical change that attends to and comports with this idea of modern power. It will be a conception that draws its inspiration from some of the ways in which Talal Asad has urged us to think about power and historical change. (I have already said that it is from Asad that I take the idea of "conscripts of modernity.") In a recognizably—though by no means reducibly—Foucauldian way, Asad focuses our attention on the constitutive and therefore productively conditioning features of power; what he sets at the center of the analysis is less the actor's volitional subjectivity (her or his agency) than the conditions of possibility for that subjectivity to be and to act. I will argue that for my purposes here, the virtue of Asad's sense of the relation between power and historical change is that it alters the question and answer complex in which the problem of New World slavery might be resituated and opens up cognitive space for new kinds of theoretical intervention in the postcolonial present.

Finally, third, I return via this detour of discussion to the text of *The Black Jacobins* and offer an engagement with some passages from the 1963 appendix, "From Toussaint L'Ouverture to Fidel Castro." The appendix is doubtlessly the best-known revision to the second edition of *The Black Jacobins*, and its importance has never been in question. It is, in many ways, James's historiographical gift to the (then) emerging postcolonial Caribbean nation-states. In my view, however, the significance of the appendix lies in its subtle alteration of the problem about slave plantation power: in the body of *The Black Jacobins* the problem of slave plantation power is located in relation to the construction of a revolutionary narrative (a longing for anticolonial revolution); in the appendix by contrast it is located in relation to the postcolonial story of the making of a civilization. And central to this story is James's depiction of the distinctive modernity of that civilization. I shall suggest that in this formulation of the problem of the slave plantation as a form of modern power his Toussaint Louverture is most usefully understood as a conscript—rather than a resisting agent—of modernity; moreover, I shall urge that his self-fashioning relation to the abbé Raynal's *Philosophical and Political History* is best read in this light as the inaugural negotiation of the colonial conscript's relation to the modern West.

The cultural-historical question of the making of the African Caribbean (and the African Americas more generally) has been dominated by two rival approaches: one focusing on African retentions, the other on Caribbean (or New World) creations. In discussing each, let me stress at the outset, I am not especially interested in the internal integrity and plausibility of the theses they advance. I am not interested in whether or not the demonstration, on the one hand, of African agency and the survival of African cultural practices in the New World, or of the invention, on the other hand, of distinctively Caribbean modes of life and thought is compelling or logically coherent on its own terms. I have a view of the matter, needless to say, but this whole anthropological—or, as the case may be, philosophical—debate has no claim on my concerns here.[27] What does interest me, however, is what the retentionist and creationist formulations are meant to do—to enable—in the respective discursive moves they make in the argument about Africans in the New World. I am interested in this because I want to show that these two approaches are in fact less rival than they are usually taken to be. And my aim in coming at this problem in this way (as I have suggested earlier) is to extract *The Black Jacobins* from the underlying preoccupation of the hegemonic paradigm these approaches have mapped together.

In a book of substantial erudition and one working both sides of the Atlantic, John Thornton has recently rearticulated the thesis of the African cultural agency of the New World slave.[28] Thornton, himself a historian of aspects of Haiti's past,[29] is particularly helpful as an instance of the neo-Herskovitsian thesis because he explicitly sees his work as a revisionist intervention in the debate about the relative roles of Africa and Europe in the making of the Atlantic world, an intervention that is, he says, both post-Eurocentric and postnationalist simultaneously. Both the Eurocentric and the nationalist views, he argues, are inadequate because neither sufficiently accounts for the active participation of Africans as makers of their own history.[30] As he recognizes, the debate about Africans in the Americas hinges "on the issue of the degree to which the exploitation of slavery and the denigration of racism crippled the slaves' ability to maintain and transmit an African culture in the New World."[31] Not surprisingly, then, his own work focuses on such questions as the following: "Did Africans participate in the Atlantic trade as equal partners, or were they the victims of European power and greed?

Were the African slaves in the Americas too brutalized to express themselves culturally and socially, and thus, to what degree was their specifically African background important in shaping Afro-American culture?" Not surprisingly, his conclusions "support the idea that Africans were active participants in the Atlantic world, both in African trade with Europe (including the slave trade) and as slaves in the New World." [32]

Thornton's argument is worked out partly as a disagreement with the direction and emphasis articulated in a famous 1976 essay by Sidney Mintz and Richard Price on the making of African American cultures. [33] In that pathbreaking essay, it will be remembered, Mintz and Price proposed an approach to understanding the African Americans, which, as they said, "refines—rather than discards or disproves—earlier approaches." [34] Synthetic though the general framework was, however, their emphasis was unmistakable. While they did not entirely reject the "retentionist" model (Herskovits is indeed warmly and frequently appreciated), they were doubtful about the formulation of claims to the distinctive "Africanness" of African American cultures. [35] It was not, they maintained, a shared African culture that made the slaves a community; rather, "the Africans in any New World colony in fact became a community and began to share a culture only insofar as, and as fast as, they themselves created them." [36] "To assume," they continue a bit further on, "that the slaves in any colony were somehow committed culturally to one or another path of development both evades the empirical question of what really happened and masks the central theoretical issue of how cultures change." For example, to attribute the form of *vodoun* initiation rites to Dahomey might be justified, on a provisional level.

> But on another, more interesting level, we still face the question of which elements of the ritual were faithfully transmitted, which lost, which modified, and by what processes, so that the Haitian rite of today may be understood for what it is: a truly Haitian innovation, constructed in particular ways and under particular circumstances by particular enslaved Africans, and perpetuated by succeeding generations—doubtless, in ever-changing form—for more than two centuries. [37]

Consequently, in their view, "the organizational task of enslaved Africans in the New World was that of creating institutions—institutions that would prove responsive to the needs of everyday life under the limiting conditions that slavery imposed on them." [38]

Thornton thinks that the emphasis here (if not the argument as a whole) is mistaken, and *Africa and Africans in the Making of the Atlantic World* is a systematic attempt to demonstrate this.[39] "African slaves arriving in Atlantic colonies," he maintains, "did not face as many barriers to cultural transmission" as is often believed. Of course Thornton does not deny that conditions on some plantations sometimes "inhibited the development and transmission of a full cultural life." This would simply be foolish. However, his point is that "where conditions permitted slaves to build their own houses and live in families and raise children, the chances for continuing African culture, creating a new Afro-American culture from the blending of African and European elements, and subsequently transmitting this culture through generations were kept alive."[40] And he continues: "It is clear that no matter how exploitative the institution of slavery was, or how traumatic the Middle Passage and subsequent enslavement were, the condition itself was unlikely to result in a permanent state of psychological shock. Furthermore, even in the most brutal of slave systems, slave communities formed, children were raised, and culture was maintained, altered, and transmitted. Clearly, the condition of slavery, by itself, did not necessarily prevent the development of an African-oriented culture."[41] Or as he puts it later on, African slaves were brought to the Americas "to work, and the slave regime often made incredibly heavy demands, pushing them to, and sometimes beyond, their physical capacity, shortening life spans, and reducing time for cultural life. Nevertheless, masters were not always willing or able to restrict cultural life, group meetings, or networks of friendship. Within the space that the slave regime allowed, the Africans re-created an African culture in America, although it was never identical with the one they had left in Africa."[42]

I HAVE QUOTED at length from both Thornton and Mintz and Price in order to give the flavor of their formulations. As I have already suggested, my interest here is not so much the relative merits of either Thornton's "retentionist" model or Mintz's and Price's "creationist" one. Indeed my interest lies less in what separates them and more in what draws them together. For while Thornton and Mintz and Price have a—perhaps radical—disagreement about how to resolve the question of Africa in black Atlantic cultures, they nevertheless share the formulation of the basic question to be answered, namely, was Atlantic slave plantation power so limiting or stultifying as to prevent or preclude the persistence of African languages, religion, kinship patterns, and so on? Notably, in other words, the debate about Africans in the Americas turns around the construction of a certain image of slave plantation power. For Thornton, no less than for Mintz and Price, slave plantation power is pictured principally as a negative or limiting force, and the central preoccupation is whether or to what extent the regime of plantation slavery restricted, blocked, paralyzed, or deformed the transformative agency of the slave. Thornton and Mintz and Price have manifestly different responses to this virtually identical picture of slave plantation power: Thornton arguing that within and against the limits of plantation slavery, African slaves reproduced their African cultures, and Mintz and Price arguing that within and against these limits the slaves invented a new and distinctively Caribbean life.

In short, both Thornton on the one hand and Mintz and Price on the other turn out to be arguing over the same problem (the genealogy of which would, I believe, well repay the effort).[43] For the one as much as for the others the problem about slavery and power is imagined in such a way as to direct our critical focus at discerning whether and how New World slaves were able to maintain some measure of their autonomous agency—whether the understanding of that agency is argued out in terms of the retention of a ground of African culture from which to act or the capacity for self-reinvention in the new and adverse circumstances of plantation slavery. In a certain sense, Thornton and Mintz and Price are equally animated by a fundamental and sympathetic humanism: the demonstration that African American cultures are, essentially, cultures of resistance. "The inescapable fact in the study of Afro-America," Mintz and Price write, expressing a sentiment Thornton would almost certainly endorse, "is the humanity of the oppressed, and the inhumanity of the systems that oppressed them."[44] Again, I want to stress that I am not saying that this humanist concern is somehow mistaken. Rather my interest is in directing our attention to what this concern obliges. And my argument here is that to construct the problem of slave plantation colonial power as Thornton and Mintz and Price do, namely, as a negative force, obliges one to look for the agency that transgresses it, survives it, overcomes it, and to look in turn for the sources (cultural or otherwise) that enabled or fed that transgression, survival, or overcoming. I am suggesting, therefore, that its critical purchase depends epistemologically on a problem-space shaped by this particular image of New World slavery, and ideologically on whether the question it answers—were enslaved Africans too brutalized by slavery to respond to it with some degree of cultural autonomy?—continues to be one worth having an answer to. My own view is that the demand constituted by this problem-space is no longer one that has a strong claim on us, and therefore we should set it aside and give up with it the question and answer problematic that animates it. My view is there are more fruitful questions to be pursued, questions that turn around a more *constructive* idea of the problem of power, and the modern power of the New World slave plantation, more specifically.

III

Especially in discussions of the worlds brought into being by the diverse transforming powers of the European colonial projects, it is hard to doubt the force of the historical salience of the problem of modernity (conceived as a complex structure of social, economic, juridical, and political relations of knowledge and power).[45] Nowhere is this question of the transforming effects of modern power more evident than in the social formations of slave plantation America. It is widely accepted that New World slavery was part of the very warp and woof of the emergence of the modern age (and it is an acknowledged fact that the seminal assertion of this is owed to *The Black Jacobins*).[46] Not only did the capital accumulation from the slave trade and slave-produced sugar help to stimulate the rise of industrial capitalism and alter the tastes of bourgeois Europe, but the slave plantations were themselves an integral (if territorially displaced) part of the larger complex of relations that constituted that modern world, and the transplanted black slaves, consequently, were integrally modern subjects. So much, perhaps, is reasonably uncontroversial. But all the implications of this depend on how the problem of modernity is formulated and characterized, that is to say, the kind of conceptual labor it is made to perform in the critical or historiographical strategy in which it is deployed. This is what interests me. Setting aside the immediate question of slavery for the moment, in what follows I sketch a contrast between two approaches to the contemporary problem of modernity—one is a prominent and widely admired approach with resonances in studies of the "black Atlantic"; the other is less well appreciated, but I am going to argue that it has a more superior purchase on the postcolonial present than the former does.

In recent years, one distinctive formulation of the problem of modernity has acquired a certain distinction in the humanities and social sciences. This is the idea of "multiple" or "alternative" or "subaltern" modernities. According to this argument—using a succinct articulation of it by Charles Taylor as an illustrative instance—the conventional view of the making of modernity is too narrow or monistic, in effect too Eurocentric in its assumption that there can only be one way to become or to be modern.[47] Insensitive to cultural difference, this conventional view believes that the rise of modernity can be described in a neutral or "acultural" narrative: the story of the development of secular or scientific reason, for example, or the growth of urbanization and industrialization, or the expansion and concentration of the functions of the state. Part of what is wrong with this view, it is urged, is that it tends to "prejudice the case against diversity," and to "predict a future of greater and greater uniformity across cultures."[48] As a consequence it fits neatly with the larger developmentalist narrative of modernity as "a point of convergence," a single end toward which we are all headed. A "cultural" theory of modernity by contrast tells the story of the rise of modernity as a kind of acculturation story, the story of innovation within adaptation. In this view, "transitions to what we might recognize as modernity, taking place within different civilizations, will produce different results, reflecting the civilizations' divergent starting points."[49] In other words, there will not be one single modernity, but multiple modernities. Taylor, it should be noted, acknowledges that "there is undoubtedly *some* convergence involved in the triumphal march of modernity," and therefore that a "viable theory of alternative modernities has to be able to relate both the pull to sameness and the forces making for difference."[50] At the same time, what is most important to focus on, he insists, is the fact that modernity is "lived from the inside,"[51] from the native's point of view, as it were. He does not dispute the fact that modernity is "wave-like" in its sweep over traditional cultures, but argues that except in cases in which the culture is completely destroyed "a successful transition involves a people finding resources in their traditional culture that, modified and transposed, will enable them to take on the new practices."[52] It may be obscure what such a "successful transition" to modernity might be, but it is clear that the focus for Taylor is on the divergence within the convergence: in short, the "invention" of modernities.

This is a very attractive argument, for obvious reasons. It is easy to recognize in it a range of social constructionist traces, some of them anthropological in affiliation, but all of them driven by a distinctive kind of subaltern oppositional desire. The argument answers the demand for an understanding of the making of the modern world that refuses the progressivist teleologies of developmentalism and the moral prejudices of Eurocentrism, and focuses our attention on the agency of the non-Western subalterns themselves and what they make with what they have. The view here is that these subalterns are not passive objects of a dominant civilizational power, merely assimilating or mimicking Europe, but rather self-conscious actors, resisting, translating, displacing, and so on, that dominant power in the course of making their own history. In its culturalist and inventionist biases, it will be immediately clear how much it comports with Thornton's idea of transplanted African culture as the underground resource or idiom of resistance, as well as with Mintz and Price's idea of the creation of new and alternative (economic, familial, social) institutions and practices as part of transgressing and subverting the dominant will of plantation power.[53] Like these stories of alternative black Atlantics, the "alternative modernities" line of argument is constructed in such a way as to issue in a narrative of subaltern agency because its objective is to displace a story of submission with a story of resistance. In the instance of *The Black Jacobins*, we would be urged to tell a story about the subaltern agency through which Toussaint Louverture and his colleagues made—or sought to make—their own version of the modern against the dominant colonial one. It might, for example, seek to explore the African cultural idiom that informed this alternative modernity, or it might inquire into the ways the rebel slaves appropriated the modern concepts and institutions they found around them and creatively turned them to their own purposes.

I am, of course, sympathetic to this oppositional desire to affirm the humanity of the subaltern, but I have a doubt that the story of resistance and agency this line of argument promotes is the best hope we have in this postcolonial present. Specifically I want to notice how the idea of alternative or subaltern modernities operates by constructing a normative expectation of resistance or overcoming. Notably it does this, at least in part, by imagining the conditions of the modern as a largely passive or negative environment merely waiting to be surmounted or mastered or translated or displaced by preconstituted subjects: modern transformations occur, and subalterns respond in more or less creative ways. Imagined in this way, what is obscured is the extent to which the transformed terrain on which these creative responses are being enacted is itself positively constituting (or rather, reconstituting) these subjects, their new objects of desire, and the new concepts that shape the horizon of that desire (it is well to recall here Bernard Yack's argument about new concepts and the creation of new expectations). In other words, the alternative modernity being made by Toussaint Louverture and his colleagues was not a prior choice they made as preconstituted subjects waking up in the middle of a world they found objectionable and in need of change; it was a choice partly constituted by that modern world and, therefore, a choice partly constructed through its conceptual and ideological apparatuses. My own view is that as we stare into the bleak face of the various dead-ended modernities constructed by the postcolonial state we ought perhaps to be less enthusiastic about the heroic story embodied in the alternative modernities thesis and more concerned to inquire into the modern concepts and institutions upon which these resisting projects themselves depended. This, I want to urge, is where the stakes for us are as we undertake to think and work our way out of the present. I am urging, therefore, that we need a way of describing the regime of slave plantation power in which what is brought into view is less what it restricts and what resists this restriction, less what it represses and what escapes or overcomes this repression, and more the modern conditions it created that positively shaped the way in which language, religion, kinship, and so on were reconstituted.

IN CONSEQUENCE I want to urge another direction for thinking about change and modernity, one as I have said that is inspired by the work of Talal Asad. Many years ago, in the course of a memorable critical engagement with Eric Wolf's epigrammatic work, *Europe and the People without History*, Asad made the following vivid remark about history and change: "Historical conditions," he said, "change like landscapes created by glaciers—usually slowly, always contingently—on which old paths that followed old inequalities simply become irrelevant rather than being consciously rejected."[54] (Note that like Wittgenstein's "sketches of landscape," Asad is employing an evocative simile here, not suggesting a natural law of historical development.) This geological image of the way historical change takes place—and of the register in which it is most useful to consider its occurrence—is instructive for thinking about the transformations that constitute the making of colonial modernities and the subjects who find themselves conscripts of that structure of power.

Part of what Asad finds unsatisfying about the kind of epic story of European expansion and the formation of world capitalism told by

Wolf is his conceptual reliance on the notion of a "precapitalist mode of production" that presupposes a theoretical "key to the secret of non-capitalist societies."[55] Not surprisingly, Asad argues that where such a notion may have a certain validity in the analysis of capitalism it has none in understanding the nonmodern world. But to my mind much the more important aspect of his objection to the kind of story advanced by Wolf (and the many others who have followed him since) concerns the place assigned to conscious agency ("the ability to bestow meanings" in Wolf's phrase), especially in the consideration of strategies of resistance to patterns of inequality. In Asad's view: "The classic conception of ideology as the glue of consciousness that holds political structures together . . . obscures the fact that the story of industrial capitalism can be told not just as the collective adventure in which all the world's peoples have combined to make their own history, but as the progress of glacial powers that have altered the conditions, the values, the desires of the peoples in our world."[56] The point Asad is seeking to illustrate about historical change by means of this geological metaphor is that as new historical conditions emerge (conditions shaped by new technologies and new rationalities, not merely new consciousnesses) the efficacy of old distinctions and old options wanes, fades, becomes obsolete. The old paths do not necessarily disappear altogether. They may well remain dimly visible along with remnants of the languages that articulated them. But their point—that is, their ability to produce salient effects—becomes attenuated. The paths now go *nowhere* because they have become not false so much as irrelevant.[57] For Asad, therefore, if there is a story to be told about the new (say, subaltern) choices people make in the course of acting historically, there remains nevertheless another story besides this one, namely, "the story of transformations that have reshaped those conditions which are not of people's choosing but within which they must make their history."[58] Notice that Asad is not thinking of this power as a merely negative power, blocking the action of already constituted subjectivities. In his view, these subjectivities are themselves constructed inside of the new relations of power. As he says: "We should not think of those conditions as though they merely set varying limits to preconstituted choices. Historical conditions construct those choices, just as distinctive choices constitute historically specific subjectivities."[59]

It is this conception of power and historical change that ought to command our attention in our contemporary discussions of modernity.

Modern power, obviously, is a crucial aspect of the story of historical change in the non-European world because the modern age unleashed forces that sought not merely to extract forms of tribute or impose asymmetrical patterns of exchange, but to forcibly—and very often violently—destroy old ways of social and moral and political life and build up new ones. Unlike nonmodern power, in other words, modern power has been concerned precisely with systematically transforming the very *conditions* in which life as a whole is organized. As Asad writes in a related essay:

> The modern world is now structured as a power domain in which political, economic, and ideological processes interact directly regardless of distance, and where historical agents in very different places are obliged to address aspects of identical problems. To say this is not to assert that the globe is socially homogeneous, or that non-European societies have lost their cultural "authenticity." Such claims have been made or denied by travellers, anthropologists, and political ideologues for generations. My point is a different one: that social and cultural variety everywhere increasingly responds to, and is managed by, categories brought into play by modern forces. If, as some anthropologists now put it, culture is always invented, if invention always opens up the possibilities for difference, then it should also be clear that the conditions of invention are no longer what they once were. More precisely, even if it is true that new cultural forms are being continuously invented in different societies, those societies now live in a single, shared world, a world brought into being by European conquest.[60]

From this point of view, then, the problem with the multiple (or invention of) modernities argument is not that it pays little attention to the conditions in which people remake their lives; after all, historical and anthropological theorists such as Mintz and Price are concerned with precisely these conditions. Rather, the problem turns on the way the relation between action and its conditions is formulated. By understanding conditions as limits or restraints on action, the multiple modernities account of modernity obscures the way in which they actively help to construct new choices which themselves are constitutive of new creative subjectivities.

I want to endorse and work with this insight. In my view, Asad's intervention registers an implicit recognition of an alteration in the cognitive-political problem-space we inhabit and, therefore, of the changed nature of the demand of criticism. He has, in effect, altered the strategic question about colonialism—and with it the salient description of colonial power—on the basis of which a critical response is solicited. In the anticolonial story, colonial power (or Western power, more generally) is understood as a force blocking the path of the colonized, a force that, having intruded, is standing—literally and metaphorically—in the way of the colonized. In this narrative, colonial power is conceived in the image of an obstruction, often a morally distorting obstruction, that seeks to materially dispossess the colonized, to exclude them from access to power, and to psychologically dehumanize them. Colonial power is therefore something to be overthrown, to be overcome, in order that the colonized can progressively retake possession of their societies and their selves. Frantz Fanon's *The Wretched of the Earth* is perhaps the paradigmatic instance of this conceptualization. We have already seen it at work in *The Black Jacobins* (see chapter 2), and I will return to it in a moment.[61] Moreover, in the period after World War II—and especially since the 1960s—this story of colonial power has gathered significant moral force among the scholarly disciplines in the humanities and social sciences. The advocacy of the native's point of view, for example, the assertion of the autonomous agency of the colonized, and the vigorous defense of their history making in acts of resistance, are all ways in which the humanities and social sciences have taken up and provided disciplinary authority for the Romantic narrative of anticolonial resistance and liberation.[62]

My point here (and in this book as a whole) is neither to disparage nor refute this anticolonial narrative, nor to suggest that this conception of colonialism is all there is to them (it would be easy to show in texts like *The Wretched of the Earth* and *The Black Jacobins* the complexity of their formulations). Rather, my point is to dissolve the compelling claim this story has on us now. I am not concerned with whether that narrative got its characterization of colonial power right or wrong. The point I am after is a more fundamental one, namely, whether the problem-space in which the narrative of (social or nationalist) liberation is constituted continues to be a problem-space whose questions ought to exercise a claim on the criticism of the present. Or to put this in another way, the point is whether the questions this anticolonial narrative sought to answer—Is colonial power invincible? How and in what ways did the colonized resist?—continue to be questions worth responding to at all. This is what I have called the *strategic* point of criticism.[63] And I want to read Asad as saying that they are not questions to which we ought (or ought any longer) to try to formulate answers. They are questions whose moment has passed, or better, whose moment over the past decade and a half has been steadily dismantled. On my reading, it is this new problem-space and demand that Asad is urging us to respond to. He is in effect demanding a new history of the postcolonial present. In particular what interests Asad is an analytical description of the form of power that altered not merely the balance of forces in the struggle between colonizer and colonized, but the glacial terrain itself on which that struggle was engaged; that altered not merely the rules of the game of social, political, and cultural life among the colonized, but the game as such in which social, political, and cultural life was organized. Where the anticolonial story was concerned to show that, its self-understanding notwithstanding, European power was never total and that the colonized always resisted, always made their own history, what is at stake here is not whether the colonized accommodated or resisted but how colonial power transformed the ground on which accommodation or resistance was possible in the first place, how colonial power reshaped or reorganized the conceptual and institutional conditions of possibility of social action and its understanding.[64]

SOMETHING OF WHAT is at stake in altering our focus on colonial power in the way that Asad is urging us to do here might be illustrated by glancing briefly at a relevant chapter in the historiography of New World slave resistance and slave revolt. Again, The Black Jacobins is one of the seminal texts (if not the inaugural one) in the archive of this historiography.[65] The chapter I have in mind is one concerned with the so-called typology of slave rebellions in the African Americas. It takes definitive historiographical shape in the 1970s and describes a historical shift between the late eighteenth century and the early nineteenth in the character, leadership, and objectives of slave revolts.[66] This is a crucial chapter in my own story of The Black Jacobins, of course, because it is precisely the modern historical moment of James's hero, Toussaint Louverture.

Told in one way—for example, by Eugene Genovese in his classic work, From Rebellion to Revolution—this is the story of the impact of the newly ascendant bourgeois-democratic ideas of the Age of Revolution in transforming the direction and scope of New World slave insurgency. Until the late eighteenth century, Genovese argues, the ideological and social-political horizon of African American slave revolt was framed largely by a commitment to the "restoration of as much of a traditional way of life as could be remembered or copied."[67] The various New World Maroon communities that emerged in the sixteenth and seventeenth centuries are of course the paradigmatic instances of this ideological orientation. In a world-historical sense (which is fundamental to Genovese's conceptual location of slavery and slave resistance as part of the making of the modern world), this period of slave revolt resembles the great peasant revolts of medieval and early modern Europe which, as he says, lacking "the material base and concomitant ideology for the projection of a new and economically more advanced society" struggled for the restoration of a lost world. However, this restorationist vision gave way in the ideologically saturated Age of Revolution, and in the New World, the French Revolution provided the conditions in which the 1791 slave revolt in San Domingo (Saint-Domingue) could become a revolution.[68] As Genovese puts it: "The revolution under Toussaint, a leader of genius, did not aspire to restore some lost African world or build an isolated Afro-American enclave that, whatever its cultural merit, could have played no autonomous role in world affairs and would have had to become a protectorate of one or another European power. Toussaint, and after his death Dessalines and Henri Christophe, tried to forge a modern black state, based on an economy with a vital export sector oriented to the world market."[69] For Genovese, therefore, the story of the San Domingo (Saint-Domingue) Revolution is the story of one crucial chapter in an interconnected world-historical and essentially transatlantic Age of Revolution.

Told in another way—for example, by Michael Craton in *Testing the Chains* (a book with a narrower geopolitical focus than Genovese's)—the story of this alteration in the character of slave insurgency is less the story of revolutionary ideology than it is part of the larger story of Afro-Caribbean creolization. For Craton, slave revolts in the Caribbean can be divided into two main phases: an "African" phase from about the sixteenth century until about 1760, and an "Afro-Caribbean" phase from the last decade of the eighteenth century until 1831–32. The early revolts, he argues (of which the greatest was the so-called Tacky revolt in Jamaica in 1760), "were essentially African in character. The rebels were mostly African led by Africans, the uprisings plotted, planned, and prepared in African style, with aims and fighting methods that owed at least as much to Africa as to the special conditions of Caribbean colonies and Amerindian precedents."[70] The early rebels, he continues, "almost invariably, dedicated themselves to the total eradication of their white oppressors and to the founding of an Akan-style autocracy in place of the toppled plantocracy."[71] In the second phase, by contrast, the revolts were organized and led by Creole slaves, and their character and objectives were quite different. Central to this Afro-Caribbean phase of revolt, Craton argues, is what he calls the "phenomenally rapid Christianization" of the slaves after 1783, especially the emergence of the nonconformist black chapels. Christianity provided social, political, and psychological "attractions" to the increasingly creolized population. But more than this, the nonconformist chapels "provided an alternative society and refuge from the plantation ethos. They were places in which slaves from different plantations could meet regularly, places that offered opportunities for self-expression and spiritual release. The chapels also created their own hierarchies independent of plantation society—though for obvious reasons, those who became the leaders in chapel were often those who had already emerged as the plantation slave elite."[72] "In sum, the rebellions occurred because the leaders were able to mobilize the slaves, harnessing their discontent, exploiting their potential for retaliatory violence, and offering fulfillment for their deepest dreams."[73] Moreover, the goal of these Afro-Caribbean rebels, Craton maintains was not to establish an African kingdom, but to become "proto-peasants." "The chief of the slaves' aspirations," Craton says, "was, naturally, to be free. Yet the freedom sought seems to have become that of an independent peasantry, a way of life about which the slaves had quite clear notions and of which, in most areas, they already had considerable experience . . . In addition the slaves worked their provision grounds using their own methods with minimal supervision, and their new status was also demonstrated by the way in which the slaves had developed an internal marketing system quite independently and had managed to enter the cash economy on their own terms. More deeply, the slaves retained and developed concepts of family and kin quite beyond the comprehension and control of the master class and a concept of land tenure that was in contradiction to that of the dominant European culture. In brief, for ordinary slaves freedom meant being free to be small farmers, working for the plantations, if at all, only for wages and on their own terms."[74]

Both of these accounts have been subjected to considerable criticism, especially by David Geggus, perhaps the leading contemporary scholar of the Haitian/Saint-Domingue Revolution.[75] Geggus shows some of the internal incoherencies in the respective work of Genovese and Craton, in particular the difficulty in applying their models to the data of Saint-Domingue. As he says of Craton's analysis, it cannot account for the fact that it was "a predominantly African Saint Domingue that produced the classic 'proto-peasant' revolt";[76] and he warns that Genovese's reliance on the policies of Toussaint Louverture as a measure of the ideological development of the Saint Domingue (San Domingo) Revolution does not sufficiently consider that "it is now known that Toussaint was not a slave . . . when the revolt broke out, and had been free and a slave-owner for at least fifteen years."[77] For Geggus, not surprisingly, what is necessary is more—and more discriminating—empirical research and less ideologically driven generalization.[78] The direction of my own concern with these attempts to formulate a conception of the transformation of types of New World slave revolt is a different one, however. This is partly because I don't share Geggus's view regarding the virtue of new data (and the underlying assumption that data come *before* theory rather than being constituted by it in important ways). But it is also because I suspect that Geggus shares with Genovese and Craton an assumption that I regard as both dissolvable and worthy of dissolution—namely, the humanist assumption of a preconstituted slave Will to Resist or Will to Freedom that studies of slavery and slave revolt are obliged to affirm and illustrate. When, for example, Genovese writes that "revolt against slavery . . . emerged as the basic assertion of human dignity and of humanity itself,"[79] and when Craton maintains that resistance and revolt were "endemic" to the slave plantation system, "merely changing . . . forms" as new kinds of opportunities presented themselves,[80] they are both working out the "culture of resistance" paradigm that reiterates the conventional questions: To what extent and in what forms did the New World slave's will-to-freedom express itself? Under what conditions was it successful, and what constraints led to failure? How are we to understand the relative frequency—or infrequency—of New World slave revolts? And so on.

Still it is clear from the material work of Genovese and Craton that, if we set aside the metaphysical assumption of a slave Will to Freedom, another set of questions about modern power potentially comes into view, questions concerned with the ways in which modern ideas about liberty (whether abolitionist, as in Craton's view, or republican, as in Genovese's) helped to transform the conceptual and ideological conditions in which a willing subject was constituted, new choices were constructed, and a new horizon of options to be assessed and futures to hope for became possible and thinkable. Again, it wasn't preconstituted slaves who took hold of Christianity and deployed it as resistance; it was slaves whose selves were (at least partly) constituted by the Christian project as it took shape in the modern conditions of Caribbean slave plantations. My point, in short, is simply this, that however many slaves preserved individual memories of nonmodern practices from their African homelands (practices of agricultural cultivation, for example, or social organization, or kinship, or interpersonal behavior) the fact is that they were all now obliged to conduct these remembered lives in conditions brought into being by the categories and institutions of the modern world, categories and institutions that were not passive or neutral but which actively sought to reconstruct the ground on which their enslaved lives were lived. It is in relation to this consideration of the problem of modernity, slavery, and historical change that I want to resituate our investigation of *The Black Jacobins* for our postcolonial present.

IV

In 1963, I have said, a new and revised edition of *The Black Jacobins* was issued in the United States by Vintage. The book had been out of print for many years and had largely—if not entirely—been forgotten.[81] But now, in a considerably altered imperial moment—the cold war, the ambiguous climax of constitutional decolonization, the collapse of the project of the federation of the West Indies, the exhilarating victory of the Cuban Revolution—it was making a reappearance and would soon establish itself as a Caribbean classic. Perhaps the best-known feature of this edition of *The Black Jacobins* is the celebrated appendix entitled "From Toussaint L'Ouverture to Fidel Castro."[82] This appendix is conventionally read as though it were an organic, seamlessly connected part of the main body of the text of *The Black Jacobins*, as though it merely takes up the story of the Caribbean where the main text leaves off. I don't think this is entirely the case. In my view there is a very suggestive *discontinuity* between the picture each draws of the relation between slavery and modern power, and I am going to argue that the new picture of this relation alters significantly the conceptual problematic in which Toussaint Louverture's relationship to modernity might be understood and in which the story of the San Domingo Revolution, as a transforming historical event, might be told as a story for our time.

The appendix is a model of narrative economy. In scarcely thirty pages, James makes a rapid sweep through the century and a half of Caribbean history separating Toussaint Louverture and his revolution from Fidel Castro and his, dividing the period into three large swathes of time: the nineteenth century, the period between the First and Second World Wars, and the period following the Second World War. Characteristically, James is less interested in rehearsing the historical details of these time periods themselves (the individual facts are known, he says impatiently) than in drawing them together and connecting them in such a way as to make them tell the story he wants to tell about Caribbean history. Essentially, this is the story of the distinctiveness, indeed uniqueness, of the Caribbean as a world-historical civilization. In "From Toussaint L'Ouverture to Fidel Castro" James tells the story of the Caribbean as a historically particular civilizational formation: the result of distinctive historical forces, it has given rise to a distinctive social and (most importantly) intellectual mentality. If The Black Jacobins was initially conceived and written with the decolonization of Africa in mind ("as is obvious all through the book and particularly in the last pages, it is Africa and African emancipation that he [the author] has in mind"), the new appendix was centrally preoccupied with the birth of a "West Indian" national identity.[83] Or to put this in another way, part of James's point is to suggest the way in which that seminal preoccupation with "the emancipation of Africa" (in the life and work of people like Marcus Garvey and George Padmore and Aimé Césaire) set the stage for the emergence of a Caribbean identity. "The road to West Indian identity," as James writes, "lay through Africa."[84]

For my purposes here, however, what is particularly interesting to note in James's telescopic narrative is the way in which he establishes the connection between Toussaint Louverture and Fidel Castro. Surprisingly, James emphatically says that their connection is not to be found in the obvious fact that they both led successful revolutions, to that point (Grenada would come—and go—somewhat later) the only two successful revolutions in the Caribbean. "Toussaint L'Ouverture is not here linked to Fidel Castro," James writes, "because both led revolutions in the West Indies. Nor is the link a convenient or journalistic demarcation of historical time."[85] The connection, in other words, is neither trivial nor the seemingly self-evident one that they both stand at the center of social and political upheavals that changed forever the course of Caribbean—and world—history. The connection between them is rather that they both struggled (and in the case of Fidel Castro, perhaps continues to struggle) with a distinctive civilizational predicament, a predicament that in James's view is paradigmatically West Indian—"of the West Indies, West Indian," as he liked to say.

> Castro's revolution is of the twentieth century as much as Toussaint's was of the eighteenth. But despite the distance of over a century and a half, both are West Indian. The people who made them, the problems and the attempts to solve them, are peculiarly West Indian, the product of a peculiar origin and a peculiar history.[86]

What is this "peculiar origin" and "peculiar history"? It is the origin and history of modernity. For James, the Caribbean begins in modernity. This is its founding; it begins in the ordering structure of power and reason that constitutes colonial modernity. The Caribbean, in other words, is not merely modern; it is modern in a fundamentally inaugural way. And it is this inaugural modernity, he suggests, that lends to the Caribbean its distinctive (perhaps distinctively paradoxical) character. For the James of the appendix it is this fact of the founding modernity of the Caribbean, more than any other, which shaped the common experience of both Toussaint Louverture and Fidel Castro. In the angle of this formulation alone, I think, one can discern that James's perspective and the substance of his preoccupations has perceptively shifted from what it was in the body of the book.

For James, the Caribbean's modernity is inaugural in at least two senses. First, unlike other parts of the colonial world (South Asia or Africa, for example), there were no nonmodern formations in the Caribbean with which the colonial powers had continuously to contend. Here James was in fact articulating a view that was of some significance in his conceptualization in the late 1950s and 1960s of the character of Caribbean nationalism and nation-building. In the island Caribbean, at least (the Guianas were a somewhat different story), the peoples native to the region were rapidly destroyed by the early colonial powers, and consequently there was no institutional background, no deeply established forms of life, with which the colonial powers were obliged to negotiate in an ongoing way.[87] He writes:

> The West Indies has never been a traditional colonial territory with clearly distinguished economic and political relations between

two different cultures. Native culture there was none. The aboriginal Amerindian civilisation had been destroyed. Every succeeding year, therefore, saw the labouring population, slave or free, incorporating into itself more and more of the language, customs, aims and outlook of its masters.[88]

It may be objected, of course, that James overstates the case here, and that the emphasis he places on the slaves "incorporating" more and more of their master's culture is another indication of his Eurocentrism. This idea of the simple assimilation of African people in the Americas to European norms is precisely what has been disputed by the revisionist historiography of the latter half of the twentieth century, and as I have indicated its contribution is undoubted. But to belabor this point, I think, is to overlook the more significant issue at stake in James's remark, namely, the idea that the Caribbean is the paradigmatic instance of the colonial encounter. And this is not merely because it was the earliest non-European instance of it, but because it has been shaped almost entirely by that founding experience.

Second, if that modernity is a founding experience for the Caribbean, then plantation slavery is the fundamental institution through which that experience is shaped and articulated. For James, the sugar plantation constituted a disciplinary and regulatory regime that, as he says, "imposed a pattern" on the West Indies, one that was neither European nor African, nor indeed American. It was a pattern, he says, that was "not native in any conceivable sense of that word, but West Indian, *sui generis*, with no parallel anywhere else."[89] In a now famous passage James argues it this way:

> The sugar plantation has been the most civilising as well as the most demoralising influence in West Indian development. When three centuries ago the slaves came to the West Indies, they entered directly into the large-scale agriculture of the sugar plantation, which was a *modern* system. It further required that the slaves live together in a social relation far closer than any proletariat of the time. The cane when reaped had to be rapidly transported to what was factory production. The product was shipped abroad for sale. Even the cloth the slaves wore and the food they ate was imported. The Negroes, therefore, from the very start lived a life that was in its essence a modern life. That is their history—as far as I have been able to discover, a unique history.[90]

I am going to spend some time on this passage, in particular on the contrast between the image it draws of slavery and power and the one we have already encountered in the body of The Black Jacobins. Moreover, I am going to connect the image of modernity in this passage with the story of history and modern change I have been commending in the preceding pages.

Let us first recall the image of slavery established in chapter 1 of The Black Jacobins, the famous chapter entitled "The Property." In that chapter, memorably, slavery appeared in the now familiar outline of a structure of repressive violence, as a regime, as James calls it, "of calculated brutality and terrorism."[91] From the capture on the African mainland through the horrors of the Middle Passage and the barbaric humiliations of sale on the auction block to the backbreaking labor and extravagant tortures on the plantations, slavery is constructed in this chapter as a daily round of naked and systemically generated dehumanization. Again, let me be clear that I am not concerned here with whether this picture is true or even plausible, but with the *function* it serves in the overall economy of James's story. That is to say, the salience of this particular image of slavery does not inhere in the transparent (empirical) truth of the image itself but in the service it renders in the building up of a moral-political historical narrative. And I have shown how this image works to provide the generative background against which a humanist epic of resistance can unfold, how it helps to set in motion the dialectic of repressive domination and revolutionary overcoming.

The appendix—and especially the passage I have quoted—offers a significantly contrasting image of slavery to the one established in chapter 1 of The Black Jacobins. It will have been noticed that in this passage the slave plantation is characterized explicitly as a force at once "civilizing" and "demoralizing." James is not meaning to be polemical here; he is being deliberately descriptive (or better, redescriptive). He means, I think, to point to the double dynamic at work in New World plantation slavery: the regime of plantation slavery had, simultaneously, negative as well as positive effects (albeit in different registers). If slavery eroded the spirit of the slaves, degraded their humanity, that is to say, had a literally negative moral effect, it also had a positively shaping effect on the slave subject. In Michel Foucault's sense of the productivity of power, the slave plantation might be characterized as establishing the relations and the material and epistemic apparatuses through which new subjects were constituted: new desires instilled, new aptitudes molded, new dispositions acquired.[92] Or, to put it another way, the regime of plantation slavery constituted a "civilizing process," in the sense of the systemic building up over time of distinctive modes of behavior and response, a distinctive mentality. In short, in James's phrase, it imposed a pattern.

But notice also, in this passage, that this civilizing pattern is an essentially *modern* one. Plantation slavery was organized through the modern technological form of large-scale agricultural production, and it obliged the slaves to relate to themselves, to each other, and to their slave masters in new and essentially modern ways: in ways that were informed by modern ideas about property, about personhood and individuality, about time and its economic organization and efficient uses, about the relationship between the religious and the secular, about the nature of government and the sources of political authority, and so on. And this entire local structure was inserted into a modern global process in a very material way inasmuch as it was through its circuits that the slaves were clothed and fed. In other words, focusing less on the justification for revolution and more on the conditions of a civilization, something else about the regime of slavery than repressive violence and dehumanization is at stake in the description in the appendix, namely the historical transformation that positively reshaped the conditions in which the lives of the slaves were lived, and which, as a consequence, reshaped both the kinds of choices available to them as well as the kinds of subjects who made choices. It is not that slavery is no longer recognized as the system of coercion that it was, but this is not the focus around which the description is organized, not the point on which it hangs. Rather, James is concerned with the new conditions of life and work constituted by the modern regime of the slave plantation, its socializing as well as its individualizing disciplines.

It is of course true that in *The Black Jacobins* James had already developed the theme of the modernity of slavery. He is one of the first theorists to do so. Slavery, James says, was an integral part of the economic life of capitalist modernity, which is why the French Revolution and the San Domingo Revolution are so inextricably interconnected from the first pages of the narrative.[93] But it is also true that in the body of the book, in the context of building up a revolutionary narrative, James's concern was to draw a parallel between the factory-like conditions of slave life and those of a modern industrial proletariat so as to be able to make out a case for the revolutionary education that comes from working in certain conditions and that prepares workers for organized political activity.

The slaves worked on the land, and, like revolutionary peasants everywhere, they aimed at the extermination of their oppressors. But, working and living together in gangs of hundreds on the huge sugar-factories which covered the North Plain, they were closer to a modern proletariat than any group of workers in existence at the time, and the rising was, therefore, a thoroughly prepared and organised mass movement.[94]

In the appendix, by contrast, James invokes modernity for what seems to me a radically different purpose; or, if you prefer, James is looking in a different direction. The issue here is no longer revolutionary consciousness and organization, as such, but the building up of a story of modern civilization. In the appendix James's concern is to underline the fact that the West Indian is, in a fundamentally original way, both an object of modern power and the subject of a modern life. This, needless to say, is not to imply any moral judgment about those conditions. It is not to suggest that they may have been other than oppressive or demeaning or cruel or unjust. James remained as deeply sensitive as anyone to the brutalizing character of slavery. It is only to insist that these conditions were oppressive or demeaning or cruel or unjust in distinctly *modern* ways. They operated, in other words, through modern disciplinary techniques, modern institutions of government, modern forms of subjectivity, and modern conceptions of rationality.

READING THE BLACK JACOBINS in this way I want to urge that for our postcolonial present what bears understanding about Toussaint Louverture is not so much that he was a revolutionary agent who made history, but that he was constrained to imagine and make the revolution he imagined and made within the conceptual and institutional terrain of modernity. This cognitive-political terrain of modernity, in other words, was not his to choose. It did not offer itself to him as one of a range of options. Rather it was the context in which his options were themselves constituted and made visible and recognizable as options-as-such. Toussaint Louverture, in short, could not choose *not* to be modern. He was not, in consequence, a volunteer of its project. He was its conscript. He was a man who had come up in a world that had been coercively reorganized by the material and epistemic violence of a modern regime of power and forcibly inserted into a global order in a state of subordination and dependence. "The image of 'conscripts,' as opposed to 'volunteers,' " Asad writes, "does not suggest merely the recruits' initial attitude, but also the nature of the army and the war it has been fighting. To instill the desire for progress in the non-European world, it was necessary to inscribe modern Western categories into the administrative and legal discourses of that world. It was through such discursive powers that people undergoing 'modernization' were compelled to abandon old practices and turn to new ones."[95]

The story of Toussaint Louverture's fortuitous encounter with the emancipationist work of the abbé Raynal and thus with the radical tradition of the French Enlightenment is therefore not to be read as an instance of his (and James's) Eurocentric aspirations, their betrayal of Africa or the subaltern. Toussaint was a modern, and the mode of the modernist revolutionary intellectual he adopted is one of the consummate ways of embodying and realizing that modernity. The appendix, "From Toussaint L'Ouverture to Fidel Castro," closes with a discussion of three contemporary Caribbean novelists, V. S. Naipaul, Wilson Harris, and George Lamming. They are, for James, three instances of a West Indian mentality, writers who exemplify the West Indian negotiation with its peculiar modernity. In this negotiation they are prefigured in Toussaint Louverture and his relationship with the abbé Raynal. The function of that mise-en-scène of modernist self-fashioning in chapter 1 of The Black Jacobins in which Toussaint discovers the image and idiom of his revolutionary persona is to mark an inaugural moment which the West Indian intellectual—indeed any intellectual of colonial heritage— can disavow but not escape. "Toussaint tried and paid for it with his life. Torn, twisted, stretched to the limits of agony, injected with poisonous patent medicines, it lives in the state which Fidel started. It is of the West Indies West Indian. For it, Toussaint, the first and greatest of West Indians, paid with his life."[96]

TO SUM UP this part of my argument and signal the direction in which I am headed from here on, I have been concerned in this chapter to begin to alter the way we read The Black Jacobins for our postcolonial time, to alter the horizon of expectations we build into our understanding of it, and consequently to alter the nature of the dissatisfactions we come away from it with. The Black Jacobins has been read inside a distinctive horizon of expectations—expectations about the cultural autonomy of Africans in the Caribbean and the moral economy of subaltern resistance—and its deficiencies have been assessed and judged against the background of these expectations. I have argued that these expectations are built into a Romantic historical problematic, one that depends upon a now past present, a present whose liberationist futures have waned. My argument is that another way of thinking about history and historical change is called for. I have urged that we give up posing the question about the past in such a way as to oblige us to construct a Romantic narrative that demonstrates the resistance of the oppressed — whether in the name of African culture or of a cultural discourse of alternative modernities. My point has not been that such arguments are, by some objective criteria, wrong, but rather that they are strategically misplaced inasmuch as they answer a question that is no longer being asked — or anyway a question whose salience is a matter of doubt. The vindicationist story of the slave's undaunted will to resist, however stirring and commendable it may be, obscures another and — in the context of our present — more important story, namely, a story about the transformed conditions (indeed the specifically *modern* conditions) in which the slaves were obliged to fight for freedom. This is the story about Toussaint Louverture that James alerts us to in the appendix to the 1963 edition of *The Black Jacobins*. The fundamental importance of this appendix is that in it James deliberately alters the focus of our attention *away* from the reverential anticolonial story of their revolutionary heroism and toward the conditions — those principally created by slavery and the plantation — that gave distinctive shape to the political projects they undertook in making the futures they made.

In the chapters that follow I continue to think against the story-form of resistance in which James has been read and into which he has written himself. But now I begin to turn my attention to that other story-form that James himself explicitly embeds in the second edition of *The Black Jacobins*, namely, the story-form of tragedy. In chapters 4 and 5 I concern myself with the ways in which this mode of emplotment might open up a new axis along which to narrate the link between our pasts, our presents, and our possible futures and enable us to reconsider what we might call the paradox of colonial Enlightenment.

# FOUR

# Toussaint's Tragic Dilemma

Perhaps for him to have expected more than the bare freedom was too much for the time. With that alone Dessalines was satisfied, and perhaps the proof that freedom alone was possible lies in the fact that to ensure it Dessalines, that faithful adjutant, had to see that Toussaint was removed from the scene. Toussaint was attempting the impossible—the impossible that was for him the only reality that mattered. The realities to which the historian is condemned will at times simplify the tragic alternatives with which he [Toussaint] was faced. But these factual statements and the judgments they demand must not be allowed to obscure or minimise the truly tragic character of his dilemma, one of the most remarkable of which there is an authentic historical record.

I

I have already suggested that the famous appendix, "From Toussaint L'Ouverture to Fidel Castro," is not the only significant revision to the second edition of The Black Jacobins that appeared in 1963. It is perhaps not even the most significant of the revisions. There are, as I have indicated, another set of revisions that seem to me of at least equal—if not more profound and far-reaching—importance. These are the seven paragraphs added to the opening of chapter 13, "The War of Independence," the last, longest, and most dramatic chapter of the book. These seven paragraphs are of special importance, I argue, because they are concerned explicitly with the poetics of tragedy, and with its relation to historical representation and political criticism.

In these paragraphs, James constructs an image of Toussaint's tragic dilemma. He sees that dilemma and the catastrophe that inexorably fol-

lows from it, as being, in part, an outcome of the irreconcilable disso-
nance between Toussaint's expectations for freedom and the conditions
in which he sought to realize them, between the utopia of his desire and
the finitude of his concrete circumstances. For Toussaint, James suggests, the problem of emancipation was, palpably, not merely a problem of ending slavery, of breaking the bondage of the slaves. Rather,
the problem of emancipation entailed also—and simultaneously—the
project of imagining and constructing a sustainable freedom within new
forms of life. Freedom, in other words, had to have both a negative and
a positive moment. Born a slave on a French colonial plantation in the
latter half of the eighteenth century, Toussaint was necessarily formed
by the relations of subordination characteristic of that particular structure of domination. Consequently, his desire for freedom was born (and
borne) out of that fundamental circumstance: enslavement. At the same
time, however, Toussaint was a relatively privileged slave, spared the
worst of the degradation and dehumanization to which his fellows were
subjected, and afforded access, moreover, to the new world of ideas of
the European Enlightenment with its great theme of the natural right
of liberty. Therefore, the positive form of his aspiration for freedom—
not simply the determination itself to be rid of slavery—was shaped by a
movement of ideas that were in confrontation with the ideas and institutions that held the old slave order in place. Toussaint, James insists, was
always a realist. But the reality that mattered to him, the idea of emancipation to which he was committed, was at odds with the constraining
forces of an old form of life that had, partially at least, made him who
he was. The paralyzing collision between his aspiration and his conditions, therefore, was not external to him. Like Hamlet, in whose image
James (partially) reconstructs him, Toussaint is the very embodiment of
the historical conflict between the old and the new. This is why the alternatives with which he was confronted—France with reenslavement or
freedom without France—were neither alternatives of his choosing nor
alternatives between which he could choose. They were, in short, tragic
alternatives. Each involved giving up values that were, for him, fundamental—that is, nonexchangeable and unexpungeable—commitments.

In this chapter I shall suggest that the seven paragraphs reorient our
understanding of Toussaint Louverture and his project of emancipation
away from the narrative of anticolonial Romance. I want to suggest that
in reframing his story as one of tragedy rather than one of Romance, and
in recasting the figure of Toussaint Louverture as one of tragic suffering

rather than one of revolutionary heroism, James is not simply altering the mood of his historical drama—much, of course, as the melancholy rendering enhances the sense of presence and historical seriousness. More than a new darkened atmosphere of foreboding and despair, more than a new tone of sorrowing pathos, are at stake here. What James is altering, I shall argue (using Hayden White's terms), is the very content of the form of the dramatic action he is setting before us. What he is altering is the mode of emplotment of the story of Toussaint Louverture and the San Domingo Revolution, and consequently—I will urge—its moral-political teaching as well.

IN THE COURSE of his well-known book, *The Death of Tragedy*, George Steiner gets at the contrast I want to draw out here between Romance and tragedy as modes of narrative emplotment. In Romance, he says, a "redemptive mythology" makes suffering, however terrible, merely a price that is paid for the promise of a later emancipation. This is the case with Christianity and Marxism, for him two of the great redemptive mythologies in which the Romanticism of the West has been conceived. In both there is the assurance of a redeeming compensation—an awakening conscience, an acquired reason—that guarantees the possibility of restoration or redress, or reform or revolution. Whatever the guiding idiom, the stubborn Romantic ideal of perfectibility lifts the soul from its degradation and points it upward in the direction of the light, however far off, in the direction of the coming dispensation, however postponed its realization may be. As Steiner says: "Salvation descends on the bruised spirit, and the hero steps towards grace out of the shadow of damnation."[1] In tragedy, by contrast, there are no such compensations. Whether Sophocles's Oedipus or Marlowe's Faustus or Shakespeare's Hamlet, the hero cannot draw back from the abyss to which his actions have led him, nor can he make a last-minute appeal to God or History to heal his wounds, to forgive his misdeeds, to assure him that, in the end, his sacrifice will not be altogether in vain. Tragedy is remorseless. As Steiner puts it, in "authentic tragedy, the gates of hell stand open and damnation is real. The tragic personage cannot evade responsibility. . . . The redeeming insight comes too late to mend the ruins or is purchased at the price of irremediable suffering."[2] Not everyone agrees with the thesis Steiner advances in this book,[3] but it will be remembered (from chapter 1) that Hayden White suggests a similar contrast between Romance and tragedy, at least as ideal types: where the Romantic mode of historical emplotment rides a rhythm of progressive overcoming and ultimate victory over the world's misfortunes, the tragic mode offers an agonic confrontation that holds out no necessary promise of rescue or reconciliation.[4]

My point, therefore, is to suggest that where the anticolonial narrative is cast as an epic Romance, as the great progressive story of an oppressed and victimized people's struggle from Bondage to Freedom, from Despair to Triumph under heroic leadership, the tragic narrative is cast as a dramatic confrontation between contingency and freedom, between human will and its conditioning limits. Where the epic revolutionary narrative charts a steadily rising curve in which the end is already foreclosed by a horizon available through an act of rational, self-transparent will, in the tragic narrative the rhythm is more tentative, its direction less determinative, more recursive, and its meaning less transparent. I mean to suggest, in other words, that tragedy may offer a different lesson than revolutionary Romance does about pasts from which we have come and their relation to presents we inhabit and futures we might anticipate or hope for. If one of the great lessons of Romance is that we are masters and mistresses of our destiny, that our pasts can be left behind and new futures leaped into, tragedy has a less sanguine teaching to offer. Tragedy has a more respectful attitude to the past, to the often-cruel permanence of its impress: it honors, however reluctantly, the obligations the past imposes. Perhaps part of the value of the story-form of tragedy for our present, then, is not merely that it raises a profound challenge to the hubris of the revolutionary (and modernist) longing for total revolution, but that it does so in a way that reopens a path to formulating a criticism of the present.

IN WHAT FOLLOWS I pursue a circumscribed ambition. I have already inquired (in chapter 2) into the dominant story-form of *The Black Jacobins*—the mode of Romance—and suggested that the critical work it does depends on the anticipation of particular futures. I have expressed the view that in our postcolonial present those futures have lost their salience, and therefore offered a doubt about the continued critical purchase of the poetics of anticolonial Romance. I have also argued (in chapter 3) that we focus our attention less on the supposed Eurocentricism of *The Black Jacobins*, and less too on its supposed elitism, and more (as its appendix alerts us) on how it understands the constitutive relationship between New World plantation slavery and modern power. I am

TOUSSAINT'S TRAGIC DILEMMA 135

urging that we concentrate less on the revolutionary agency of Toussaint and more on the modern epistemic conditions that shaped his actions. Against this background, I endeavor to do three things. First, I try to gain a grasp of the uses James himself makes of tragedy. Specifically, I am interested in two related questions: How might one characterize the conceptual and ideological problem-space in which James turns to tragedy as a dramatic mode of emplotment? (Remember that my argument here is that the 1938 edition of The Black Jacobins is not, first and foremost, a tragic text.) And what does James mobilize this dramatic mode to do in his uses of it? In other words, what ends does tragedy serve in James's revised story? It will be noticed, therefore, that I am less interested in the "meaning" per se of tragedy in James's work than in the demand to which its uses respond and the purposes it is conceived to render. Second, I examine the conceptual sources of James's analytic of tragedy (if I can go so far as to call it an "analytic") in the seven paragraphs on tragedy in The Black Jacobins. As we will see, James takes his cue from the standard philosophical canon on tragedy—namely, Aristotle and Hegel—and from a fundamental reading of Shakespeare (especially Hamlet) and Herman Melville (especially Moby-Dick). And third, I endeavor to suggest the ways in which the moral-political teaching of The Black Jacobins is effectively altered by this reemplotment—how, in other words, tragedy enables a way of connecting pasts, presents, and possible futures that avoids the dilemmas of anticolonial Romance for our postcolonial time.

II

When the second edition of The Black Jacobins appeared, a quarter of a century after the first, the book had been out of print for many years. James, thirty-seven years old when he first published it, was now sixty-two. In the passing years between 1938 and 1963 much had changed about the world in which James lived, and likewise much had changed about James. How might we usefully describe the new conceptual-ideological problem-space out of which he wrote the 1963 revisions? Or better, what can be said about the cognitive-political distance that separates this moment in the early 1960s from the late-1930s space in which the first edition of The Black Jacobins was fashioned and published? These are questions of considerable complexity and could themselves be the subject of book-length treatment. In the late 1940s and early 1950s James's thought underwent substantial transformation, and I am going to suggest that a central aspect of this transformation—one might even say its theoretical key—is the new conceptual place he assigns to tragedy.

In recent years, of course, the story of James's intellectual and political itinerary between his arrival in the United States in the fall of 1938 following the publication of *The Black Jacobins* and his forced return to Britain in the spring of 1953 under cold war U.S. immigration orders has become well-enough known.[5] It is, to be sure, a remarkable story—of travel and displacement, self-fashioning and political agitation, passionate love and theoretical renovation, and, above all, absorbing and self-sacrificing commitment to the project of social transformation. These fifteen years represent, so many of his best commentators assert, James's most fertile period of intellectual growth, theoretical writing, and political activity. This may well be so. But it is not my concern here to take a position on the relative value of the earlier as against the later James. My purposes are at once narrower and broader than the field of questions in which this preoccupation is located: narrower in the sense that I am only interested in the career of a single idea of James's in this period (that of tragedy) and broader in the sense that what interests me are less the details of James's intellectual biography than in seeing what his understanding of tragedy might yield for rearticulating the relationship between colonial pasts and postcolonial futures. And hence for my purposes here I need do no more than sketch a usable outline, one that will enable me to foreground the contrast between the problem-space that produced the work of the 1940s and the one that produced the work of the 1950s.

Already a figure of some note in the Trotskyist Marxist Group of the Independent Labour Party in Britain, as I have indicated earlier (see chapter 1), James was invited to lecture in the United States by James Cannon, leader of the newly formed Socialist Worker's Party (SWP).[6] Part of the purpose of his visit was to contribute to SWP discussions on the "Negro Question," and to this end he traveled to meet and hold discussions with Trotsky in Coyoacan, Mexico, in March 1939.[7] In the wake of the Hitler-Stalin Pact of that year, however, serious divisions emerged within the SWP, and one wing—led by the maverick Max Shachtman—split away to form the Worker's Party in 1940. James and a small group around him—a tiny cell of intellectually gifted and politically committed Marxists that came eventually to be known as the "Johnson-Forest Tendency" or, later, simply the "Johnsonites"[8]—followed Shachtman out of the sw p. Both James and Shachtman disagreed with Trotsky's (and Cannon's) view that Stalin's Soviet Union remained essentially a worker's state and to that extent warranted defense against the aggression of the political representatives of international capital. However, the relation with Shachtman immediately produced its own conflicts and difficulties. Where Shachtman argued that the Soviet Union had become a "bureaucratic collectivist" state that, while falling short of socialism, was nevertheless in advance of capitalism, James and his colleagues developed the alternative thesis that the Soviet Union had in fact mutated into a historically new capitalist formation they called "state capitalism."[9] Moreover James began to develop a critique of the Bolshevik conception of revolutionary organization and to sketch the philosophical ground for a new conception of the self-emancipation of the working masses.[10] It was, in short, a period of tremendous revolutionary optimism, and for James and his colleagues the 1940s were a decade of remarkable productivity and conceptual renovation within Marxism.

But it was not to last; perhaps indeed it couldn't last. As James himself has noted, like many radicals of his generation he expected the war to be followed by world revolution.[11] But by the end of the 1940s it was clear that the confidently forecasted and fervently hoped-for revolutions were not going to materialize. Moreover, with the defeat of Nazi Germany and Imperial Japan, the new structure of bipolar global relations, constituted by the rise of the United States to civilizational dominance and the rapid growth of the Soviet Union as an economic and military force, introduced an increasingly cramped and hostile ideological atmosphere for anti-Stalinist revolutionary politics. In 1948, in an attempt to forge a unified Trotskyist movement, James took his Tendency back into the sw p. However it was already clear that he and his colleagues had moved too far outside the mainstream of Trotskyist ideas to fully assimilate, and in 1951 they finally broke altogether with official Trotskyism.[12]

By this time, however, James had turned his mind toward a larger set of cultural-critical themes—the relation between historical movements and personalities, the character of modern society, the popular arts, and the problem of criticism, and all of this in relation to the framing question of the character of American civilization. To be sure, from the early 1940s, the question of "America" had been central to James's thinking about Marxism: he had, famously, urged the development of a Marxism appropriate to America's history, what he thought of as an "Americanization" of Bolshevism.[13] But increasingly there emerged a

dimension of this thinking concerned less with the minutiae of revolutionary theory and organization and more with coming to terms with the
loss of revolutionary momentum and with gauging the tempo and direction of large-scale historical change. By itself, this shift was not novel.
Many "heterodox" or anti-Stalinist Marxists of the postwar period—
T. W. Adorno, Herbert Marcuse, Jean-Paul Sartre, and Raymond Williams among them—were similarly turning their attention to the problem of the failure of the working class in the industrial West to rise to
revolutionary proletarian consciousness.[14] Marxists, so it now seemed,
had failed to understand something very fundamental about human life,
about the contingencies that sometimes undo its purposes, about the
unpredictable vagaries of consciousness and the subtleties of personality, about the opacities of culture, and about the general impossibility
of simply reading subjectivity off the modes of economic organization.[15]
James would frame this concern around the question: "What is it that the
people want?" It is in the context of this preoccupation that he begins
to discuss the historical and conceptual significance of tragedy.[16]

JAMES'S FIRST ELABORATE discussion of tragedy takes place in the
1949–50 manuscript that was published posthumously (in 1993) as
American Civilization.[17] Above all, American Civilization is a work of synthesis made possible not only by James's prodigious learning (a learning
that expanded enormously in the United States), but by the distinctive
angle he brought to his vision of America. As James himself later noted,
unlike many American and European critics, his colonial background
gave him a special angle from which to view the United States.[18] American Civilization grew out of a conviction James had formed by the middle
1940s that the age of European civilization had effectively come to an
end. Europe was moribund. The horrific destructiveness of the war and
the cynical ideologies that sought to justify it were proof enough. The
creative energies that had produced its literary, philosophical, and scientific breakthroughs of the eighteenth and nineteenth centuries were
now exhausted. Little that was new could now be expected from it, and
its internal contradictions—and in James's mind, its gloomy, subjec-
tivist, existential literary and philosophical tendencies confirmed this—
were such as to point it in the overall direction of decline. By contrast,
the Unites States pointed in the opposite direction: incline, invention,
expansion. America was all capacious potential. It was not that James
wrote to simply or naively celebrate the United States. He was a profound

critic of its social and political flaws. It is rather that *American Civilization* is a work of moral imagination: James was not merely writing an analysis; he was issuing a warning to a civilization, which, even while rushing headlong to its doom, contained in an immanent way the possibility of regeneration.[19] Central to James's positive appreciation of the potential of the United States was its relaxed untheoretical relation to popular culture, meaning by this, Hollywood, comic strips, radio drama, baseball, and so on—that is, what some of his European contemporaries disparaged as "mass" culture. (In this, of course, he differed substantially from his Frankfurt School contemporaries, Max Horkheimer and T. W. Adorno.)

It is this sense of a historical crisis that led to James's considerations of the relation between ancient Greece and modern, industrial America and to his reflections on the role of tragedy in transformations of civilization. "During the last thirty years," James writes of the analogy between America and ancient Greece, "*mass production* has created a vast populace, literate, technically trained, conscious of itself and of its inherent right to enjoy all the possibilities of the society to the extent of its means. No such social force has existed in any society with such ideas and aspirations since the citizens of Athens and the farmers around trooped into the city to see the plays of Euripides, Sophocles, and Aeschylus and decide on the prize-winners by their votes."[20]

Greek tragedy, James emphasized, was a popular art, and the tragic poets were spiritual and social leaders. The tragedies of the fifth century were performed as part of the great spring festival in honor of Dionysus, son of Zeus and god of fertility, wine, and ecstasy, and it was an occasion, as James says, on which "practically the whole of the able-bodied population of the free citizens of Athens went to the theatre to see the plays and decide by their votes who was the prize-winner. Generals, statesmen, artists, tanners, sausage-sellers, workers, peasants, who lived in the countryside near and beyond the city-state, these were the audience and the judges."[21] The historical relation between tragic drama and political democracy particularly impressed James. The "great period of Athens," as he called it, between the defeat of the Persians at Marathon (490 BC), Salamis (480 BC), and Plataea (479 BC) and the collapse and capitulation to Sparta (404 BC) is simultaneously the age of the democratic polis and the age of tragic drama. Prior to the fifth century, the cult of Dionysus was celebrated by public performances of song and dance known as dithyrambs. (Pindar, for example, was one of the famous poetic composers in this form.) But, as James writes, "when Athens won the great victory over the Persians and after years of struggle had established the new democracy, suddenly overnight as it were, Aeschylus created practically single-handed the Athenian drama."[22]

Of the three tragic poets—Aeschylus (526–456 BC), Sophocles (495–406 BC), and Euripides (480–406 BC)—whose extant work shapes our understanding of Athenian tragedy, it is the eldest, Aeschylus, who most held James's attention. This is because what interests James is that moment when old social and political forms of life are giving way to new ones. This veteran of Marathon and Salamis transformed the innovations introduced by the chorus-leader Thespis in the latter half of the sixth century (these were, principally, the insertion of spoken verse and the use of an actor who assumed the role of one of the characters in the song) and created what we now recognize as tragic drama.

> Aeschylus added another speaker to the man who led the chorus at the religious festivals and then added another; and the Greek drama was born, to last for a century and then to collapse with the collapse of the democracy. Aeschylus passionately loved the new democracy as did the great body of the people. Somehow Aeschylus understood the new society well enough to know that it wanted, it terribly wanted a new way to express the new moral, social and political process which had been created by the new democracy and which alone could make it work. He introduced these new speakers and transformed the religious ritual into political plays, political plays in the highest sense, the Greek sense of that word. The chorus he kept to act as commentator on the drama, representing the people.[23]

Aeschylus's intuition, James suggests, was that the old forms of politics and the old forms of art were exhausted and that with the emergence of the new political order, new forms of aesthetic expression were needed. And embodying, as he did, both the old and the new, having lived through the collapse of the old tyranny and the emergence of the new democracy, he was best placed to carry out the innovations. In the uncertainty of the new democracy, Aeschylus's tragedy provided a form in which it could examine—and criticize—itself. As James acutely says:

> The tragic hero was a distinguished man. He usually suffered from some weakness—a kind of personal pride to which the Greeks

gave a special name—hubris. And any man who sought too much power, too much distinction, to remove himself from the normal, then the tragic destiny was likely to fall upon him. It was a warning to the democracy to maintain a certain balance, a certain proportion.[24]

It is not hard to see the figure of Toussaint Louverture in this image of the potential doom of the distinguished-man-as-hero.

Thus in 1949–50, against the backdrop of the changed fortunes of the revolutionary project, James is constructing a conception of historical—or rather civilizational—transformation, at the very center of which is the idea of tragedy. James is impressed by the relation between the rise of the Athenian democracy and the origins of tragedy; he is impressed by the "commonness" of the Dionysian scene of Athenian tragic drama; and most of all he is impressed by tragedy's dramatic ability to contain and represent moments of historical transformation, moments when possible futures seem less certain than they have been, and when heroic personalities embody both the old and the new in ways that lead to both grandeur and catastrophe.

### III

If the 1950s brought altered conditions of radical politics in the United States it did so also in the Caribbean, to which James returned his attention in the aftermath of his forced return to Britain in 1953. James, of course, did not cease being a revolutionary. Nor did relations with his "Johnsonite" comrades in the United States come to an end (or at least not all of them; Raya Dunayevskaya, the erstwhile "Freddy Forest," broke with James and established a rival group of Marxist-Humanists). These trans-Atlantic relations, continued through collective theoretical projects (most especially *Facing Reality*) and their new paper, *Correspondence*, did much to sustain him in the bleak early years of his new life in London. Indeed, the revolutionary uprising in Hungary in 1956 (and especially the formation of the self-emancipatory workers' councils) only served to underline and justify the hard years of slow and careful Marxist theoretical revisionism James and his colleagues had begun in the 1940s.

But London must also have seemed a different place than he had left in 1938. And not just because of the physical devastation resulting from the German blitz, or the pathetic state of the Left during the creeping years of the Cold War. The "Windrush" revolution was underway; West Indians were pouring into Britain by the boatload, fleeing the depression of postwar Caribbean economies and taking advantage of the demand for labor in the mother country.[25] As Louise Bennett so memorably put the paradox in her poem of the period, West Indians were "colonizing England in reverse."[26] Importantly, this movement of colonial peoples to the metropolitan center brought workers as well as students and writers (indeed many of the latter had to make a living among the former). And while it's likely not many of them would have immediately recognized C. L. R. James if they passed him on the street (there is a famous occasion on which James recognizes George Lamming in the London Underground, not the other way around),[27] together they provided him with a new context of cultural-political discussion, debate, and activism: that of Caribbean nationalism and the politics of decolonization and West Indian federation. James quickly became a central part of this movement.

In what he has described as a momentous occasion for him, James was urged to return home to Trinidad in 1958 by Eric Williams, founder and leader of the People's National Movement (PNM) and premier of Trinidad and Tobago.[28] It was a moment of great hope for James: it would be the first time in more than a quarter of a century that he would be back in the Caribbean. And here, once again, loomed the prospect of participating in a revolutionary transformation—not a socialist one, to be sure, but still a transformation all the same from an old social and political order to a new one. It was not to be. Invited by Williams, his former student and a historian by training (his classic study of slavery abolition, *Capitalism and Slavery*, was deeply indebted to James and *The Black Jacobins* in particular), to attend the inauguration of the Federal Parliament in Port of Spain, he was soon asked to take over the editorship of the weekly paper of the PNM, the PNM *Weekly* (soon to be renamed the *Nation*) as well as the secretaryship of the West Indies Federal Labour Party, the political party leading the movement for a federated and independent West Indies.[29] The world of the Caribbean was now vastly different from the one James had left in March 1932. In the intervening twenty-odd years much had happened to transform the social and political landscape and with it the horizon of expectations of his fellow West Indians in and out of the region. First of all, the nationalist movements had grown out of the labor riots that were sweeping the Anglo-Creole Caribbean in the late 1930s even as James was completing the first edition of *The Black Jacobins*.[30] And by the late 1950s all the larger Anglo-Creole territories—Jamaica, Trinidad, British Guiana, Barbados—were in various stages of constitutional decolonization and gathering momentum for the hoped-for federal nationhood. So that while formal political independence was an only vaguely conceivable ambition when in the 1930s James wrote his tract on Captain Cipriani and the demand for self-government, it was now a visibly approaching reality.[31] A great victory had been won. The Union Jack was everywhere coming down. A new day of sovereignty was dawning.

At the same time, however, it was palpably not the kind of new day that James would have hoped for. The cold war had had its curtailing effects not only on James's political activities in the United States. It had also had a major effect on the Left within the anticolonial nationalist movements in the Caribbean—dramatically in Jamaica where the Marxists were expelled from N. W. Manley's People's National Party in 1952 and even more dramatically in British Guiana where Cheddi Jagan's Marxist People's Progressive Party was thrown out of government in 1953 after one hundred days in office.[32] More importantly, James's own experience in Trinidad was to sharply underscore the compromising and vacillating character of the nationalist movements and the spinelessness and opportunism of the middle class from which their leadership principally came.[33] Quickly becoming absorbed in the work of reorganizing the intellectual apparatus of the PNM, James advanced the argument that whereas in "advanced" countries the party was an anachronism (this, famously, was the conclusion arrived at in the United States by the Johnson-Forest Tendency at the end of the 1940s), in "underdeveloped" countries such as those of the Caribbean it was a fundamental necessity in guiding and shaping the coming into being of the new nation. In the Caribbean the formation of an independent outlook among the soon-to-be sovereign citizens was crucial, and in this essentially pedagogical process the most important organs of the nationalist party were its publications, first and foremost its newspaper. To this end James worked hard at transforming the *Nation* (looking forward to its becoming a daily) and at seeking to reconstitute its relation (and with it, that of its editor) to the PNM. However, his suggestions for what was in effect the fundamental reimagining of the relation between the party and the nation only threatened and antagonized Williams's colleagues and doubtlessly alarmed Williams himself. So almost as soon as he was enjoying the prospect of participating concretely in the regional project of decolonization he was unceremoniously shut out of favor and out of contact ("There is nothing to discuss" was Williams's rude reply to James's attempt to open a discussion about his predicament and his decision to resign).[34] Moreover, in the wake of his split with James, Williams (following the lead of Alexander Bustamante's Jamaica) withdrew from the federation to pursue single-nation sovereignty for Trinidad. To James this was retrograde. As he ruefully remarked, "the whole politics of independence has pushed the people back not forwards."[35] If something had been won with the coming independence, then, poignantly, something had also been lost. As he was to say, West Indians went to independence as to a funeral. Bitterly disappointed, but at least without loss of his dignity and his sense of purpose, James returned to London to continue his own work.

IT IS IN this context that James writes the book that is often thought of as his finest literary-political achievement, *Beyond a Boundary*. And again, Greek tragedy forms the central fulcrum around which the argument in it turns.[36] This book, though substantially complete by 1957 (James was writing in Spain), was published in the same year as the revised edition of *The Black Jacobins*, 1963.[37] As he seeks to do with the United States in *American Civilization*, so in *Beyond a Boundary* James is sketching an outline of the civilizational structure of the Caribbean, the constitutive relations between culture, society, and politics; and similarly, he is doing so in order to formulate an answer to the fundamental question: "What do men live by?" This indeed is the title of one of the central chapters of *Beyond a Boundary*, that chapter in which part of the context for understanding the style and achievement of the great batsman, W. C. Grace, is set out. In this chapter James suggests how in the wake of the nonmaterialization of the proletarian revolution and the rise of the bureaucratic-totalitarian state he reorganized his Marxist ideas "to cope with the post-war world."[38] This, he says, was "a matter of doctrine, of history, of economics and politics" and was fought out in public debates with collaborators and rivals. But in another register he was, as he puts it, "traveling in a different direction" from many of these interlocutors. He was posing a question most Marxists had not much troubled themselves with. "In my private mind," James writes, "I was increasingly aware of large areas of human existence that my history and my politics did not seem to cover. What did men live by? What did they want? What did history show that they had wanted? Had they wanted then what they want now? The men I had known, what had they wanted? What exactly was art and what exactly culture? I had believed that, more or less, I knew."[39] In the context of Britain and the British colonial Caribbean these questions led in the direction of a consideration of the significance of sports. The Trotskyists no less than other Marxists had proceeded as though sports were a deflection from the important world of politics. "With my past," James says, "I simply could not accept that."[40] But to understand the cultural-political importance of sports required, first of all, that he "get Greece clear."[41] And getting Greece "clear" was, importantly, about tragedy.

"The first recorded date in European history," James tells us, "is 776 B.C., the date of the first Olympic Games."[42] The symbolic significance of this is enormous for the reorientation he wants to effect. Like the Marxists of his own day, the ancient Barbarians were astonished and perplexed that the Greeks should spend so much time in such childish pursuits to the detriment of more serious and worthy affairs. "Forty thousand pilgrims would assemble, including the most distinguished members of Greek society. Plato and Pythagoras were always in the front seats. Socrates, Anaxagoras, Demosthenes, Pindar, Herodotus, and even Diogenes came to the games."[43] Not only were the games an integrated aspect of the intellectual, political, and aesthetic life of Greeks, they became a public space in which orators and poets read to the audience. "It was at Olympia that Herodotus tried out the new art of history by reading his early chapters to the crowd."[44] At the same time, James urges that the social character of the games ought not to be overstated; they were essentially a festival of the feudal aristocracy. When the democracy came to power "it lifted another type of celebration to a position of eminence to which the games soon took second place."[45] This new celebration was dramatic tragedy. And what is important to James is that by contrast with the games it was a *popular* form.

> By the time the democracy had definitively established itself Aeschylus had written the first genuine tragedies. Original and never to be surpassed, they were popular. The dramatists and actors were subsidized by the state or under the aegis of the state. The people did not have to travel anywhere. They paid a few pennies and took their seats. The Athenian drama was competitive, and the populace who attended were moved to laughter and tears, ter-

ror and pity; but also they applauded their favourites and howled down their dislikes in much the same way as did the crowd at the Olympic Games.[46]

On James's account, the Caribbean form that corresponded to this was cricket. Cricket, for James, is not merely a game but an aesthetic—almost narrative—form. It is, as he said, "first and foremost a dramatic spectacle. It belongs with the theatre, ballet, opera and the dance."[47] Of its dramatic character he writes as follows:

> It is so organized that at all times it is compelled to reproduce the central action which characterizes all good drama from the days of the Greeks to our own: two individuals are pitted against each other in a conflict that is strictly personal but no less strictly representative of a social group. One individual batsman faces one individual bowler. But each represents his side. The personal achievement may be of the utmost competence or brilliance. Its ultimate value is whether it assists the side to victory or staves off defeat. This has nothing to do with morals. It is the organizational structure on which the whole spectacle is built. The dramatist, the novelist, the choreographer, must strive to make his individual character symbolical of a larger whole. He may or not succeed . . . The batsman facing the ball does not merely represent his side. For that moment, to all intents and purposes, he is his side. This fundamental relation of the One and the Many, Individual and Social, Individual and Universal, leader and followers, representative and ranks, the part and the whole, is structurally imposed on the players of cricket. . . . Thus the game is founded upon a dramatic, a human, relation which is universally recognized as the most objectively pervasive and psychologically stimulating in life and therefore in that artificial representation of it which is drama.[48]

If tragic drama was the institutional form that enabled the integration of the individual and the community in democratic Athens, then in the Caribbean (the Anglo-Creole Caribbean, at any rate) a similar role fell to the institution of cricket.

IN SHORT THE ideological background against which the new edition of *The Black Jacobins* emerges is nothing if not a profoundly paradoxical and ambiguous one. If the book was originally conceived and written at the outset of great optimism for a revised Marxism and an anti-Stalinist revolutionary movement led by Trotsky, it was now being reissued when Trotskyism had largely failed to produce a coherent theoretical and organizational alternative, and when (especially in the wake of Hungary, 1956) the international expansionism of the Soviet Union seemed never more secure. And if the book was originally conceived and written at the outset of the nationalist assault on British colonial rule in the Caribbean (and indeed as a vindication of black self-determination generally),[49] it was now being revised and reissued when that 300-year-old project was both drawing to a close and opening onto a time of intense uncertainty and anxiety. Here, therefore, was the story of the first and greatest struggle for freedom and independence in the Caribbean being revisited in a moment, at once of unparalleled exhilaration and weariness, fervent hope and certain betrayal. Conceptually the problem-space was characterized by the loss of the purchase of the categories that had given the revolutionary story its point (those categories that organized the progressivist relation between history, subjectivity, and social transformation) and by the demand for a theoretical renovation. By the 1950s, therefore, tragedy came to have the status of a key theoretical tool for James, and in *American Civilization* and *Beyond a Boundary* he deploys it as a way of reconceptualizing the relation between art, history, and politics in a moment of considerable historical crisis and uncertainty.

These are the ideological conditions, it seems to me, in which the importance of the revisions to the 1963 edition to *The Black Jacobins* comes forcefully into focus. These revisions and additions, as I have already indicated, are of special significance for the reading-for-the-present of it that I want to commend, for they underline less the grand story of heroic resistance and revolutionary agency than the problem of colonial modernity and, furthermore, the colonial modern *as* a problem of tragedy. It is to these revisions and additions that I now want to turn.

IV

Let us first recall the setting. It is early 1802. The drama is very nearly over as James closes the penultimate chapter, "The Bourgeoisie Prepares to Restore Slavery." In it we have been watching Toussaint Louverture descend to his worst. No longer the man of unambiguous, unshakable purposes, we see him hesitating, faltering, vacillating, misjudging, and veering sharply—almost determinedly—in the direction of the impending disaster. He has recently had his nephew (and probable rival), the much-beloved Moïse, shot on charges of treason as a result of the rebellion in the North against his leadership. He is growing more and more unsure of himself. While he knows he must act—and act decisively—to right the wrong, he is unable to take a clear position on anything, and each action now only adds to his undoing. As James unflatteringly puts it, he has been "busy sawing off the branch on which he sat." [50] More than this, his effusive and careful letters to France have not been able to stay Napoleon's design of reenslavement. A seemingly inexorable process has been set in motion, and the coming catastrophe is now visibly at his door. The French fleet of reconquest has already set sail under Bonaparte's brother-in-law, General Leclerc, and we look on as Toussaint watches with helpless anguish the first detachment of 12,000 men sail into the harbor at Samana Bay. In James's hand, the moment is intensely vivid and superbly poignant. Here is Toussaint finally come face to face with himself, alone with the angel of fortune standing in the path upon which, it seems, his whole life has been moving with such uncanny certainty since he sat reading his abbé Raynal at Bréda late into his consoling nights of revolutionary hope. He has, to borrow a darkly felicitous phrase from Derek Walcott, "circled every possibility to come to this." [51] Defeat is now almost palpable. The abyss is beckoning. Nothing of his stoicism, of his dignity and determination, is lost, but his dejection is complete. As he returns to his staff to give the orders of engagement he utters the famous words of heroic futility: "We shall perish. All France is come to overwhelm us." [52] And James, never for an instant deserting his doomed hero, and as though turning from this sad spectacle to address his readers, writes feelingly in Toussaint's defense: "It was not fear. He was never afraid. But certain traits of character run deep in great men. Despite all that he had done he was at bottom the same Toussaint who had hesitated to join the revolution in 1791 and for one whole month had protected his master's plantation from destruction. Only this time it was not a plantation and a few score slaves but a colony and hundreds of thousands of people." [53] Here was a man who, as Nietzsche said of Schopenhauer, had the courage to be himself, to stand alone without the men at the front or the nod from above.[54] Toussaint was standing alone at his crossroads, James seems to be saying, but it was Napoleon and not Laius in the chariot.

In the 1938 edition of *The Black Jacobins* chapter 13 moves on from here directly into the stages of the extraordinary military campaign against Bonaparte's forces. The narrative plunges us straightaway into the tumult of the decisive struggle against French colonialism: the pathetic letters from Leclerc to Bonaparte pleading for reinforcements; the negotiated settlement and Toussaint's retirement; Toussaint's arrest, deportation, and imprisonment and eventual death in France; the rise of Dessalines and Christophe; and finally, the victory of the revolution in 1804. By contrast, the 1963 edition opens recursively, reflectively, and meditatively with what I think of as a long, conceptually reframing author's note. Sustaining and deepening the tragic mood and disconsolate temper of the previous chapter's ending, James steps back from the cut and thrust of the impending action and, with a magisterial hand and complete solemnity and utter compassion, underscores the shape of the tragedy we are witnessing and the abject features of the tragic hero who bears the action forward to its unhappy conclusion. I shall have to quote at length here.

The defeat of Toussaint in the War of Independence and his imprisonment and death in Europe are universally looked upon as a tragedy. They contain authentic elements of the tragic in that even at the height of the war Toussaint strove to maintain the French connection as necessary to Haiti in its long and difficult climb to civilisation. Convinced that slavery could never be restored in San Domingo, he was equally convinced that a population of slaves recently landed from Africa could not attain to civilisation by 'going it alone.' His tergiversations, his inability to take the firm and realistic decisions which so distinguished his career and had become the complete expression of his personality, as we watch his blunders and the inevitable catastrophe, we have always to remember that here is no conflict of the insoluble dilemmas of the human condition, no division of a personality which can find itself only in its striving for the unattainable. Toussaint was a whole man. The man into which the French Revolution had made him demanded that the relation with the France of liberty, equality, fraternity and the abolition of slavery without a debate, should be maintained. What revolutionary France signified was perpetually on his lips, in public statements, in his correspondence, in the spontaneous intimacy of private conversation. It was the highest stage of social existence that he could imagine. It was not only the framework of his mind. No one else was so conscious of its practical necessity in the social backwardness and primitive conditions of life around him. Being the man he was, by nature, and by range and intensity of new experiences such as is given to few, that is the way he saw the world in which he lived. His unrealistic attitude to the former masters, at home and abroad, sprang not from any abstract humanitarianism or loyalty, but from a recognition that they alone had what San Domingo society needed. He believed that he could handle them. It is not improbable that he could have done it. He was in a situation strictly comparable to that of the greatest of all American statesmen, Abraham Lincoln, in 1865: if the thing could be done at all, he alone could do it. Lincoln was not allowed to try. Toussaint fought desperately for the right to try.

If he was convinced that San Domingo would decay without the benefits of the French connection, he was equally certain that slavery could never be restored. Between these two certainties, he, in whom penetrating vision and prompt decision had become second nature, became the embodiment of vacillation. His allegiance to the French Revolution and all it opened out for mankind in general and the people of San Domingo in particular, this had made him what he was. But this in the end ruined him.

Perhaps for him to have expected more than the bare freedom was too much for the time. With that alone Dessalines was satisfied, and perhaps the proof that freedom alone was possible lies in the fact that to ensure it Dessalines, that faithful adjutant, had to see that Toussaint was removed from the scene. Toussaint was attempting the impossible—the impossible that was for him the only reality that mattered. The realities to which the historian is condemned will at times simplify the tragic alternatives with which he was faced. But these factual statements and the judgments they demand must not be allowed to obscure or minimise the truly tragic character of his dilemma, one of the most remarkable of which there is an authentic historical record.

But in a deeper sense the life and death are not truly tragic. Prometheus, Hamlet, Lear, Phèdre, Ahab, assert what may be the permanent impulses of the human condition against the claims of organised society. They do this in the face of imminent or even certain destruction, and their defiance propels them to heights which make of their defeat a sacrifice which adds to our conceptions of human grandeur.

Toussaint is in a lesser category. His splendid powers do not rise but decline. Where formerly he was distinguished above all for his prompt and fearless estimate of whatever faced him, we shall see him, we have already seen him, misjudging events and people, vacillating in principle, and losing both the fear of his enemies and the confidence of his own supporters.

The hamartia, the tragic flaw, which we have reconstructed from Aristotle, was in Toussaint not a moral weakness. It was a specific error, a total miscalculation of the constituent events. Yet what is lost by the imaginative freedom and creative logic of great dramatists is to some degree atoned for by the historical actuality of his dilemma. It would be a mistake to see him merely as a political figure in a remote West Indian island. If his story does not approach the greater dramatic creations, in its social significance and human appeal it far exceeds the last days at St Helena and that apotheosis of accumulation and degradation, the suicide in the Wilhelmstrasse. The Greek tragedians could always go to their gods for a dramatic embodiment of fate, the *dike* which rules over a world neither they nor we ever made. But not Shakespeare himself could have found such a dramatic embodiment of fate as Toussaint struggled against, Bonaparte himself; nor could the furthest imagination have envisaged the entry of the chorus, of the ex-slaves themselves, as the arbiters of their own fate. Toussaint's certainty of this as the ultimate and irresistible resolution of the problem to which he refused to limit himself, that explains his mistakes and atones for them.[55]

These are magnificent passages. To my mind, they are among James's most poignant sentences ever. And yet they bear rereading several times over not only for their somber quality of beauty, but for their attempt to refigure our understanding of Toussaint Louverture and the predicament he engaged. In what follows I want to explore the understanding of tragedy they embody and the conception they articulate of the relation between a certain kind of dramatic art and the narrativization of historical events.

"MY IDEAS OF art and society," James wrote in a letter in June 1953 (a decade before the publication of the revised edition of The Black Jacobins), "like my specifically literary criticism, are based upon Aristotle and

Hegel." [56] In fact, in the course of his reflections on art and society in the 1950s, James discusses Hegel far less explicitly than he does Aristotle, though, as we will see, Hegel's place in James's thinking on tragedy, especially on Shakespeare and Melville, is in actuality no less important, and perhaps more.

James was severely critical of the literary criticism of his day (the 1950s). In his view, this criticism had, in its narrow professionalization, become so sterile that it was meaningful only to academic literary critics. Whereas it had "piled up . . . mountains of information" and "discovered a variety of technical instruments," it was incapable, he said, of something more important, namely integrating all this "into any coherent system or method." [57] It was James's opinion that the failure of modern literary criticism (and among the critics he has in mind here are such luminaries as F. R. Leavis and L. C. Knights) had chiefly to do with the forgetting of Aristotle, "the first and still the greatest of literary critics." [58] And forgetting Aristotle, he says, they have forgotten the *worldliness* of literature; unlike him, contemporary critics "do not root their criticism in the world in which they live." [59] On James's account, for Aristotle literature conceived for a popular audience was more difficult than literature conceived for a cultivated audience. This is how he reads the Aristotelian emphasis in the *Poetics* on plot construction, Aristotle's famous remark regarding the superiority of poetry over philosophy, and his affection for tragedy over epic. "Where the modern critic from Saint Beuve to T. S. Eliot conceives of literature as a form of culture for the cultivated and popular art as some form of relaxation or anodyne for the common people, Aristotle choosing between the epic (which was narrated before a cultivated audience) and tragedy (performed before a popular audience) came down squarely on the side of tragedy as artistically superior." [60] In James's view, therefore, the first virtue of tragic drama—whether in its classical Greek or Elizabethan forms—was that it spoke in the language of the people, and to their vital concerns.

In the new opening passages to chapter 13 of *The Black Jacobins* James specifically invokes Aristotle's elusive idea of *hamartia*. It will be remembered that in chapter 13 of the *Poetics* Aristotle defined tragedy—for him the supreme form of poetic drama—as a *mimesis* (imitation or representation) of a certain kind of human action, specifically one organized in such a way as to evoke fear and pity, and through this, to produce a distinctive effect: *catharsis*. In his schematic (or, as James might say, "integrated") account, while a tragedy was made up of a number of objective constituent elements, he gave primacy to plot, the ordered sequence of events that, in their totality, make up the action performed in the drama. Tragedy, Aristotle said, is principally a mimesis of actions not persons.[61] And therefore a well-formed plot is more important to the production of the overall effect of tragedy than the dispositions of the character whose life it depicts.[62] It is in the context of his discussion of the "best kinds of tragic plot" that Aristotle talks about hamartia. In these passages, Aristotle is expressing his views about the devastating reversal that constitutes tragedy; he is arguing that the best kind of tragic plot is neither one in which a decent person undergoes a change of fortune from good to bad, nor one in which a depraved person undergoes a change from bad to good fortune, nor again one in which a wicked person falls from good to bad fortune. Rather, the best kind of tragic plot involves a person "intermediate" between these. "This is the sort of person who is not outstanding in moral excellence or justice; on the other hand, the change to bad fortune which he undergoes is not due to any moral defect or depravity, but to an error [hamartia] of some kind."[63]

The ambiguity of the concept of hamartia has long been argued over, whether what is meant is a moral or an intellectual weakness.[64] Part of the ambiguity stems from the fact that Aristotle's view that the heroes of the best tragedies are not outstanding in virtue seems to contradict the fact that the heroes of the tragedies he greatly admired (those of Sophocles, most especially) are precisely of this kind. The hero of a tragic plot, says Aristotle, will be "one of those people who are held in great esteem and enjoy great good fortune, like Oedipus, Thyestes, and distinguished men from that kind of family."[65] However, Malcolm Heath has usefully suggested that this ambiguity might be satisfactorily resolved if one thinks that Aristotle meant neither a serious moral depravity (such as wickedness), nor mere miscalculation or negligence. In any case, as he says, moral and intellectual errors are not so cleanly separable as that distinction suggests. Intellectual miscalculation or negligence often has a moral aspect or moral consequences and to that extent may indeed be blameworthy. Hamartia, he suggests therefore, is better thought of as including "errors made in ignorance or through misjudgement; but it will also include moral errors of a kind that do not imply wickedness."[66]

Speaking of Toussaint's hamartia, James gives the conventional gloss of "tragic flaw" and goes on to indicate that what is meant thereby is not a "moral weakness" but a "specific error, a total miscalculation of the constituent events." In doing so James seems to be cautioning against the view that Toussaint's catastrophic fall may have been due to a morally unworthy blemish of some sort, some corruption of character, say, or some perversity of intention, that has at length turned back upon him in a tragic reversal and precipitated his suffering. This is not the case. There is no depravity in Toussaint's soul. His "flaw" was in a different register, more intellectual or cognitive than moral. Or perhaps, following Heath, both cognitive and moral together, inasmuch as what Toussaint was faced with was a situation of choice between ends that were not commensurable. Toussaint, James says, totally miscalculated. But it is important to grasp that these miscalculations were not mere arbitrary lapses of judgment, a momentary negligence in an otherwise clear and efficient mind. They would in that case hardly rise to an occasion of tragic suffering. If they did not stem from a perversely divided soul, neither were they the simple result of a poor choice—as though, had he been more vigilant or more thorough or more reflective, or had he the opportunity to do it all over again with the benefit of hindsight, he might have chosen otherwise, and better. Toussaint's error, as James says in an earlier and very profound passage (to which I return in the following chapter), "sprang from the very qualities that made him who he was."[67] He could not have chosen otherwise; there was no otherwise on the basis of which he could have exercised choice—and as James goes on to say, tellingly, there would have been no otherwise for us (his readers) to choose either. We—colonial and postcolonial moderns ourselves and constituted (or conscripted) in precisely the same predicament—could not have chosen better, more successfully, in Toussaint's place.

Toussaint was a whole man, James argues. His errors were inseparable from who he was. That is to say, they were a part of the single fabric from which his political subjectivity was constituted. And therefore they were inseparable from what had enabled him, in the first place, to conceive what he conceived and how, inseparable from what he had been able so magnificently and with so little to accomplish. The singular achievement and the utter failure of his political subjectivity, then, are the sides of one and the same coin. They were part of the single framework—in James's words—of his mind. They are derived from a single cognitive universe, a cognitive universe that had produced both the modern Atlantic world of the sugar plantation in which Toussaint found himself a modern slave and the French Revolution that gave him a revolutionary modernist language in which to criticize it. Toussaint's error, in short, derived from the fact that he inhabited a cognitive universe he could neither simply claim as his own nor completely disavow. It was the error of a conscript.

AS I HAVE suggested, James's conception of tragedy in these 1963 paragraphs is indebted not only to Aristotle, but also, indeed perhaps more profoundly so, to Hegel.[68] I have already quoted James as saying that his understanding of the relation between art and society is "based upon" Aristotle and Hegel. And it is interesting that he follows this remark immediately with another referring to his intense reading and rereading of Aeschylus and Shakespeare because it is chiefly in relation to the latter — and as we shall see, especially in relation to *Hamlet* — that his Hegelian understanding of tragedy is constructed.[69] If, as Peter Szondi has expressed it, there has been a "poetics" of tragedy since Aristotle (that is, an interpretive account of the essential elements of successful tragic drama), Hegel's reflections on the subject form a decisive contribution to the "philosophy" of the tragic that emerged in German thinking toward the end of the eighteenth century as part of a revolt against the dualisms and formalisms of Kant's philosophy. ("Composed as an instruction in writing drama, Aristotle's text strives to determine the elements of tragic art; its object is tragedy, not the idea of tragedy.")[70] But whereas the *Poetics* presents a compact schema (however much of the original text may be lost) of his "theory" of tragic drama, Hegel's reflections on tragedy are scattered over many of his substantial works: from the early theological writings to the later aesthetic ones.[71] Indeed arguably — and in spite of the title of A. C. Bradley's famous lecture (to which I return in a moment)[72] — Hegel has no *theory*, as such, of tragedy, in the comprehensive or systematic way that Aristotle does, only a number of very profound and interconnected observations regarding the nature of the tragic and its relation to the dialectic in ethics, aesthetics, and history.[73] For Hegel, the tragic was a constituent aspect of the division-in-unity or difference-in-identity of which the historicity of ethical life was produced in its perpetual striving for reconciliation. In Szondi's significant phrase, in Hegel, "the tragic and the dialectic coincide."[74]

By contrast with Aristotle's conception of tragedy, in Hegel the analytical focus is directed less to the formal organization of emplotted action, or to the pity and dread that derive from the spectacle of the hero's tragic suffering, and more to the relationship between action and character, especially the collision of contending actions. It is this collision that is conceived to generate the tragic suffering, the catastrophe that often accompanies it, and "the sense of reconciliation which the tragedy affords by the glimpse of eternal justice."[75] For Hegel, the best tragedies center less on the question of the flaw that disfigures and finally destroys the hero or heroine than on tragic conflict. Or to put it another way, the distinctive suffering and catastrophe that interests Hegel is that which derives from a particular kind of action, the kind of action in which a collision or conflict of incommensurable wills or purposes or forces or obligations or powers takes place (between family and state, for example, or ruler and ruled, or parent and child).[76] And for Hegel this is not necessarily a conflict between a neatly divided good and evil, but rather between relentlessly and intransigently one-sided positions adopted by the antagonists. This one-sidedness constitutes the real ground of the collision. And from this point of view he urged that Sophocles's *Antigone* was "the most magnificent and satisfying work of art."[77] For neither Creon nor Antigone are embodiments of unambiguous "ethical substance," neither is wholly good nor wholly bad—even if, on the whole, Antigone's virtues are more attractive than Creon's. Rather what is important for the tragedy is the collision of the inflexible conceptions of the good held by each: their "false one-sidedness," to use Hegel's term. In consequence of this, Hegel writes, "there is immanent in both Antigone and Creon something that in their own way they attack, so that they are gripped and shattered by something intrinsic to their own actual being."[78]

Hegel is of particular interest also because he sought to think the difference between classical and modern tragedies, between ancient and what he sometimes called "romantic" poetic dramas. If conflict and the "tragic steadfastness" that forms its basis are to be found alike in both ancient and modern tragedy, what sets the latter apart from the former is its distinctive conceptualization of character. In ancient drama characterization is more typical and representative than specific and subjective. So that whereas in ancient drama, the tragic heroes, as Hegel puts it, "come on the scene" as "representatives" of the "essential powers that rule human life," in modern drama "the principal topic is provided by an individual's passion, which is satisfied in the pursuit of a purely subjective end, and in general, by the fate of a single individual and his character in special circumstances."[79] It is, needless to say, in the tragedies of Shakespeare that Hegel found paradigmatic instances of the most profound and psychologically penetrating elaboration of the tragic character. And of these tragedies it is of course above all in Hamlet that he finds

Shakespeare's supreme dramatization of this conception of character as tragic self-consciousness. *Hamlet* shares with certain of the tragedies of Aeschylus and Sophocles a plot in which the King is murdered and the Queen marries the murderer, but the modern tragedy turns on the predicament of "character in special circumstances." In *Hamlet*, Hegel says, "the collision turns strictly . . . not on the son's pursuing an ethically justified revenge and being forced in the process to violate the ethical order, but in Hamlet's personal character. His noble soul is not made for this kind of energetic activity; and, full of disgust with the world and life, what with decision, proof, and arrangements for carrying out his resolve, and being bandied about from pillar to post, he eventually perishes owing to his own hesitation and a complication of external circumstances."[80]

The foremost Hegelian theorist of Shakespearean drama in the early twentieth century was A. C. Bradley.[81] In the same year that James was born — 1901 — he delivered a lecture entitled "Hegel's Theory of Tragedy" in which he focused on the place of collision, especially internal ethical conflict, in that philosopher's conception of tragedy. "The essentially tragic fact," he wrote, "is the self-division and intestinal warfare of the ethical substance, not so much the war of good with evil as the war of good with good."[82] His classic work, *Shakespearean Tragedy*, was published in 1904, and since then has been the object of considerable critical appraisal.[83] For Bradley a Shakespearean tragedy is typically a story in which a prominent or conspicuous person undergoes a reversal of fortune that usually ends in his or her death. But what is important, Bradley says, is less the death than the suffering that "conducts" toward it. This suffering, he says, is of a distinctive sort: it does not merely happen to the hero or heroine; it does not simply befall him or her. Rather this suffering and catastrophe is a direct consequence of his or her actions. As he wrote in the remarkable chapter on "The Substance of Shakespearean Tragedy":

> We see a number of human beings placed in certain circumstances; and we see, arising from the co-operation of their characters in these circumstances, certain actions. These actions beget others, and these others beget others again, until this series of interconnected deeds leads by an apparently inevitable sequence to a catastrophe. The effect of such a series on imagination is to make us regard the sufferings which accompany it, and the

catastrophe in which it ends, not only or chiefly as something which happens to the persons concerned, but equally as something which is caused by them. This at least may be said of the principal persons, and, among them, of the hero, who always contributes in some measure to the disaster in which he perishes.[84]

For Bradley, therefore, tragedy turns centrally on the relation between action and character. In a tragedy, what we are witness to are "deeds" being performed, and in a deed what unfolds is, so to speak, character-in-action, action in other words that is fully expressive of character.[85] This is why Bradley writes, in one of his most memorable summations: "The centre of the tragedy . . . may be said with equal truth to lie in action issuing from character, or in character issuing from action."[86] But equally important is the relation between character, action, and something else, namely, ineluctable contingency. In tragedy we also see the ways in which acting in the world obliges us to expose ourselves to conditions and consequences not entirely of our own choosing. Tragedy, in other words, raises significant questions about the extent to which we are — entire and whole and perfectly — the masters and mistresses of our ends. As Bradley wrote: "That men may start a course of events but can neither calculate nor control it, is a *tragic* fact."[87] This indeed is a crucial feature of tragedy that we will return to.

It is not hard to build a connection between Bradley's Hegelian conception of tragedy and James's.[88] In a curious way, these two — Bradley (who was James's elder by exactly half a century) and James (who arrived in Britain three years before Bradley's death, and at a time when his work was overshadowed by negative criticism and misunderstanding) — seem, however unlikely, very much contemporaries of the imagination, at least of the literary-philosophical imagination. Victorian Romantics both, they came at the world with a palpably vivid sense of the dialectical interplay between character (especially heroic character) and action. When, for instance, James writes in a letter to the Russian critic Jay Leyda that what he has done in his ostensible book on Herman Melville, *Mariners, Renegades and Castaways*, is to "put forward a theory of *characters in great fiction*," he could well have expected a nod of recognition and appreciation from Bradley's ghost (emphasis in original).[89] Needless to say, however, what sets James's Hegelian theorization of character apart from Bradley's is his Marxist historicization of it, his understanding of the way in which each great character is, as he put it, "rooted in his own age." [90] In the same letter to Leyda, James goes on to argue that if previous generations of critics could ignore the "social and political assumptions of the work," this is no longer possible or acceptable. As he says with emphasis:

> Now, I repeat, a modern critic has to begin there. If he does not he does not belong to our age. Hazlitt did not have to, nor Coleridge, nor Bradley. They lived in an age in which concern with individual character was part of the total intellectual climate. They did very fine work. Those days, however, are over; that work is done. We have to begin with the social ideas. I do not say that a critic has to write about that aspect. God forbid. He writes about what he pleases. But this is the mental framework of our age. The critic who ignores it will find himself pursuing single aspects until he finds himself way out of contact with anything or anybody, other than his own coterie. I cannot go into it here except to repeat (with Melville) that the age of individualism is over. The intellectual must once more be incorporated with the universal. It is a profound subject today. [91]

It is this attention to the historical location of the distinctive conflicts particular tragic characters embody that will be important to James's reading of Hamlet and, moreover, to his understanding of Toussaint Louverture as a kind of Hamlet.

In a significant way, then, James builds his conception of tragedy around a Hegelian understanding of collision or conflict. In his own thinking about Shakespearean tragedy, and Hamlet in particular, he argued that this collision involved a clash between competing and irreconcilable conceptions of society. As he put it: "All great tragedies deal precisely with this question of the confrontation of two ideas of society and they deal with it according to the innermost essence of the drama—the two societies confront one another within the mind of a single person." [92]

> It seems that at very great crises in human history, and they must be very great, an author appears who becomes aware that one great age is passing and another beginning. But he becomes aware of this primarily in terms of new types of human character, with new desires, new needs, new passions. The great writer, at least each of the three greatest writers the author of this book knows [Aes-

chylus, Shakespeare, and Melville], conceives a situation in which this character is brought right up against things that symbolize the old and oppose the new. The scene is set outside the confines of civilization. What is old is established, it has existed for centuries, it is accepted. But the new will not be denied. It is not fully conscious of itself, but it is certain that it is right. A gigantic conflict is inevitable.[93]

For James (as for Hegel), Shakespeare's genius lay in his incomparable grasp of the conundrums of individual character, and (again, as with Hegel) it is in the figuring of Hamlet more than any other of his characters that this genius is realized. If *Othello* is the tragedy in which Shakespeare has mastered the "problem of human personality," James says, it is in *Hamlet* that, more profoundly and more poignantly than anywhere else, the idea of collision is embodied and given acute expression. This, he says, is because in *Hamlet* the antithesis is not external to the protagonist's character (like Iago to Othello); it is a constitutive part of that character, namely Hamlet, around whom the entire drama centers. James writes:

> Hamlet has a situation to deal with, a situation that is far clearer than the one Mark Antony handled with such success. In his mind he knows what he ought to do. His position, his training, his sense of duty, his personal affections and the spirit of his father, embodiment of the old regime—all are telling him what he ought to do. But he himself, his sense of his own personality, is in revolt, against this social duty. That in itself, however, would not be sufficient to make *Hamlet* what it is—the central drama of modern literature. What gave Shakespeare the power to send it expanding through the centuries was that in Hamlet he had isolated and pinned down the psychological streak which characterised the communal change from the medieval world to the world of free individualization.[94]

If *Hamlet* is "the central drama of modern literature," it is not merely because Shakespeare gave embodiment to a notion of collision of ideas or commitments, but because (as, in another moment, Melville did in *Moby-Dick*) he gave enduring form to a specific social mutation, a specific historical transformation, one indeed through which he was himself living at the end of the sixteenth century and the beginning of the seventeenth.

And this form has endured for us precisely because that transformation is one we now think of as marking the emergence of the modern world.

As Marcellus expresses it with great agitation, as he and Horatio seek to comprehend the ghost's appearance and its appeal to the young and already morbid Hamlet: "Something is rotten in the State of Denmark." Hamlet straddles a time of collapse of one kind of society and the inchoate emergence of another—the change "from the medieval world to the world of free individualization." A later Marxist critic, Victor Kiernan, has argued similarly, contrasting the young Hamlet with his murdered father as men facing different historical directions: "They were different personalities, offspring of discordant eras. One is a warrior, of the age of chivalry, whom we hear of fighting Poles, Norwegians, Englishmen, but doing little else. It is in martial guise that he returns to earth, in full panoply of arms. The other is a young man of modern and speculative turn of mind." [95] Hamlet, he goes on to say, is "stranded between two eras, two conceptions of right conduct," between the old and crumbling order represented by the ghost of his father that demands revenge and the new commercial and jurisprudential order that is emerging.[96] It is as though Hamlet was "suddenly waylaid by a resurrected past and its imperatives, which men of the new age were trying to shake off." [97]

But more than this, for James, Hamlet inaugurates a "new type of human being," namely, the modern intellectual, in whom this collision of obligations (the demands of social responsibility on the one hand and the individual commitment to freedom of thought on the other) is at once poignantly conscious and unmasterable. This is the meaning for James of Hamlet's famous lament as he seeks to secure his friends' pledge to secrecy: "The time is out of joint. O, cursed spite, / That ever I was born to set it right!" As James says: "This colossal change in the organisation of social function was the very basis of individual personality. But from the start it was inseparable from a tension between individual freedom and social responsibility. To the extent that any modern man thought at all, he was subject to this tension. And it was nowhere greater than in the man for whom freedom of thought and speculation became a socialised function—the intellectual." [98] If for the ancient Aristotle thought is subordinate to action, for the early modern Hamlet thought is his conception of action.

The habit of thought was no flaw in Hamlet's character. It was his character. If it was a flaw, it was a flaw in the whole construction of civilisation from the sixteenth century onwards. And inevitably, with this polarisation of action and thought in social function and personality, there developed in the men of thought a sense of isolation, of impotence, of melancholy, because you wandered through eternity, you voyaged in strange seas of thought, alone; that is to say, with an ever-growing consciousness of the divorce between the boundless exhilaration of thought and . . . reality.[99]

Hamlet's obsessive self-regard, his melancholy distraction and frustrated indecisiveness, his feverish preoccupation with the grounds of his action (or inaction), however exaggerated they may seem, are not moral distortions of character or psychological weaknesses of personality. Or rather, to paraphrase Bradley's marvelous expression, if they are indeed exaggerations they are exaggerations of a vital truth about the age in which he lived—an incipiently modern age in which new conflicts (between social duty and freedom, between action and reflective thought) were coming to define the space of public and individual life.[100] If Hamlet continues to be vivid to us today—as of course he does—it is because these conflicts remain profoundly our own.

IT IS THROUGH this Hegelian conception of tragedy as collision, and especially this (Marxist) historicization of the figure of Shakespeare's Hamlet as embodying a specific social mutation, that in the second edition of *The Black Jacobins* James seeks to reimagine his revolutionary hero, Toussaint Louverture.[101] For James, Toussaint like Hamlet embodies a social crisis, the collision of embattled and irreconcilable social forces. Moreover, like Hamlet, Toussaint too is lived by this historical conflict; he is not merely its external product. And as with Hamlet this social mutation, which Toussaint lives as the very integument of his life, has to do with the forms of the modern, in this case the *colonial* modern. Toussaint embodies the collision of, on the one hand, the old order of slave plantation San Domingo, and on the other, the new order represented by the Enlightenment ideals of revolutionary France. And living this conflict in the way he does, Toussaint like Hamlet marks also the emergence of a new type of human being, in this instance, however, not merely the modern but the modern *colonial* intellectual. It is in this sense that for James Toussaint is the first West Indian; he is the paradigmatic instance of a figure that has become very familiar to our postcolonial age. Again like Hamlet, Toussaint has a situation to deal with, one which his closest associates—Dessalines, Christophe, Moïse—would have dispatched without delay, but which he is unable to decide on, and which as a consequence of his irresolution leads to his doom.

For Toussaint, the alternatives with which he was confronted were at once absolute and impossible. As James endlessly repeats, he could choose neither a return to slavery nor a San Domingo without France. He lived the collision of these alternatives, and the values they represented, as a reality to which he was condemned, which, in other words, he could not evade. But Toussaint's dilemma, of course, consists in the fact that these alternatives were not abstractions—they were neither morally equal nor lived in a historical vacuum. On the one hand, as an ex-slave who had fought so long and so desperately for freedom, a return to the degradation of slavery was inconceivable and therefore nonnegotiable. At the same time (and this is the point about the inaugural modernity of the Caribbean) there was no *before* slavery to return to either. The lives of the African slaves (as I have argued in chapter 3) had been irrevocably transformed in a modern direction by the relations of power of New World plantation slavery. The choice, insofar as there was a choice, was not between modernity and something else, but *within* modernity. And from where he stood he was inspired by modernity's highest ideals. Consequently, on the other hand, as the embodiment of a modernist intellectual who had come to recognize himself in the vision of the French Revolution, the ideals of the European Enlightenment constituted the only horizon on which he could imagine a possible future. At the same time this Europe that had made him see what he saw with such clarity was assiduously preparing his betrayal and destruction. So that whereas the pasts (whether slavery or Africa) seemed to hold no possible futures, the possible futures he had long anticipated in the Enlightenment project seemed increasingly like a trap. In this sense, therefore, *The Black Jacobins* is not only about the profound connection between tragedy and modernity for someone like Toussaint Louverture; it is about the ways in which, for someone like Toussaint Louverture, the modern is confronted *as* a tragic condition, a condition in which there are, as James puts it, *only* tragic alternatives.

To read *The Black Jacobins* in this way is to read it as being acutely sensitive to the vagaries of fortune and the contingencies of circumstance that acting in the world inevitably exposes us to. It is to read it as honoring the simple but often obscured fact that as human beings we never begin in conditions of our own choosing. And being the mortals that we are, fettered, limited, partial, never fully transparent to ourselves, never fully self-present to our rational consciousnesses, never fully self-determined in our behaviors, we cannot ever totally overcome these circumstances. Nor do the virtues of character and intellect bring us any nearer the complete mastery of our conditions. And as a consequence we cannot evade our finitude. Toussaint Louverture lived that inseparableness of luck and reason, circumstance and virtue. Born a slave on an eighteenth-century New World slave plantation, Toussaint came of age in a deprived subject-position in a coercive structure of social relations. These were his ineluctable circumstances. And this simple contingent fact established the framework of his world and the idiom in which possibilities became conceivable as possibilities. If his choices were impossible ones, he nevertheless had to choose—to act—and to live with the consequences of his choice. On this reading, Toussaint's greatness consists less in his agency than in the example of his courage in facing up to and acting within the impossible circumstances with which that agency was confronted.

V

I would like to suggest that the seven paragraphs on Toussaint Louverture's tragic dilemma explicitly introduce into the 1963 edition of *The Black Jacobins* a refiguration of its dominant mode of emplotment. These seven paragraphs on tragedy, I suggest, interrupt the revolutionary Romanticism in which the original 1938 edition of the book is principally cast and by so doing offer a revised standpoint from which to consider the narrative relationship between the colonial past and the postcolonial present and future. It is not, obviously enough, that James is changing the ending of his story of Toussaint Louverture—from a good to a bad one, from a happy to an unhappy one—to comply with the strictures of the new genre he is employing. James, after all, is writing history here, not fiction. The basic facts of the case therefore remain as they are: Toussaint is arrested and deported to France where he dies in a fortress in the Jura Mountains in 1803. Rather, what James is altering with these seven paragraphs is the narrative or interpretive framework in which the overall point or significance of the story is given shape.

In the dominant mode of emplotment, as we have seen (in chapter 2), the story of Toussaint Louverture and the San Domingo Revolution is narrated as Romance, as a story of anticipated overcoming in which past, present, and future are arranged in a progressive series or dialectical succession in such a way that we are driven ever forward in the direction of a utopian horizon. Even as Toussaint falters and falls, the new hero—Dessalines—steps forward to complete the anticolonial process and to assure thereby the unbroken continuity of the revolutionary momentum. In this emplotment, the temporality of history has a steady rhythm and a regular and progressive direction. In it, the present is a transitory resting place between where we have come from and where we are going, and the future, we know, will always reprise the past. In George Steiner's lyrical phrase, "Salvation descends upon the bruised spirit, and the hero steps towards grace out of the shadow of damnation." By contrast, the seven paragraphs suggest a somewhat altered historiographical focus and temporal rhythm. They insert a genealogical moment, so to speak, a recursive moment in which the narrative drive folds back on itself in an attitude of self-questioning. If they do not literally rewrite the story they nevertheless oblige us to adopt a certain skepticism to what has gone before and a certain caution in how we judge the remainder of the story to come (it is an interesting fact that the seven paragraphs are placed at the beginning of the last chapter rather than at the end as a concluding reflection). In them the progressivist rhythm of Romance is interrupted, and our attention is centered on the dire conflict that constitutes the dilemma out of which Toussaint's catastrophe unfolds. That dilemma is such as to suggest that past, present, and future are not to be understood as moments of epic succession; they do not line up neatly as though history were heading somewhere: from bondage to freedom, from despair to triumph. Moreover, the colonial past here is not constituted in them as a state of injury that the anticolonial revolution will heal in a redemptive act of salvation, moral-political vindication, and therapeutic regeneration. For tragedy, history is not leading us anywhere in particular. And if the past is a wound, it is one that may not heal; it cannot be evaded or cleanly overcome. It doesn't go away by an act of heroic agency. Nor is there a rational calculus that will guarantee the navigation of the contingencies that inevitably appear in the tragic hero's path. History, in short, is not a series of neat resolutions; the future does not grow triumphantly out of the wicked turmoil of the past.

In the seven paragraphs of the second edition of *The Black Jacobins*, we have before us a reflection on the contingency of human action and the ultimate catastrophe and suffering to which such action sometimes conducts its agent. Toussaint Louverture is a man who, like all great men (James says), straddles historical eras: he looks simultaneously to the past and to the future; and therefore he is, in a sense, an embodiment of both and the resolution of neither. In San Domingo Toussaint has embarked upon a dangerous course of action, in cooperation with some and in dire conflict with others. The course of action is particularly perilous and uncertain because it is unprecedented and as a consequence Toussaint cannot entirely, and in advance, define the ends he pursues. But he acts, nevertheless, and with willful determination because it is the only way to meet the circumstances he faces, to open a way from the past to the future he glimpses. One self-consciously formulated action follows another, which in turn serves to generate another in an interconnected series of actions until he comes to his end in a catastrophic downfall. But that catastrophe, when it comes, is a catastrophe only insofar as it is not merely an event that befalls Toussaint. His conduct in some way helps to lead to it. Again, to paraphrase A. C. Bradley, the tragic fact is that while we can (and often must) embark upon courses of action, we can neither completely calculate nor control them. And if this is so, then what tragedy is suggesting—and what I think James is urging in these paragraphs—is that we should give up the consoling idea that past, present, and future can be plotted in a determinate causal sequence. The contingent relationship between character, action, and circumstances always leaves us open to the possible incursion of tragedy.

WHATEVER THE MOTIVATIONS that led James to insert those seven paragraphs, they add an immeasurably significant dimension to the figuration of his hero Toussaint Louverture and offer a challenge to our contemporary thinking about James's story of the San Domingo Revolution. Framed by Aristotle's conception of hamartia or "tragic flaw" and Hegel's idea of tragic "collision," these paragraphs urge us to read *The Black Jacobins* less as a Romantic narrative of anticolonial overcoming than as a tragedy of colonial modernity. For through them we are led to reimagine Toussaint not so much as the hero of an unfolding epic of liberation but as the embodiment of colliding historical forces, a man confronted with impossible alternatives. This situation of "tragic choice" is by no means an abstract one, however; it is not merely one instance of a universal and mythic theme (though it is also profoundly this). Rather this situation of tragic choice is for James a real outcome of the real transforming effects of modernizing forces on the nonmodern and colonized world. Toussaint is a tragic subject of a colonial modernity to which he was, by force, conscripted. His tragedy inheres in the fact that, inescapably modern as he is obliged by the modern conditions of his life to be, he must seek his freedom in the very technologies, conceptual languages, and institutional formations in which modernity's rationality has sought his enslavement.

It may be true, as Hayden White argues, that there is no simple deterministic relation between historical moments and modes of historical representation. The historian, he famously maintained, is indentured to a choice and chooses from among a range of tropic possibilities. I want to hold on to this insistence on the relative autonomy of narrative. But it may be equally true, as White came later to believe, that as devices of critical illumination certain modes of emplotment comport better than others with the histories they seek to construct. This for me is a question of strategy. That is to say, certain modes of emplotment may answer more adequately the challenge posed by the presents they inhabit. Consequently, the critical value of a mode of historical representation has to be judged, neither absolutely, nor arbitrarily, but in relation to its ability to meet a demand in the present in which it is deployed. I have suggested that the mode of Romance answered an anticolonial demand. It comported well with a historical present in which transformative horizons were still visible—and not only visible, but plausible.

For better or worse, we no longer inhabit that present, and consequently Romance no longer answers a critical demand. I want to suggest that the mode of emplotment of tragedy comports better with a time of postcolonial crisis in which old horizons have collapsed or evaporated and new ones have not yet taken shape. It seems to me that it is this potential that draws James's attention to Aeschylus and Shakespeare and Melville. They wrote in ambiguous moments of historical crisis and transformation, when old certainties were coming apart, when old securities were disappearing, and their tragedies capture the paradox of conflicts that offer no guaranteed resolution. In *The Black Jacobins*, the seven paragraphs on Toussaint's tragic dilemma do not, it is true, entirely displace the dominant Romantic—and vindicationist—figuration of the revolutionary hero, but their agonistic juxtaposition is enough to suggest in outline the direction such a displacement might take. By interrupting the teleologies of Romance and focusing our attention on the paradoxical inscriptions of pasts within the present, on the persistence of contingencies within freedom, on the intransigence of failure within success, tragedy may help us better than Romance to cope with so unyielding a postcolonial present as our own.

# FIVE

# The Tragedy of
# Colonial Enlightenment

Yet Toussaint's error sprang from the very qualities that made him what he was. It is easy to see to-day, as his generals saw after he was dead, where he had erred. It does not mean that they or any of us would have done better in his place. If Dessalines could see so clearly and simply, it was because the ties that bound this uneducated soldier to French civilisation were of the slenderest. He saw what was under his nose so well because he saw no further. Toussaint's failure was the failure of enlightenment, not of darkness. It needed another 150 years before humanity could produce and give opportunity to men who could combine within their single selves the unrelenting suspicion and ruthless ferocity necessary to deal with imperialism, and yet retain undimmed their creative impulse and their respect for the attainments of the very culture they fought so fiercely.

I

If *The Black Jacobins* is a book about enlightenment, still, as these sentences suggest, it is a book about the paradox of enlightenment, not its pathos. It is a book about the enigma of enlightenment, not its transparence. *The Black Jacobins* is a book about enlightenment's recalcitrant ambiguity, the collocation of vision and blindness, knowledge and ignorance, illusion and reality. And Toussaint Louverture, C. L. R. James's doomed hero, is the embodiment of this irrepressible illusiveness of enlightenment. For James, Toussaint's is the gift of enlightened self-consciousness. He possesses this gift in a way that Dessalines does not. And consequently he lives the imagination of the revolution and its possible ends in a way that Dessalines cannot. This is not a question, obviously, of their relative moral value as human beings, as slaves who demand to be free. It is that less encumbered by the specific experience of his circumstance Toussaint can, as Dessalines cannot, partially step back from what he has been made into by those conditions and think more abstractly, more generally, more theoretically, and through a more self-reflexively encompassing vision of what might be. For James, in short, Toussaint Louverture is a modern intellectual who lives the tangled relation between thought and action—and with it the conflict of moral options and the negotiation of contingencies—in a way that Dessalines cannot.

But there is a price of suffering exacted for Toussaint's gift of enlightenment. The cost of his wisdom, his unerring ability to discern the deepest truths about the world in which he lives and which he is trying so desperately to change, is an adequate understanding of the most basic, the most pressing, the most self-evident realities and dangers that lie immediately before him. His privilege of insight, a seeming benediction, is paid for with a terrible blindness. What he holds is in fact a fatal gift. Free of the prescripts that constrain and narrow the horizon of a man like Dessalines, that faithful adjutant, that simple soldier, Toussaint is nevertheless a conscript of a larger and more profound condition that simultaneously enables and disables him, that is at once the source of his strength and his weakness, a condition whose script is barely legible to him because it is written in a language whose familiarity is both recent and coerced, and which, in consequence, he cannot clearly recognize, much less fully command and master. The first and greatest of West Indians, as James so liked to repeat, was a man of unimpeachable dignity and certain genius, a man of impeccable humanity and extraordinary determination, who overcame great odds and whose achievement is monumental by any standard of measure, and yet for all that a man of the most astonishing ignorance and seemingly willful self-deception.

This is the story of Toussaint Louverture in *The Black Jacobins* that I want now to turn my attention to. I am going to argue that this story is a version of the classic myth of the tragic hero of enlightenment. James's Toussaint is imagined on the myth-model of the tragic World Redeemer. In arguing this, of course, I am only reiterating and underlining my view (set out in chapter 1) that James's *The Black Jacobins* is a mythopoetic text. Like Michelet's *History of the French Revolution* and Trotsky's *History of the Russian Revolution*, it is a work of narrative imagination that draws its inspiring significance from its embodiment of a generative and archetypal myth-model—an exemplary story about a past and its relation to the present we inhabit and a future we might look forward to. James is an anticolonial mythmaker, doubtlessly one of the most remarkable of his generation. Again, we are reminded that The Black Jacobins is more than an estimable book of social history (which in any case it never ceases to be); it is first and foremost a book of political instruction and of moral vision. It not only tells us about what happened in the past to those slaves who rose up and shook off their chains; it discloses to us a world of suffering and blight, and the wonder and will and courage and sacrifice and determination and hope it took to confront and change it. Unlike Michelet's and Trotsky's histories, however, James's story of revolution in The Black Jacobins depends for its evocative power and compelling force on the deployment of a version of the classic myth of the hero. James's historical imagination, for all its democratic sensibility and popular ethos, leaned ever in the direction of the heroic man of destiny, the man of world-historical will. Indeed, I have suggested (in the prologue) that in a curious and fascinating way The Black Jacobins depends on two latent figurations of the mythic hero, one of Romance and one of tragedy. We have already seen (in chapter 2) something of the narrative work of the Romantic figuration of Toussaint Louverture, the vindicationist moral it helps to point, and the politics of revolutionary overcoming it helps to urge. In this chapter, following on my discussion in chapter 4 of the framework of "tragic dilemma" through which James revises the emplotment of his story in the second edition of The Black Jacobins, I am going to suggest that reading the career of Toussaint Louverture as a tragedy of enlightenment may offer us some guidance in reconceiving the moral-political predicament of a postcolonial present not only drained of the fervor of the anticolonial revolution and the certainties of the first decades of nation-state sovereignty, but one also confronted by the seemingly intractable dilemmas of modernity.

ONE PARADIGMATIC MODEL of the myth of enlightenment, as is well known, is the story of Oedipus in Sophocles's tragic drama, Oedipus Tyrannus. There is no evidence that James was specially attracted to Oedipus, but there is a good deal in the internal rhythm and structure of the rise and fall of Toussaint Louverture, as he tells it, that conforms to the Sophoclean paradigm of tragic heroism. The setting is the familiar one: It is a Dark Time of Troubles, not of Plague but of Revolution, not in ancient Thebes but in modern colonial San Domingo. Our hero, too, has a recognizable outline: an outcast, a man of doubtful origins and lowly status, who rises to become a much-revered leader. He is, moreover, a man of almost unblemished perfection, selfless courage, and unfathomable compassion, who embodies the great hope of his people for salvation. But most of all, he is a man of singular knowledge and insight, a man who, having solved the riddle of the Sphinx, having attained enlightenment, has earned thereby an entitlement to command. At the same time, however, he is equally a man of pride and ambition, and a man of unbending, even arrogant, willfulness. He believes that his knowledge is the key to freedom, and he employs it in the achievement of his farsighted aims. He is warned, however, and repeatedly, that he may be mistaken about this knowledge; that it may be ill-conceived; that it may yield more—and less—than the freedom he imagines it guarantees. But he heeds no one's advice. He trusts fundamentally, absolutely, to his enlightenment. With it he believes he can subdue or even evade the coming catastrophe. And he does for a time, and with much success, found and sustain the ideal republic of his dreams. Almost immediately, though, the tide begins to change, and he comes to see that his evasions are a mere illusion, that every step taken to avoid his encounter with Fate only draws him closer and closer to his day of reckoning. With crushing clarity he realizes that his great knowledge is also a great ignorance. But it is already too late. The fatal price has been paid. Read this way, Toussaint is a kind of Oedipus.

However, there is another model of the tragic hero of enlightenment, an older one, one that was doubtlessly close to James's mind as he wrote his history of the uprising of the San Domingo slaves. This is the myth of Prometheus as represented in Aeschylus's *Prometheus Bound*, the first and only surviving part of his trilogy on this ancient heroic figure. James, I have noted (in chapter 4), had a tremendous affection for Aeschylus's tragedies, the *Prometheus* particularly, but the *Oresteia* as well. And we have also seen James draw attention to the similarity—and dissimilarity —between Toussaint and Prometheus. (James asserts, remember, that whereas Prometheus is one of the pantheon of "truly tragic" figures, "Toussaint is in a lesser category" because his "splendid powers do not rise but decline.")[1] Oedipus and Prometheus are two great signifiers of the incommensurable paradox of enlightenment. But the myth of Prometheus is especially interesting here because at least since Shelley (that most unrepentantly visionary of the English Romantic poets) it has entered into the modern imagination of the liberation of the oppressed. Prometheus, stealer of fire, was the champion of the wretched of the earth. In his courage and endurance, in his "patient opposition to omnipotent force," he was, said Shelley, "the type of the perfection of moral and intellectual nature, impelled by the purest and the truest motives to the best and noblest ends."[2]

James's disavowal of his genuinely tragic character notwithstanding, it will not be hard to see the parallels between the tragic enlightenments of Aeschylus's Prometheus and his own Toussaint. The Time is the Beginning (or near to it) when mortals are being held in subjection and ignorance by the tyrannical gods. Our hero, mothered by Earth and fathered by one of the gods, is the only Titan to be given the rational gifts of enlightenment and foresight, and the moral virtues of compassion and love of freedom. In the great battle among the gods for supremacy, a battle between the old dispensation of Force and the new one of Reason, he takes the side of the latter, knowing in advance that the future belongs to it, and believing implicitly in reason's rightness. But he is mistaken. The new ruler turns out to be no less cruel toward the mortal children of Earth and plans in fact their destruction. Our hero cannot abide this. He is, after all, himself a child of Earth and feels a profound sympathy for their plight. He steals fire from the heavens and brings it back for Earth's mortals, and by teaching them the material and rational arts of civilization he enables them to liberate themselves from the arbitrary will of the gods and the contingencies of nature. This incenses the chief of the gods, however, and he has the hero captured by Strength and Violence and exiled to a remote mountain where, as a punishment for his audacity, he is impaled and bound forever.

For C. L. R. James, Toussaint like Prometheus is an inaugural figure of an emancipatory enlightenment. Like Prometheus he is confronted with the relationship between bondage and ignorance and, consequently, with the redemptive relationship between knowledge and freedom. But Toussaint's specific world-historical importance resides in the fact that he was confronted with a challenge that would, from that moment on, forever frame the colonial and postcolonial encounter with Europe's modernity: how to use the enlightenment that is his inheritance—and which as a consequence he cannot disavow—to secure and sustain the only image of freedom intelligible to him. For James, Toussaint is the first and greatest of West Indians because he is the paradigmatic instance of the heroism that faced up to the immense ambiguities of this challenge. There is a sense in which he succeeded, and a profound sense in which he failed in meeting this challenge. But as James so presciently understood, we, with all the benefits of hindsight (the early- to mid-twentieth-century anticolonial movement; the late-twentieth-century making of the postcolonial nation-state), could have done no better in his place. Not because we are no wiser than Toussaint was, but simply because there is no overcoming this ambiguous inheritance of enlightenment. There is only the everlasting negotiation with it. For us, no less than for Toussaint, it is a permanent part of what it means to be a conscript of modernity. This is our tragedy as much as it was Toussaint's. In the reading I want to commend, this tragedy is the fundamental story of *The Black Jacobins*. And part of what makes this work of James's of such enduring value is that it remains the fundamental story of our time.

IN THIS CHAPTER, I want to use *The Black Jacobins* to stage an engagement with this problem of the paradox of colonial enlightenment. First, I shall briefly revisit some aspects of the very important contemporary debate about Europe's Enlightenment, and the participation in it of claims about the nature of colonialism and postcolonialism. The question of the significance of the European Enlightenment has, needless to say, been a persistent theme in the very often divisive intellectual discussions about the modern (and "postmodern") world: on the one hand are the poststructuralists inspired by Michel Foucault who take a generally dismissive approach to the Enlightenment, and on the other are the critical theorists who, inspired by Jürgen Habermas, seek the completion rather than the rejection of the Enlightenment's project. Not surprisingly, postcolonial theorists often align themselves with the former against the latter. I will want to urge that while there is something at stake in the question of the Enlightenment for a moral-political criticism of the postcolonial present, this ought not to take the form of either a simple embrace or a simple dismissal.

Second, I inquire into aspects of the quite fascinating discussion about the uses of Greek tragedy as an interpretive framework for reconceiving conventional (largely Kantian) assumptions about moral agency and its implications for our understanding of justice, community, identity, history, and so on. This work has been particularly instructive in its consideration of the ways in which tragedy unsettles, problematizes, and subverts the mastering (and self-mastering) ambitions of civilization and the knowledge/power drive of enlightenment without offering a simple rejection of its claims. What is distinctive about the perspective of tragedy, we will see, is the way it reflects upon the inversions and reversals that constitute the relationship between mastery and chance, between invulnerability and fragility, between knowledge and ignorance, between action and contingency, between achievement and failure. Tragedy poses the questions: What is the connection between, on the one hand, the indispensability of enlightenment to the resistance of tyranny and domination and, on the other hand, the inevitable costs that attend a relentless and unheeding sort of enlightenment thinking? What is the relationship between the invaluable human desire for freedom and the impoverishment that is often the consequence of the attempt to seal ourselves off completely from any risk of contingency and plurality?

And third, I shall return, via this detour, to a reading of *The Black Jacobins* as a tragedy of enlightenment, and more specifically, a tragedy of colonial enlightenment. We will see James establish the figure of his hero, Toussaint Louverture, through familiar images of mastery and self-mastery. His life will be made to unfold through a conventional series of trials and challenges, obstacles and temptations, each one of which he will meet and one by one overcome until at length he meets with a contingency that is, alas, unmasterable, that masters him. The rhythm and plot of the myth-model in which James inscribes his story is archetypal, but James's agenda has a specific historical drive. In the end, Toussaint is neither Oedipus nor Prometheus; he is old Toussaint, former slave on a sugar plantation in the eighteenth-century French colonial Caribbean. The form and content of his enlightenment, therefore, are partly governed by the distinctive colonial circumstances of its achievement. By this I do not mean that it is colonial just by virtue of the accident of its geohistorical location; it is colonial because it is conditioned by the distinctive structure of domination in which it emerges and to which it responds. Toussaint Louverture, as I have said, was a conscript of modernity. And his enlightenment, as a consequence, is partly shaped by the subordinate place he occupied within the relation of power that constituted the modern colonial empire. In James's narrative this history is grist for his mythmaking story of tragedy. Perhaps all enlightenments are shadowed by domination, but my point is only that in this specific instance of that truth James offers a very poignant story with which—and through which—to reflect upon some aspects of the predicament of our postcolonial time. I will suggest that *The Black Jacobins* provides a promising vantage from which to consider the ways in which tragedy potentially complicates our understanding of the constitutive ambiguities of colonial enlightenment in a manner that opens up space for ethical-political theorizing about the postcolonial present.

II

In recent years, an attitude of suspicion toward the modern Enlightenment has become a familiar and indeed prominent feature of the contemporary landscape of social, cultural, and political theory. The eighteenth-century European Enlightenment, so it is argued, constituted a universalizing project aimed aggressively and systematically at displacing the varied traditions of rationality and morality that characterized the nonmodern world and at imposing in their place a singular standard or calculus of instrumental reason. In this view, the Enlightenment's rationalism, historicism, individualism, and foundationalism has had an impoverishing effect on our moral, intellectual, cultural, and political worlds. Far from initiating a period of unparalleled freedom and toleration, as its protagonists believed, the Enlightenment merely opened a new and more far-reaching chapter in the history of domination.[3]

Needless to say, not the least of the most outspoken antagonism toward the European Enlightenment has come from that ensemble of critical strategies known collectively as "postcolonial theory." Speaking broadly, and in a way designed to encompass the vast (and not always cohesive) array of disciplinary and thematic concerns at work in this field, the retheorization of colonialism and the postcolonial over the past two decades or so has been considerably invested in the enterprise of attacking the Enlightenment project. This is not hard to understand. After all, Empire and the Enlightenment developed hand in hand. European colonial rule, while obviously predating the eighteenth-century Enlightenment, became a beneficiary of the transformations in the rationalities, mentalities, and technologies of power in the late eighteenth century and the early nineteenth—in particular those that sought the dismantling of the traditional structures of the social, political, and economic life of the colonized, and the implanting in their place of conceptions and institutions based on *modern* power. Moreover, the Enlightenment underwrote the idea of the privilege of normative European conceptions of thought and behavior over what its visionaries and statesmen were pleased to call the "superstitions" and "customs" of non-European peoples. Not surprisingly, the work of Michel Foucault has been central to this postcolonial enterprise of anti-Enlightenment critique, the Foucault, especially, of *Discipline and Punish*. His notion of the constitutive relation between knowledge and power, his genealogical practice of demonstrating that authoritative configurations of knowledge have in fact been assembled within specific relations of power and specific games of truth, both inspired and helped to shape postcolonial theory's concern to unmask the pretensions of the European Enlightenment. Armed with Foucault, it has been easy to demonstrate, for example, the ways in which the enlightened reform of legal, administrative, and economic policy in the early nineteenth-century British Empire (from Jamaica to Sri Lanka) was only part of a new dispensation of colonial prejudice and a new order of colonial exclusion. In the work of Enlightenment thinkers like James Mill and Jeremy Bentham, the new utilitarian rationalism of the eighteenth century simply provided the clarifying justification for more deeply entrenched, more sweeping, and more efficient practices of subjectification, surveillance, regulation, and discipline.

Part of the aim of this chapter is to raise a doubt about the adequacy of this strategy of criticism of the Enlightenment. I don't entirely disagree with its analytic of suspicion, of course. Indeed, it would be easy enough to show me to have been one of its protagonists.[4] But I am concerned that something about our present may be obscured by continuing to hold—or hold rigidly—to this particular strategy of unmasking the Enlightenment. Therefore, I want to be attentive to those critics who have expressed a concern that attacks on what is called "the Enlightenment Project" often depend upon a demonological reification of the idea of the Enlightenment.[5] It seems to me that rethinking the postcolonial present requires less an either/or and more a both/and approach to the problem of the Enlightenment. And here again, not surprisingly perhaps, Michel Foucault (the much later Michel Foucault) might provide some useful guidance. It is well-enough known that in his early work—on madness, the clinic, the general structures of knowledge, prisons—Foucault was a scornful critic of modernity's progressivist autobiography, its arrogant belief in its enlightened self-consciousness, and much of his work aimed at undermining the assumptions that sustained this view. In his later years, however (as he negotiated criticisms of his work; as he recognized the intersections between his work and that of others such as Horkheimer and Adorno; and especially as he sought to rethink the relation between politics and ethics), he altered this dismissive and one-dimensional assessment of the Enlightenment, and of Kant as its theorist par excellence. (This alteration has of course puzzled and dismayed a number of his critics and commentators who find in it little more than unresolved contradictions.[6] But it has also stimulated a number of other critics and commentators to new appreciations of his work.)[7] On at least three occasions in the last decade of his life, Foucault returned to Kant's famous 1784 essay, "An Answer to the Question: What Is Enlightenment?"[8] On each of these occasions he drew out different dimensions of Kant's essay, but on all of them he sought to rethink the relationship between the Enlightenment criticism, the present, and modernity.[9]

In the essay that will particularly concern me here—"What Is Enlightenment?"—Foucault is looking for a way of thinking about the problem of the Enlightenment that avoids the normalizing drive to take a position "for" or "against" it. This is what he so felicitously calls "the 'blackmail' of the Enlightenment": the coercive demand to respond to a "simplistic and authoritarian alternative: you either accept the Enlightenment and remain within the tradition of its rationalism (this is considered a positive term by some and used by others, on the contrary, as a reproach); or else you criticize the Enlightenment and then try to escape from its principles of rationality (which may be seen once again as good or bad)."[10] Foucault aims to disengage this drive. This is not to say that he discounts the Enlightenment as a transforming historical event or process; that he denies its historical formation "as a set of political, economic, social, institutional, and cultural events on which we still depend in large part." To the contrary, this is precisely the point. Insofar as we are "historically determined, to a certain extent by the Enlightenment" it remains, unavoidably, one of the conditions of the analysis of ourselves. At the same time, Foucault argues, there is another idea of the Enlightenment that ought to command our attention, namely, the Enlightenment as a kind of "attitude," a kind of philosophical "ethos." What is at stake in our relation to the Enlightenment, he urged, ought not to be "faithfulness to doctrinal elements, but rather the permanent reactivation of an attitude—that is, of a philosophical ethos that could be described as a permanent critique of our historical era."[11]

It is the formulation of this attitude or ethos that Foucault finds adumbrated in Kant's 1784 essay, "What Is Enlightenment?" The novelty of this essay, he suggests, lies in its inauguration of a mode of philosophic reflection on the present, posing the question: "What difference does today introduce with respect to yesterday?"[12] Kant's conception of enlightenment as an "exit" from a state of "immaturity" urged the cultivation of the courage and the will to adopt an attitude of criticism of authority in the public use of our reason. This is what is captured in his motto of enlightenment, *Sapere Aude!*[13] But again, characteristically, Foucault is less concerned here with fidelity to Kant and more concerned with the programmatic translation of Kant's "negative" attitude of critique into a "positive" mode of historicocritical inquiry into the present. This mode of investigation—what he calls a historical ontology of ourselves—consists, he says, of a "historical investigation into the events that have led us to constitute ourselves and to recognize ourselves as subjects of what we are doing, thinking, saying."[14] It is, above all, an experimental (rather than a metaphysical or transcendental) mode of investigation, aimed at grasping the limits of who we are, what we have become, what we have made of ourselves. In this sense, it is neither "global" nor "radical" in its scope or ambitions, but is characterized as "historico-practical test of the limits that we may go beyond, and thus as work carried out by ourselves upon ourselves as free beings."[15]

Here, it seems to me, is an approach to the problem of the Enlightenment that students of the postcolonial might learn from. Like the early Foucault, in part guided by him, the criticism of the postcolonial present has been seduced by the "blackmail" of the Enlightenment. But perhaps today the critical return on this blackmail is less compelling than it once was, and perhaps we can ourselves (critics of the postcolonial) put aside the Romantic longing for overcoming that made its allure so attractive and seek instead to cultivate an ethos more open to our ambiguous and paradoxical (and at any rate permanent) relation to the Enlightenment. Foucault's disavowal of the obligation to either affirm or disaffirm a normative commitment to the Enlightenment's idea of itself while at the same time acknowledging that the very terrain of that disavowal, the very mode of critique that sustains it, is part of his inheritance of the Enlightenment, is a recognition of the paradox of enlightenment and a useful place to begin. This attitude, moreover, comports well with my idea, expressed in chapter 3, of the postcolonial paradox of modernity; namely that the contemporary postcolonial problem about modernity ought to be formulated in such a way as to enable us to appreciate both the historical fact of our constitution as modern subjects on a terrain of modern institutions and social relations, and the theoretical justification for a suspicion of any normalization of modernist values and ethos. I want now to suggest that the literary genre of tragedy constitutes a useful framework in which to consider this paradox of Enlightenment. Indeed, as we will see, Foucault has himself been taken to be a tragedian of sorts.

III

In his remarkable book of a number of years ago on Sophocles's extant work, Charles Segal developed a fascinating thesis on the relationship between tragedy and civilization.[16] Greek tragedy, Segal argued, Sophoclean especially, is particularly preoccupied with the precariousness of civilization (by which he means the totality of human social and political organization and cultural attainments).[17] The work of civilization, the exertion and cultivation of our moral and intellectual capacity for mastery over nature (including our own natures), our ability and desire to transform ourselves and our worlds to suit our ends and purposes— all this is constantly open to the threat of disaster from the impersonal forces of nature (including, once again, our own natures), and from the remote and often arbitrary will of the gods.

In the view of the Greek tragedians, our achievements, just because they are *human* achievements, are exposed, vulnerable, and perishable. They are mutable, reversible, and susceptible of inversion, collapsing into dust and nothingness on little more than adverse contingency: the wink of the gods. In their paradoxical vision, greatness and degradation, knowledge and ignorance, fame and infamy are often collocated antinomies. And of the Greek tragedies, Segal argues, it is Sophocles's work that is most acutely attuned to this paradox.[18] This is especially true of the *Oedipus*, Sophocles's great tragic drama of destiny and identity. "No other figure in Greek drama," Segal writes, "more powerfully and tragically embodies the paradoxes of man's civilizing power than Oedipus. Ruler of a great and ancient city by virtue of his intelligence, vanquisher of a mysterious monster itself half-human and half-bestial, Oedipus sums up all that man can attain by mind alone. And yet this solver of riddles does not know the most fundamental thing about himself. He lacks the basic information about his origins that gives man his human identity and sets him apart from the undifferentiated realm of nature and the anonymous, unindividuated realm of the beasts."[19] Oedipus, full of confidence in human reason's power of understanding and control, soon finds this reason powerless to tell him what he most needs to know. As we will see in a moment, the *Oedipus* (and especially this approach to it) has been of particular importance to political theorists seeking to use Greek tragedy as a vantage from which to revise our formulation of the problem of enlightenment, and as I have already suggested it will be central to the reading of *The Black Jacobins* as a tragedy of colonial enlightenment I shall propose.

Martha Nussbaum has made the theme of the unresolvable antinomy between human mastery and human exposure to contingency central to her splendid work on the ethics of Greek tragedy.[20] Her exploration of the continuities and discontinuities between the ways in which Greek tragic poets such as Aeschylus and Sophocles and Euripides, on the one hand, and philosophers such as Plato and Aristotle, on the other, grappled with the fact of contingency in human life is especially interesting, I will suggest, in counteracting the predominance in contemporary theory—both "liberal" and "radical"—of a social and cultural constructionism. As Nussbaum argues, tragedy is centrally concerned with our constitutive openness to luck, to fortune, to chance. It shows us in a dramatic and vivid way our very mortal vulnerability to the contingencies of our worldly life and of our physical embodiment. It urges us to appreciate that we cannot make ourselves entirely immune to the vagaries of misfortune, to calamities, say, or loss or bodily desire. We cannot do this because we are not entirely the authors of our lives. Rather, tragedy presents us with a picture of ourselves as simultaneously authors of our ends and authored by forces and circumstances over which we have no—or little—rational control. In other words, we are at once makers and made, at once active and passive creatures, positively shaping our experience and receptively yielding (or being obliged to yield) to the world's contingent demands on us. It is not that tragedy doubts the formidable capacity of human beings to reason and plan, to order values and ends and make decisions between their relative worth. Indeed it is part of tragedy's point to pay special attention to precisely this compelling aspect of being human. But tragedy's doubt is whether this rationality is such as to be able to make us *completely* immune to the incursions of fortune, to keep us *entirely* beyond the claims of unpredictability and exposure to chance. Tragedy's doubt, in short, is that contingency can be altogether banished or overcome.

For tragedy, the fact of the plurality of values and ends does not present an occasion to affirm a rational calculus on the basis of which to choose the best way to proceed. What interests the tragedians are those instances in which the plurality of values is such that it is impossible to choose satisfactorily—to choose without remainder—between rival goods. This is the kind of conflict over which tragedy wishes to ponder. For some valued goods are not commensurable with each other. And therefore it is not rationally possible either to have them both or to choose neatly between them. They are incommensurable; and in such circumstances one may be obliged to choose a value that is false to other just as deeply held values, an end that damages or diminishes other important ends. In such circumstances choice is tragic. This was the predicament of Toussaint Louverture.

As Nussbaum describes it, this was also Agamemnon's predicament in Aeschylus's tragedy that takes its name from that hero, *Agamemnon*. The fleet is gathered at Aulis about to set out on the expedition against Troy that has been demanded by Zeus to revenge a crime against hospitality. But another god, Artemis (sister of Apollo and goddess of the hunt), has becalmed the winds and the fleet is unable to set off. Starvation is imminent. The seer of the Greek armies, Calchas, divines that the situation can only be resolved by the sacrifice of Iphigenia, Agamemnon's daughter. Here, Agamemnon is faced with a tragic choice. He has not come to this terrible dilemma as a consequence of some blameworthy act. He has been placed there, so to speak, by the contingency of the gods. It comes to him from outside. Zeus and Artemis have imposed on him a situation in which no guilt-free choice is open to him. If he does not sacrifice his daughter, Iphigenia, the fleet will not be able to depart and the defeat of Troy will go unaccomplished. As a result he will have violated Zeus's demand. At the same time, if he carries out the act of child murder he will have violated his filial duty; he will have failed in a particularly horrible way to protect his own child against danger. Both courses of action, therefore, are guilt-bearing. Whichever way he chooses he will violate a prior value and obligation. But choose he must, and choose he does. And Nussbaum writes:

> Agamemnon is allowed to choose: that is to say, he knows what he is doing; he is neither ignorant of the situation nor physically compelled; nothing forces him to choose one course rather than the other. But he is under necessity in that his alternatives include no very desirable options. There appears to be no incompatibility between choice and necessity here—unless one takes the ascription of choice to imply that the agent is free to do nothing at all. On the contrary, the situation seems to describe quite precisely a kind of

interaction between external constraint and personal choice that is found in any ordinary situation of choice. For a choice is always a choice among possible alternatives; and it is a rare agent for whom everything is possible. The special agony of this situation is that none of the possibilities is even harmless.[21]

Nussbaum's *Fragility of Goodness* is explicitly formulated as a criticism of Kantian ethics. She is rightly worried about the widespread influence Kant's ideas have had on contemporary moral-philosophical discussions.[22] Kantians, as she says, believe that the domain of moral value can be—and should be—conceived of as being immune from luck, safe from the unpredictability of contingency (as well as the unreliability of human fancy). Kant's idea of the "categorical imperative," in the *Grounding for the Metaphysics of Morals* (1785), for example, is directed at securing the invulnerability of the domain of moral value by imposing on it an absolutely rational criterion of determination, namely, the a priori reasoning of the autonomous moral agent. It is not, of course, that Kant was unaware of the vagaries of human sentiment. On the contrary, it is *because* (like Plato) he is acutely aware of the human inclination to inconsistency, to be swayed in our judgment by an authority other than our own independent reason (what he called heteronomy), that he so zealously seeks to found his moral imperative on universal and inviolable grounds. The accent in this approach to ethics, noticeably, is squarely on the sovereignty of the autonomous agent to construct her or his world of moral value (only in this way could it be conceived as genuine) and on the moral agent's cognitive ability (and indeed responsibility) to stand back from its given circumstances, from what, so to speak, it finds in itself, and to choose otherwise: to remake itself in accordance with its revisable notion of the good. This Enlightenment view has had an enormous impact on social, cultural, and political theory, especially on the social constructionism that has virtually become the norm in the past two decades or so in the humanities and social sciences in the North Atlantic academy (and elsewhere, no doubt). It has been as fundamental to Rawlsian liberalism as to varieties of postmodernism, feminism, and of course postcolonial theory. They all endorse the idea that we are, above all, self-making creatures. Quite apart from its appeal to Kantian liberals (and Kant, as we have already noted, was a great advocate of the criticizing force of public reason), part of the attractiveness to radicals of a moral self only superficially touched by contingent determinations is that it supports a theorization of resistance in which, being what we have made, we have the sovereign will to change. As Ian Hacking has suggested in his book on social constructionism, "it has been a constant thrust in moral theory, from Immanuel Kant's categorical imperative to John Rawls's theory of justice and Michel Foucault's self-improvement, to insist that the demands of morality are constructed by ourselves, as moral agents, and that only those we construct are consistent with the freedom that we require as moral agents." [23]

Nussbaum's Aristotelian formulations are aimed at disputing this. Tragedy, she suggests, invites us to doubt the Kantian conception of human being and human action and the moral aspiration to rational self-sufficiency and heroic invulnerability it embodies. In her view, it is central to the ethics of Greek tragedy that sometimes we can *only* choose badly even as we are obliged to choose. We may be essentially good people, have good characters, but acting in the world necessarily presents us with situations that are anomalous or that make conflicting and incommensurable demands on us. Tragedy is a meditation on the nature and consequences of action in such circumstances. But more than this it is also a *normative* evaluation of such action. For Greek tragedy, it is not only that life is such that we cannot seal ourselves off from chance, but that seeking to rid ourselves of contingency positively *impoverishes* us. We choose; and in being obliged to choose between impossible options we sometimes choose badly. And in so doing we often participate in our own downfall. Yet it is precisely in this fact of our exposure that the poignant beauty of our humanity lies. It is our vulnerability, our fragility in the face of fortune, that lifts us from ordinariness to the sublime. This, I am going to suggest, is the tragic beauty of James's Toussaint Louverture. What makes him so eternally an instance of the tragic sublime is the singular and courageous way in which he dared at the highest cost to believe in the freedom he sought, and the unflinching way he faced up to his obligation when the time came to choose between what he knew were impossible—because they were incommensurable—options.

IN RECENT YEARS there has emerged a very suggestive attempt to link this conception of the ethics of Greek tragedy to a renewal of political theory or political criticism. J. Peter Euben and Christopher Rocco, for instance, have sought to show that not only was Greek tragedy historically central to the shaping of classical political philosophy but, more

than this, it also can provide a vantage from which to reconceive or reorient the political criticism of the present away from the current stalemate
in which it is trapped. The point of their work has not been to introduce
a new reductionism, to collapse tragic drama and political philosophy
into one another, for example. Rather, the drift has been tentative, exploratory ("experimental," Foucault might say), a seeking out of points
of contact between the tragic and the political.

Euben's point of departure is to take issue with the view that tragedy
and philosophy (or political theory) are necessarily opposed.[24] (It will be
noted that in this regard he shares something with those concerned with
rethinking the relation between myth and philosophy.[25]) This view of
the antagonism between philosophy and tragedy, Euben maintains, rests
on a narrow reading of Plato's *Republic*, one that takes it as the autho-
rizing text of the West's antimythic political tradition. On this reading,
he maintains, Plato's explicitly dismissive attitude toward poetry (tragic
poetry especially) is understood too transparently, too unambiguously.
Against this reading, Euben argues that the *Republic* is in fact a recursive
and contingency-laden text: not only are there important continuities
between it and the tradition of tragic poetry that should not be overlooked in a proper appreciation of Plato, but also "a case can be made
for the *Republic* as a philosophical tragedy."[26]

Furthermore, Euben argues, the claim that tragedy and philosophy
are antithetical to each other depends on a view of each that warrants
criticism and revision. On the one hand it depends on a foundationalist,
ahistorical, and antitraditional view of philosophy, according to which
what distinguishes philosophy from other forms of knowing is its privileged access to "reality" or "truth." However, with the linguistic, pragmatic, and hermeneutic turns in Anglo-American and Continental philosophy, this view is less convincing and harder to sustain than it once
was. On the other hand, the opposition between philosophy and tragedy
depends equally on a view of Greek tragedy as emotional rather than
intellectual, and conservative rather than critical. Again, Euben urges
that this is a mistaken, or anyway an overstated and therefore misleading
view. In the first place, he argues, Greek tragedy was an important public institutional dimension of the democratic life of fifth-century Athens
and as such participated in the cultivation of the cognitive virtues of
citizenship, fostering insight, and enhancing judgment. In the second
place, Euben argues that contrary to the conventional view, tragedy was
neither critical nor conservative, but *both* together. Tragedy, he suggests,

provided a performative occasion where the city's traditions could be simultaneously reflected upon, questioned, and sustained. In this view then, the important point about tragedy is precisely that as a discursive and institutional form it embodied in a compelling way a distinctive capacity for ambiguity and paradox, a capacity to look in several competing directions at once—in the direction of a self-appraisive reflexivity and in the direction of an appreciation of the constitutive ground of tradition. And this is why Euben finds in it the resources for raising a doubt about the inflation of deconstruction and the tone of antitraditionalism that pervades contemporary constructivist theorizing. He is not sure, he says, in a very valuable comment, whether "critics are attentive enough to the practical implications of what it means for 'us' to believe that we are the creators of our own purposes, values, and natures, and whether they are as appreciative of the mythopoetic Nietzsche as the deconstructive Nietzsche."[27]

In developing his argument, Euben draws attention to the work of Michel Foucault and to similarities between the labor of genealogy and the labor of tragedy. This at first sight might appear anomalous. Euben is of course very much aware of Foucault's open contempt for the place of classical Greece in the story of who we moderns are. "We are much less Greek than we believe," he famously said. "We are neither in the amphitheatre, nor on the stage, but in the panoptic machine, invested by its effects of power."[28] Foucault's suspicion of the Greeks is part of his antihumanist suspicion of any straightforward relation between knowledge and freedom. But, as Euben says, dismissive as he is of this tradition, there are strong similarities between his genealogy and tragedy. The dilemmas genealogy poses for contemporary political theory are analogous to those tragedy posed for classical political theory. Foucault raises hard questions, as he says, about progressivist stories, stories that move from "darkness and chaos to light and freedom, from disease, madness, and transgression to health, sanity, and salvation, or from monstrosity to normalcy."[29] Like Foucault's genealogy, "tragedy does not present otherness as a disease to be cured but leaves the other as other. The great Sophoclean heroes and heroines remain liminal figures, saviors and polluters, touching gods and beasts at once. They do not instigate a third term in which warring principles are fully subsumed and silenced."[30] And Euben goes on: "To the degree tragedy confronted its audience with the fictive aspects of its otherwise lived past and warned of the mind's propensity for theoretical closure, it was itself a genealogical activity.

But it was also a warning about genealogy's insufficiencies. The tragedians tend to portray discourses that fix, define, center, and ground us
as simultaneously closing us off from other possible modes of speaking
and acting and giving us place and identity."[31]

For Christopher Rocco, similarly, Greek tragedy offers a way of gaining a productive purchase on the impasse in contemporary political
theory.[32] But while he shares much with Euben in the critical impulse
that shapes his disquiet, his angle of approach diverges somewhat, and
in helpful ways. Rocco is perhaps less convinced than Euben that Foucault offers an adequate model of criticism. Or rather, to gain the desired
theoretical uptake, Foucault's genealogy will itself have to be folded into
another strategy. For Rocco, Foucault is less a way out of the impasse
that confronts us than a constitutive part of it. The genealogical criticism that aims to perpetually unmask the conceits of modernity is in
his view as relentlessly one-sided as the Habermasian critical theory that
seeks to correct and complete the project of modernity. Rocco's hope is
that tragedy will offer us the resources—the epistemological as well as
the moral resources—necessary to give up the paralyzing either/or implied in this Habermas/Foucault opposition and encourage us to adopt
a more both/and attitude to enlightenment. Can we, he asks, develop a
stance "that combines the quest to fulfill the emancipatory aspirations
of enlightenment with an unrelenting critique meant to disturb its normalizing and disciplinary effects?"[33]

Rocco urges that Greek tragedy, and especially Sophocles's *Oedipus
Tyrannus*, shows us that it is possible to develop such a stance, a different, more complicated relation to enlightenment, and that indeed it is
morally and politically important that we do so. Like Segal, to whom he
is clearly indebted, Rocco reads the tragedy of Oedipus as a tragedy of
enlightenment: Oedipus is a paradigmatic civilizing hero whose attainments—as solver of the Sphinx's riddle, as savior and leader of the city
of Thebes—are inseparable from his transgression of the norms of the
very civilization he embodied, and therefore from his downfall. In this
way, he argues, Sophocles makes a contribution to a kind of enlightenment thinking that sustains and even celebrates enlightenment virtues
while at the same time opposing enlightenment hubris and the enlightenment drive to normalize and discipline the very subjects it seeks to
emancipate and empower.[34] But more interesting still is the way Rocco
uses *Oedipus Tyrannus* as a frame through which to reread and resituate
Max Horkheimer's and Theodor Adorno's *Dialectic of Enlightenment*. First

published in the 1940s (and in English translation in 1972), *Dialectic of Enlightenment* came to define the attitude of the early Frankfurt School to modernity.[35] This was an attitude characterized especially by their attentiveness to modernity's contradictions and ambiguous legacy. Rocco wants to show that at the heart of this work is a tragic sensibility that bears comparison with Greek tragedy. *Dialectic of Enlightenment*, he urges, "reinserts the ancient sense of the tragic into contemporary theorizing in a way that alerts us to the tremendous losses suffered in the name, and for the sake, of modernity—losses that liberal and radical theorists alike have largely ignored."[36] Rocco sees Horkheimer and Adorno as "playwrights of a sort, composing a drama about the vicissitudes of enlightenment."[37] He reads *Dialectic of Enlightenment* as a modern tragedy, as he says, a work of tragedy in an antitragic time. It is an example of how the themes, style, and language of Greek tragedy can provide a point of reference and a source of inspiration for theorizing in and about the present. Like Sophocles's *Oedipus Tyrannus*, then, *Dialectic of Enlightenment* is a tragedy of enlightenment.

In this reading, *Dialectic of Enlightenment* offers a way of holding the contradictions of modernity in a more productive nonreductive tension than either Habermas's version of critical theory or Foucault's genealogical critique accomplish by themselves. On one side, like Habermas, Horkheimer and Adorno are looking for a critical and emancipatory rationality, a form of reason that does not suffer from the limitations of the instrumental and administrative reason that has so disfigured modern life. But unlike Habermas, they are more worried about how straightforward the elaboration of such a reason might be; they are attuned to modernity's inversions and reversals and therefore they harbor the suspicion that modernity's gift and modernity's curse might in fact be inseparable. And this is why "*Dialectic* continually invokes the lives that have been damaged, lost, or destroyed, the experiences that have been repressed, subjugated, or smoothed over by the functionalist coherence of a system that must either expand or perish."[38] As a consequence, on the other side, Horkheimer and Adorno, like Foucault, are alive with doubts about the celebratory rhetoric of enlightenment. They have a sense of the relationship between knowledge and power, and they do not believe in a neat fulfillment of the modern Enlightenment's promise. At the same time, however, their view is that freedom is not possible without enlightenment. "*Dialectic* thus pursues a relentless critique of reason that nonetheless refuses to give up the ideas of justice and freedom to further functionalization by the general systems analysts and their managers."[39] This ability to hold the paradoxes of enlightenment without either diluting or prematurely resolving them, Rocco argues, owes to the form of immanent critique it shares with the Greek tragedians, and Sophocles in particular—a form of criticism that is able to acknowledge a debt to the mythic traditions that nourish it while at the same time distancing itself from that tradition.

The wager here, therefore, is that folding *Dialectic of Enlightenment* into this pronouncedly recursive space opened up by *Oedipus Tyrannus* lifts it out of the dead-end quarrel between critical theory and poststructuralism and refocuses our attention away from the paralyzing either/or— either embrace the project of modernity or reject it—into which that debate has inserted us. (As we have already seen, in rejecting the "blackmail of the Enlightenment" this is precisely the point Foucault uses Kant to argue, though it is hard not to see Foucault worrying about the implications of the theme of alienation at work in Horkheimer and Adorno.) It is a move that urges us to read *Dialectic of Enlightenment* as inviting neither a complacent acquiescence to the totalizing languages of modern reason, nor the fantasy of an exit or escape from the modern conditions that have contributed definitively (if not comprehensively) to making us who we are. It invites, moreover, a suspicion of the constructivism according to which we are the autonomous authors of choosing, alterable selves, and neatly commensurable and revisable ends, and honors more poignantly our vulnerability to chance and intractable contingencies, our exposure to surprises and luck, and the ineluctable ways in which our mastery is undone by our fragility and our pasts extend their shadows over our presents. "In tragedy," as Segal has memorably written, "truth has many voices."[40] And consequently, this folding of *Dialectic of Enlightenment* through a poetics of tragedy potentially inspires the cultivation of an idea of politics and of ethical-political action that depends less on the heroism of the sovereign revolutionary subject and the renewal of humanity it promises to initiate, and more on a receptivity to the paradoxical reversals that can unmake and corrupt our most cherished ideals.

IV

As I have said, I want to read the story of Toussaint Louverture in *The Black Jacobins* as an elaboration of the classic myth of the tragic hero of enlightenment. At least as James tells it, Toussaint's fabled career, from

slave to revolutionary leader and from statesman to ignominious pris-
oner, maps an archetypal path that takes him on a familiar symbolic journey—from Call through Travail to an Overcoming and Apotheosis that
leads on, inevitably, to Disaster. In the penetrating luminosity of its depiction of the limits of enlightened knowledge and the catastrophic reversals of fortune that often accompany the greatest accomplishments,
I have moreover suggested, *The Black Jacobins* bears traces of the *Oedipus* of
Sophocles; and in its compassionate portrait of the suffering and doom
that is sometimes the lot of those whose splendid and selfless lives have
been dedicated to the emancipation of the oppressed, there is a strong
echo of the *Prometheus* of Aeschylus. In turning now to a discussion of the
"dialectic of enlightenment" at work in *The Black Jacobins* I should stress
that my concern is to work with the complex moral density with which
the figure of Toussaint Louverture is constructed in it, both in terms of
the moral substance he is made of and the way he deals with the circumstances in which he finds himself. Like any tragic dramatist James
does not seek to simply evade reductions of either character or plot but,
rather, to use them creatively in establishing the tensions and intensities
his historical drama depends on.

I have said that *The Black Jacobins* is a tragedy not only of enlightenment,
but specifically of colonial enlightenment. As we will see, the images
through which James figures his tragic hero, Toussaint Louverture—the
image of the man of exceptional knowledge, courage, skill, compassion,
and so on—are the recognizably conventional images of the mythic hero
of enlightenment. James is a mythmaker, it bears repeating. At the same
time, these images are given a concrete historical location, namely, the
slave plantation formation of the French colonial Caribbean at the end
of the eighteenth century, and a distinctive embodiment in the person
of Toussaint Louverture, former slave. The constraints on, as well as the
possibilities available to, Toussaint were shaped by the specific conditions of modern slave society in David Brion Davis's "Age of Revolution."
Toussaint's enlightenment and Robespierre's, while astonishing in their
own right, were not strictly symmetrical. They were shaped by a differ-
ential access to both the new knowledges of critical reason and freedom
and to the power that gave the new discourse its political and institutional force. This, of course, is precisely James's point. The tragic enlightenment of Toussaint Louverture may be structurally subordinate,
but it is not morally inferior. Toussaint's tragic enlightenment, moreover, is paradigmatic in the sense that standing as it does at the begin-

ning of the encounter with European modernity it fashions the model for a journey which postcolonial intellectuals have never ceased—and perhaps can never cease—traversing.

In reading *The Black Jacobins* in the way I propose, I am especially interested in drawing out the moral and political lessons to be learned from its reflection on the inversions and reversals that constitute the relationship between mastery and contingency, light and dark, invulnerability and fragility, knowledge and ignorance in Toussaint's career. As I suggested earlier, I am concerned with James's sense of the connection between, on the one hand, the indispensability of Toussaint's enlightenment to resisting colonial tyranny and domination, and on the other hand, the inevitable costs that accompany relentless and unheeding enlightenment thinking. I am interested also in the way *The Black Jacobins* establishes the relationship between the inestimable human desire for freedom and the moral and intellectual poverty that derives from the attempt to seal ourselves off completely from any risk of contingency and plurality of perspectives.

WE FIRST MEET Toussaint Louverture in *The Black Jacobins* in the context of James's discussion of the character of slavery in the opening chapter on "The Property." Among other things James is setting out the conditions of Toussaint's emergence as leader of the San Domingo Revolution and, in effect, the conditions that will make his later summons to destiny intelligible, compelling. It will be the earliest indication we have of his exceptional status, his singularity, his difference. This is simultaneously a particular and a general story: "The leaders of a revolution are usually those who have been able to profit by the cultural advantages of the system they are attacking, and the San Domingo Revolution was no exception to this rule" (BJ, 11 [19]). In this chapter, in a famously vivid description, James sketches a picture of slavery as not merely a system of physical brutality and even torture, but a system that degrades the soul and numbs the mind. He offers that a small elite group of slaves escape this treatment, but these largely become loyal and obedient to their masters. A very few of them, however, make use of their opportunities to transform themselves in another direction. One of these is the memorable Henri Christophe, the waiter who will later become a famed emperor of Haiti.[41] But the exemplary, unsurpassed instance of this is to be found only in our hero, Toussaint Louverture. It is Toussaint Louverture, a man without equal, who will surmount and exceed his limiting personal and social circumstances in an unprecedented—and in the end tragic—way.

In a series of rapid strokes and condensed formulations James gives us a glimpse of our hero's unusually supportive and nurturing family background. Toussaint, we are told, was a generation removed from Africa, where his father had been a "petty chieftain" who, when brought to San Domingo, was "bought by a colonist of some sensibility" who "allowed him a certain liberty on the plantation and the use of five slaves to cultivate a plot of land" (BJ, 12 [19]). From his father Toussaint gained knowledge of medicinal plants and so forth, and from his "godfather" he learned French and some Latin. In short, Toussaint was born in conditions that enabled him to gain not only practical knowledge but also *intellectual* knowledge as well. He grew up in conditions that made possible the cultivation of a reflective intelligence, an active, questioning, thinking—in short, enlightened—mind. Eventually this brings him to the attention of his master, and he is elevated to the position of coachman, a position, James says, that "brought him further means of comfort and self-education" (BJ, 12 [20]). Soon Toussaint is further promoted to the position of "steward of all the live-stock on the estate—a responsible post which was usually held by a white man" (BJ, 12 [20]). These circumstances then bring "into his hands" some of the great texts of the French Enlightenment, including the abbé Raynal's famous book, *Philosophical and Political History of the Establishment and Commerce of the Europeans in the Two Indies* (BJ, 16 [24–25]). Toussaint will famously find his destiny inscribed in Raynal's prophetic remark that "a courageous chief only is wanted."

It is significant to note here that James is stripping the story of Toussaint Louverture's origins bare of the sentimentalism and racial moralizing that could easily attach to it. It would be a mistake to believe that in this description James is merely showing us the beginnings of a Eurocentric sycophant. James has another and I think more profound agenda here. What is important to see is that Toussaint is partly the product of contingencies, of conditions he does not and cannot himself choose: on the one hand, enslavement and all the limitations that this is understood to imply; on the other hand, an innate intelligence and relatively fortunate circumstances of birth. As James puts it in an eloquent turn of phrase: "If Toussaint's genius came from where genius comes, yet circumstances conspired to give him exceptional parents and friends and a kind master" (BJ, 12 [20]). We are urged, therefore, to see a man who was gifted with the exceptional aptitudes and unusual dispositions that make for genius but whom chance had also afforded the good fortune to live in circumstances that would enable him to take full advantage of these aptitudes and dispositions and develop them in a direction denied most others who shared his general conditions of life. Here in other words was a man, born where he was, in the extreme and lowly conditions that misfortune had given him to be born into, whose circumstances, however, dire as they were, were still such as to spare him the worst of the privations and degradations that befell most of those who shared his lot, and whose gifts and natural talents were of a sort as to enable him to make the best of what he was given and raise him far beyond what he was. It is really only a prelude: the outline of a promise which is yet to be fulfilled. But preliminary though it is, the signs are there for the future coming of our hero and the powers he will bring to remaking his world.

It is against the pregnant background of these contingencies that when we meet Toussaint Louverture for the second time (in chapter 4, "The San Domingo Masses Begin"), James spends a number of passages establishing the contours of intellect, character, and will through which our hero exhibits his capacity for mastery and, especially, his capacity for self-mastery. Between our first encounter with Toussaint and the one we are about to have, in which he will begin his mythical journey and make his entrance into history, James has drawn a complex portrait of the social, economic, and political circumstances, both local and international, of the time. He has described in some detail the slave-owning class, their indulgences, their viciousness, their demoralization, their isolation, their ignorance. And he has given us a breakdown of the distinctions among them, between big whites and small whites, between mulattoes and free blacks, and between whites and nonwhites. The discussion of all this is important because it prepares us for the shifting alliances and affiliations that will occur during the course of the revolution. Furthermore, the inverse relationship between the misery of the slaves and the prosperity that formed the justification of the existence of San Domingo is underlined: "If on no earthly spot was so much misery concentrated as on a slave-ship, then on no portion of the globe did its surface in proportion to its dimensions yield so much wealth as the colony of San Domingo" (BJ, 33 [46]). It is well known, and hardly needs repeating, that The Black Jacobins is one of the first to acknowledge and draw out the implications of San Domingo's world-systemic location, in particular metropolitan France's dependence on the wealth it derived from it. This wealth would provide the economic basis for the dissatisfactions that gave rise to the French Revolution, news of the beginning of which arrives in the colony in September 1789. As the events in France begin to unfold we watch the agitations in the French Assembly and San Domingo of the movement for equal political rights among the wealthy mulattoes and its eventual savage defeat (especially the torture and execution of the mulatto leaders Chavannes and Ogé in the public square at Le Cap in October 1790). However, as James writes, "phases of a revolution are not decided in parliaments, they are only registered there" (BJ, 63 [81]). It will be the black masses of San Domingo who, having watched and prepared themselves for two years, now take matters into their own hands and, following the legendary meeting at Bois Cayman, move into insurrectionary action in the north on August 22, 1791, under the leadership of the *hungan*, Boukman. With destructive force, the slave rising begins. And as James writes, with absorbing dramatic tension, it isn't long before Toussaint Louverture is called to his great undertaking: "It is at this period, one month after the revolt had begun, that Toussaint Bréda joined them, and made an unobtrusive entrance into history" (BJ, 69 [90]).

In the description of Toussaint Louverture that follows (and it is in fact a deeply sensitive one), James begins to outline a portrait of his hero's astonishing powers of intellect and character. Above all, he shows us a man who is the embodiment of perfectly enlightened self-consciousness. The very name he adopts soon after joining the revolt, "Louverture" (the Opening), signals this self-consciousness of enlightenment. Toussaint-the-Opening is the man who has come to cast his light upon the dark and troubled landscape and open the redemptive way to freedom. His every action is predicated on, and characterized by, an exceptional degree of reflective forethought, a studied deliberation, and a carefully measured calculation. We have the sense, as we observe him preparing his future, of a slightly aloof and profoundly cerebral man, without Hamlet's playful sense of irony perhaps, but nevertheless constantly aware of the most minute tilt and movement of his mind, of its every cognitive process. As James writes:

> The man who so deliberately decided to join the revolution was 45 years of age, an advanced age for those times, grey already, and known to everyone as Old Toussaint. Out of the chaos that existed then and for years to follow, he would lay the foundations of a Negro State that lasts to this day. From the moment he joined the

revolution he was a leader, and moved without serious rivalry to the first rank. We have clearly stated the vast impersonal forces at work in the crisis of San Domingo. But men make history, and Toussaint made the history that he made because he was the man he was (BJ, 70 [90–91]).

Here, in the unlikely figure of a Wise Old Man, is the revolutionary crossing the threshold and going forth to meet his Destiny.

As steward of his master, Toussaint occupied a position that gave him "experience in administration, authority, and intercourse with those who ran the plantation." (BJ, 71 [91]). This was his practical education. He also cultivated his mind, reading "Caesar's Commentaries," which gave him "some idea of politics and the military art," as well as the "long volume by the abbé Raynal on the East and West Indies" which educated him in global economics and politics (BJ, 71 [91]). Toussaint, then, is a man with an intense—indeed, with a relentlessly obsessive—intellectual relationship with himself and the world in which he lives. He is transparent to himself, fully in charge of himself, fully in command of his intentions and his ends. Given his circumstances, his "superb intellect had therefore had some opportunity of cultivating itself in general affairs at home and abroad: from the very beginning he maneuvered with an uncanny certainty not only between local parties in San Domingo but between the international forces at work" (BJ, 71 [91]).

But Toussaint was not merely distinguished by the capacity of his mind, extraordinary as that by itself was. He was also distinguished by the almost flawless excellence of his character. The following passages are worth quoting at length:

An important thing for his future was that his character was quite unwarped. Since his childhood he had probably never been whipped as so many slaves had been whipped. He himself tells us that he and his wife were among the fortunate few who had acquired a modest competence and used to go hand in hand and happy to work on the little plot of land which some of the slaves cultivated for themselves. Besides his knowledge and experience, through natural strength of character he had acquired a formidable mastery over himself, both mind and body. As a boy he was so frail and delicate that his parents had not expected him to live, and he was nicknamed "Little Stick." While still a child he determined to acquire not only knowledge but a strong body, and he strengthened himself by the severest exercises, so that by the time he was 12 he had surpassed all the boys of his age on the plantation in athletic feats. He could swim across a dangerous river, jump on a horse at full speed and do what he liked with it. When he was nearly 60 he was still the finest rider in San Domingo, habitually rode 125 miles a day, and sat his horse with such ease and grace that he was known as the Centaur of the Savannahs.

As a young man he had run after women. Then he decided to settle down. Refusing to live in the concubinage which was so widely prevalent among all classes in San Domingo, but particularly among the slaves, he married a woman who already had a son. She bore Toussaint one child, and he and his wife lived together in the greatest harmony and friendship, when he was master of all San Domingo just as in the days when he was an ordinary slave. . . .

From childhood he had been taciturn, which singled him out among his countrymen, a talkative, argumentative people. He was very small, ugly and ill-shaped, but although his general expression was one of benevolence, he had eyes like steel and no one ever laughed in his presence. His comparative learning, his success in life, his character and personality gave him an immense prestige among all the Negroes who knew him, and he was a man of some consequence among the slaves long before the revolution. Knowing his superiority he never had the slightest doubt that his destiny was to be their leader, nor would those with whom he came in contact take long to recognise it (BJ, 71–72 [92–93]).

Toussaint, moreover, is as self-sufficient as he is self-conscious. He needs no counsel but his own. In a fundamental sense, he is always alone. Nor does he allow himself to trust anyone. He has several secretaries taking the same instructions so as to guard himself against being tricked or betrayed. He holds himself aloof from every human need. He is invulnerable to the most elementary wants. We hear repeatedly that he rarely sleeps. He succumbs to no transports of lust or violence or irrationality. There is indeed nothing passional about him. In this way, as a consequence, he seems completely invulnerable to any extraneous intrusion that might undo the settled concentration to which his disposition inclines him. Short-term ends, let alone irrational or impulsive ones, never distract him.

It is this enlightened, reflective self-consciousness and self-sufficiency, above all else, that separates him from the other notable leaders of the revolution. None of them—not Jean François nor Biassou, not Dessalines nor Moïse—possess, in any proximate measure, Toussaint's virtue of self-consciousness and self-command. To be sure, each of these is a man of considerable talent in leadership who inspired those he commanded during the unfolding insurrection. But they are separated from Toussaint by a fundamental qualitative gap. The contrast with the earlier leader, Mackandal, is instructive here, because although this indomitable Maroon chief was a remarkable man in many respects—in intelligence, in fortitude, in organizing ability—he was not what Toussaint was, namely, an *intellectual*. He did not live *in mind* as Toussaint did. In 1751, it will be remembered, Mackandal had conceived the "bold design" of uniting all the blacks and "driving the whites out of the colony." In eloquence, fearlessness, and vigor, he was no doubt Toussaint's equal. Still, there was between them an essential difference. Mackandal's methods, as James says, were those of a "terrorist." "An uninstructed mass feeling its way to revolution, usually begins by terrorism, and Mackandal aimed at delivering his people by poison" (BJ, 13 [21]). He conceived an elaborate plan and built up a massive organization over six years; but it all came to nothing when the plan was discovered in 1757 and he was executed. "His temerity was the cause of his downfall. He went one day to a plantation, got drunk and was betrayed, and being captured was burnt alive" (BJ, 13 [21]). We are made to feel, with a certain force, that this could not have befallen Toussaint. Toussaint is not moved by such meager, instrumental motivations as hatred—he was a man "quite untouched by the ordinary human passion of revenge" (BJ, 168 [204]). It is not merely that he is unfamiliar with such urges. It is that his foresight affords him an acute awareness of their limited scope. Toussaint is moved, rather, by completely rational ends he has self-reflectively prepared in advance. And consequently, he is never blindly precipitated into action.

This is not to say, of course, that James shows Toussaint to be a man without feeling. To the contrary, Toussaint is repeatedly presented as an unusually sensitive man. Indeed, the contrast is everything. All his personal relations—with family, friends, and enemies alike—are characterized by consummate compassion, forbearance, and generosity. James gives the example of his very devoted relationship with his wife and children; he tells us of an occasion when Toussaint is on his way to prosecute some important purpose or other when his path is crossed by a lost child and he turns back to leave the child with his wife. And there are, of course, the innumerable instances when he intervenes to save the life of some enemy of the revolution. But this sensitivity is also unmistakably of a certain sort. It is not, like Rousseau's pity, spontaneous sentimentality. It is deeply cognitive; it is measured, restrained, and even-tempered. Again, there is nothing emotional about Toussaint Louverture, nor anything excessive or effusive, nothing that is not already mediated—and mastered—by mind.

One of the most dramatic and remarkable illustrations of this self-command comes early in the story when Toussaint has not yet become the great man we know he will, over the next several years, become. It is indeed the more arresting for that because we are afforded a fascinating glimpse of this turn of mind as it seeks to negotiate a relatively minor but profoundly consequential contingency. This is that famous moment of Toussaint's hesitation to join the insurrection—it is the almost obligatory pause in the myth of the hero when the protagonist seems to stall to consider his impending action, as if by some premonition he knows that beyond this threshold there is no return. The slave uprising has been gathering momentum, the plantations are being put to the torch, and the whites are fleeing en masse to the relative safety of Le Cap on the north coast of the island. Toussaint's benevolent master, Bayou de Libertas, has joined a camp of armed planters not far from his property. And Toussaint, instead of immediately putting his oppressors to death, destroying or appropriating their belongings, and joining the insurrectionary forces himself, as his fellow revolting slaves are doing, stays behind to protect his master's wife, Madame Bayou de Libertas, and their property.[42] It seems an unaccountable action for a slave! But Toussaint, of course, is not like other slaves. Note that it is not ignorance that stalls him. He is fully aware of the state of affairs; he has, after all, been in communication with the leaders. Indeed it is precisely *because* he is aware that he hesitates. The reason, rather, is that he himself is not ready. He needed time to reflect on the nature of his undertaking. James's comment makes this clear:

> Toussaint, then as always master of himself and of all near to him, maintained this untenable situation for over a month. But as the insurrection grew, worn out by the strain of defending the property, his master and his mistress, and learning that Madame de Libertas' life was now in danger, he decided that the old life

was over and a new one had begun. He told Madame de Libertas that the time had come for her to go to Le Cap, packed her and some valuables in a carriage and sent her off under the care of his brother, Paul. He sent his own wife and the two children of the household into a safe spot in Spanish San Domingo. Then he slowly made his way to the camp of the revolted slaves (BJ, 70 [90]).

A great deal of the complexity and nuance of Toussaint's character is contained in this wonderful passage. We are made to see a man who, even in moments of hesitation, seeming uncertainty, remains completely and perfectly in control of his actions, balanced, impervious to unreasoned impulses. And when, later, he once again hesitates, this time fatally, James draws the connection between the quality of his doing and quality of his doubt: *deliberation*. Even at this moment of his "greatest uncertainty," James says, "so different from his usual clarity of mind and vigour of action, Toussaint showed himself one of those few men for whom power is a means to an end, the development of civilization, the betterment of his fellow-creatures. His very hesitations were a sign of the superior cast of his mind. Dessalines and Moïse would not have hesitated" (BJ, 235 [281]).

His hesitation, in other words, is the mark of his enlightenment. It underlines the fact that this is a rational act of the will, not the eruption of anxiety; it is a task that Toussaint is, with profound and difficult forethought, undertaking. Unmoved by the galvanizing passions of the insurrectionary moment, he is not merely unwilling to act irrationally, but he is invulnerable to any desire to act against an antecedently held principle. We recognize in him, therefore, a grave and fastidious commitment to an idea of himself, an idea which he is unwilling either to compromise or to yield to the frenzy of destruction. And we notice that even when he does decide that the time has come to give up his position, it is not because he feels that the principle has proven wrong, nor even simply that he has reconsidered the circumstantial forces and determined that they are no longer such as to enable him to maintain his position. It is because he has finally arrived at the decision to pursue his undertaking. In this we also see a man of perfectly ordered mind. There is no clutter about Toussaint's thought; there is nothing but tidiness. As James says: "Nothing could be imagined more calculated to revolt his orderly mind than the spectacle which the slave camp presented" (BJ, 72 [93]). And so it is with great reluctance that he eventually goes out to impose his will on the chaos and disorder and wretchedness of the incipient revolutionary movement.

Another significant moment that underlines this remarkable self-consciousness comes not long after this hesitation when Toussaint Louverture is a member of one of the bands — Biassou's — of revolted slaves. This is perhaps his first great trial when his mettle is really tested. The Spanish offer the bands an alliance against the French revolutionary government which has recently executed the king. All the insurgent bands accept the offer, but Toussaint, beginning to impose his will on the course of events, negotiates his agreement as an independent leader. And James writes: "Like all the other blacks, Toussaint attacked the godless kingless republic and fought in the name of royalty, both Spanish and French. *But for him, already, these slogans were merely politics, not convictions*" (BJ, 99 [124]; emphasis added). Again, this is what sets the temper of Toussaint's mind apart from that of his fellow leaders. What distinguishes him is not merely discipline or courage or even military skill, but the strategic gift of farsightedness. Whereas the other leaders, James says, were satisfied with their positions, Toussaint "alone of all the black leaders, with freedom for all on his mind" (BJ, 92 [116]) has his sights set on a further horizon.

IT NEEDS TO be underlined that James draws this austere picture of a faultless Toussaint Louverture with perfect seriousness and complete devotion to the integrity of his hero. There is no trace of condescension or irony in this picture of Toussaint's omnipresence, or deliberate mysteriousness, or his cultivation of the virtues of civility and courtesy, taste, politeness, courage and bravery, and tolerance. We are not invited to laugh at Toussaint, to mock him, as from the position of those who already know his fate. James does not adopt a superior pose in relation to his hero-protagonist. But, at the same time, if James shows us this seamless embodiment of enlightenment, he also invites us to consider the cost of sustaining this conception of the human good and the conceptions of political order, community, and justice that accompany it. If we can see the advantages of the enlightened committed action that Toussaint embodies we are soon made acutely aware of the disadvantages, the pitfalls, the losses. Or rather we are soon made aware of the extent to which the disadvantages are, paradoxically, immanent within the advantages themselves, the weaknesses immanent within the strengths, the ignorance immanent within the knowledge. No sooner are we witness to

Toussaint's magnificent display of self-mastery and enlightened perfection than we begin, disturbingly, to see its paradoxical consequences in disfiguring blindness. This is perhaps nowhere better illustrated than in the nature of the threat his nephew, Moïse, posed to him and the manner in which he dealt with it.

If James has presented Toussaint Louverture as a Promethean hero who aims courageously at the emancipation of his people from tyranny, he also presents him as a kind of Sophoclean Creon who presides with single-minded authority over the political order of freedom he has established. In the classic myth-pattern of tragic reversal, the hero-as-World Redeemer becomes the hero-as-Tyrant. Toussaint governs by an unswerving attachment to certain rational principles of justice and order. By the light of them, he seeks to promulgate humane laws by which the people are to be ruled; he tries to instill a conception of fairness and to cultivate a new public spirit of liberty. Toussaint is no narrow-minded despot: he wants light where once there was darkness, he wants prosperity where once there was need, he wants happiness where once there was sorrow, he wants right where once there was wrong.

> Personal industry, social morality, public education, religious toleration, free trade, civic pride, racial equality, this ex-slave strove according to his lights to lay their foundation in the new State. In all his proclamations, laws and decrees he insisted on moral principles, the necessity for work, respect for law and order, pride in San Domingo, veneration for France. He sought to lift the people to some understanding of the duties and responsibilities of freedom and citizenship. It was the propaganda of a dictatorship, but not for base personal ends or the narrow interests of one class oppressing another (BJ, 207 [247]).

There is nothing either cynical or instrumental in any of this. We see Toussaint acting consistently out of a profound sense of conviction and direction. He believes deeply and sincerely that his way—the restoration of the rationality of a plantation economy—is the only way to reestablish the economic viability of the colony. And he believes with convincing faith that it is only by reestablishing this viability that the freedom from slavery that has been won with blood can be secured and preserved.

> The ultimate guarantee of freedom was the prosperity of agriculture. This was Toussaint's slogan. The danger was that the blacks

might slip into the practice of cultivating a small patch of land, producing just sufficient for their needs. He would not allow the old estates to be broken up, but bound the interests of the labourers to their work by giving them their keep and a fourth of the product. . . . He confined the blacks to the plantations under rigid penalties. He was battling with the colossal task of transforming a slave population, after years of licence, into a community of free labourers, and he was doing it in the only way he could see. On behalf of the labourers he saw to it that they were paid their quarter of the produce. This alone was sufficient to mark the change from the old to the new despotism (BJ, 201 [242]).

None of this, taken by itself, is worthless. But at the same time it is coldly remote. We feel the chill air of its Platonic abstractness, its rigid conformity to a principle of Form. And in his drive to banish any sign of dissent or plurality from the body politic of his new Republic, Toussaint refuses to hear the voices of other values and other commitments. He is deaf to them. He cannot, for instance, hear the voices that came to find their representative in Moïse, his commandant in the North Province. Toussaint, James says, had instituted a rigid discipline that was "hard, but it was infinitely better than the old slavery" (BJ, 231 [275]). The "old revolutionary blacks," however, objected less to this aspect of Toussaint's regime (the reinstitution of a regime of plantation work) than to the fact that they were often obliged to work for whites, sometimes for their old slave masters who Toussaint had invited back to their plantations. This was a bitter pill to swallow. More than a physical blow, it was an insult; it was like rubbing salt into an old and yet unhealing wound. Moïse was sensitive to this outrage.

In the narrative economy of *The Black Jacobins*, the figure of Moïse works like a kind of counterpoint to Toussaint and Dessalines. In James's imagination of the problem of leadership (shaped as it was in the context of the unfolding catastrophe of the Russian Revolution) Moïse is to Toussaint and Dessalines as Trotsky is to Lenin and Stalin. He was the people's tribune. Like Antigone's demand that there are attachments and obligations that are being violated by her uncle Creon's autocratic refusal to bury her brother, Polynices, who has died fighting against Thebes, Moïse was urging that certain kinds of solidarities and commitments were being dishonored by Toussaint's demand that the exslaves serve under their old slave masters. "Whatever my uncle may do,"

James has him declare, "I cannot bring myself to be the executioner of my colour. It is always in the interests of the metropolis that he scolds me; but these interests are those of the whites, and I shall only love them when they have given me back the eye that they made me lose in battle" (BJ, 231 [275]). Where Toussaint wanted to keep the old plantations intact Moïse wanted to break them up and redistribute them among the junior officers and the subalterns. Moreover, while Moïse (unlike Dessalines in this regard) was not antiwhite, he favored an alliance between blacks and mulattoes against the French, whereas Toussaint sought always to appease the white Creoles and the French.[43] Consequently the insurrection in the North is a deep threat to Toussaint. It exposes him to unsettling contingencies that his mode of thinking cannot abide. "He was afraid," James writes, "that Moïse might supplant him" (BJ, 232 [277]). But it is not merely that Moïse might take his place, it is that the moral and social values Moïse represented were incompatible with his understanding of what rule required. So he has him shot (at Port-de-Paix on November 24, 1801). It is in some ways the beginning of the end of the revolution. But Moïse, even at the moment of his death, is undaunted, and speaks his last heroic words from the ungovernable grove of those alternative values. "He died as he lived," James writes. "He stood before the place of execution in the presence of the troops of the garrison, and in a firm voice gave the word to the firing squad: 'Fire, my friends, fire' " (BJ, 232 [277]).[44] The irony in the remark is brutal.

Again, it is important to see here that, fatal though his actions, Toussaint is not guided by a simple blameworthy self-interest. There is no question in James's mind that the execution of Moïse was inexcusable.

> Toussaint explained nothing, and allowed the masses to think that their old enemies were being favoured at their expense. In allowing himself to be looked upon as taking the side of the whites against the blacks, Toussaint committed the unpardonable crime in the eyes of the community where the whites stood for so much evil. That they should get back their property was bad enough. That they should be privileged was intolerable. And to shoot Moïse, the black, for the sake of the whites was more than an error, it was a crime. It was almost as if Lenin had had Trotsky shot for taking the side of the proletariat against the bourgeoisie (BJ, 237–38 [284]).

But for James it would also be an error to perceive in this Toussaint harboring and acting out of some perverse preference for his white ex-masters. "It is Toussaint's supreme merit that while he saw European civilisation as a valuable and necessary thing, and strove to lay its foundations among his people, he never had the slightest illusion that it conferred any moral superiority" (BJ, 227 [271]). In such passages, James is very keen, I think, that we see that however far he leans in the direction of the interests of the whites it is not self-hatred that motivates him but the working out of a detached and single-mindedly held principle. What Toussaint harbors, rather, is a Hegelian dream that a synthesis or reconciliation is possible, that the old conflicts can be resolved in a higher unity among blacks, whites, and mulattoes. What he is committed to is a humanist hope for a civic compact conceived on the basis of racial harmony. His hope is to transcend the old animosities and prejudices, the old hatreds and wounds, and to join the old divisions together in making an enlightened Republic guided by the abstract principles of liberty, equality, and fraternity.

Toussaint does not see that some wounds and injuries are more recalcitrant to healing than others; that some assaults or injustices cannot simply be papered over or made good by the application of an enlightened rational calculus however well-meaning it might appear. And consequently, Toussaint's course of action, at first sight the very embodiment of enlightened values and ideals, leads in the end to a new form of barbarism. Rigidly one-sided, these values and ideals propel him into actions that are, in fact, the antithesis of his cherished hopes for liberty. As James describes the crisis that would lead almost immediately to military dictatorship, Toussaint's mind is "so set" in its ways that "he could only think of more repression." He did not think, for example, as he might well have paused reflectively to do, to ask whether there might have been praiseworthy reasons for the popular support of Moïse, reasons he might have casuistically accommodated to his own larger emancipationist purposes. "That question he did not stop to ask or, if he did, failed to appreciate the answer." Instead he releases a reign of terror. "In the districts of the insurrection he shot without mercy. He lined up the labourers and spoke to them in turn; and on the basis of a stumbling answer or uncertainty decided who should be shot. Cowed by his power they submitted" (BJ, 233 [278–79]). This is the beginning of the end of Toussaint Louverture: once the savior of the revolution, now the revolution will need to be saved from him.

In short, Toussaint pays a terrible price for the fixed, unbending adhesion to the prescriptive order of values he holds and rules by—the loss of such important values as those defended by Moïse and his support-ers. It is an immeasurable, irreparable loss. In Toussaint's inability (or rather, unwillingness) to admit the virtue of other values—those values, in particular, that register the injurious traces of the past of slavery, that are an embodiment of a people's collective memory of degradation—we are made poignantly aware of the impoverishment that accompanies so remote and so rigid a conception of the good, however well-meaning, however farseeing. To seek, as Toussaint has sought, to seal himself off from exposure to the ordinary vagaries (of impulse, of passion, of friend-ship) and likewise to seal his moral-political order off from those stub-born contingencies and hard-to-heal wounds that are the past's legacy to the present is to reduce the world of value to little more than a cipher. It is to refuse to see that there are perhaps some values that are more unyielding than others, that touch us more deeply than others, and that, as a consequence, are not simply available for revision or uprooting by the revolutionary principles of enlightenment. In that moment of tragic conflict with Moïse, we are made to recognize, with a startling and hum-bling clarity, the arrogant simplicity of Toussaint's sophisticated and cosmopolitan world of value. In a moral-political world in which all other values exist only to be overcome or subordinated to a single over-arching principle, while we may gain much from the vision and certainty, we also impoverish our readiness for accommodation, for reception, for openness, for yielding. And from this angle of comprehension, it is hard not to reach the conclusion that Toussaint's brilliant enlightenment is merely the condition of his surpassing blindness; his intellectual free-dom little more than the obverse side of his bondage to ignorance; his astonishing success the mirror of an appalling failure.

READING THE BLACK JACOBINS as a tragedy of enlightenment, I'm sug-gesting, obliges us to rethink some of our cherished assumptions about political order, about justice, and about community as well as some of our conventional conceptions about agency, responsibility, and freedom. This is because such a reading teaches an untimely lesson about the constitutive ambiguities of enlightenment, about the paradox of mas-tery and self-mastery enlightenment confronts us with. As it urges us to appreciate the yield of enlightened thinking in terms of insight and critical judgment, it also shows us the impoverishment into which we are led by the arrogance of a one-sided reason that seeks to disavow or disallow any space for contingency and chance, for the ineluctable ways in which the past lays its claims upon the present. Through Toussaint's great achievement and failure (indeed, through the dialectical connection between his achievement and his failure), we are poignantly warned about the doubleness of knowledge: how it can obscure even as it reveals, how it can disable as much as it enables, how it can imprison at the very moment that it emancipates. It seems to me that in a postcolonial world drained of the determined fervor of anticolonial revolution and the passionate certainty of the first decades of sovereignty, there is an untimely timeliness about these lessons. They draw our attention away from the nostalgia and clinging resentment that attaches to the fading narrative of anticolonial Romance and invite us to consider, with more humility perhaps, the paradox of the conjuncture in which we find ourselves.

In the example of the tragic heroism of Toussaint Louverture we meet, at one and the same time, the yield and the limit of enlightenments — we meet enlightenments at their best and at their worst, in what they open as well as in what they close. And we meet this yield and this limit of enlightenments not as separate goods between which it is possible to choose, but as constitutive aspects of a single framework of cognitive and moral understanding. As James so deftly suggests, Toussaint's weaknesses sprang from the very qualities that gave him his strengths, his insight from the same qualities that blinded him. What he could imagine, and what he could not, were part of a single whole. The farsighted self-consciousness that enabled him to keep certain features of his world before him, that enabled him to analyze with such clarity and judge with such decisiveness, was but one side of a nearsighted rationalism that prevented other features of that world from coming into view. The acute self-awareness through which he sought to master himself, through which he endeavored to shut out distracting quotidian demands and extraneous forces and guard against exposure to unwanted irrational intrusions, made him more, not less, susceptible to miscalculation and instrumental reductiveness. In this perspective, the tragedy of enlightenments is that what lies immediately before one is often obscured by the very fact that one can see what lies in the distance — seeing the forest, sometimes, obscures the trees. I want to stress, though, that on this reading of The Black Jacobins the point is not that, consequently, the trees are more important than the forest, the subaltern than the elite, Dessalines than Toussaint. The point rather is the harder one that enlightenments have their costs, costs that cannot simply be evaded, postponed, or overcome by the application of one rationalism or another, costs, in other words, which can often be tragic.

But Toussaint's failure to seal himself off from exposure to vulnerability, his failure to completely master every dimension of his circumstance, every possible contingency, does not diminish the poignant grandeur of his heroic vision and the stoic dignity with which he faced his doom and endured his suffering. "In overthrowing me," he said, as he stepped aboard the boat that would take him into imprisonment in France, "you have cut down in San Domingo only the trunk of the tree of liberty. It will spring up again by the roots for they are numerous and deep" (BJ, 277 [334]). Toussaint Louverture remains, in James's resounding phrase, the first and greatest of West Indians. The phrase is not merely rhetorical—nor, in fact, is it to be limited to this particular area of the postcolonial world. Aimé Césaire once said it is our great misfortune to have encountered "this particular Europe on our path." [45] And James's point is that the paths of Toussaint Louverture are a paradigmatic instance of the negotiation of that encounter, a paradigmatic instance of paths we have all since negotiated—the paths of our conscripted encounter with European modernity. The enduring greatness of Toussaint Louverture is that he took up this challenge and traveled these paths without the benefit of precedent, without the lamp of the gods to whom the Greek tragedians could turn for hindsight. His, therefore, is the paradigmatic story of our encounter with the enlightenments of colonial modernity. It is how we began. And we have never ceased—and perhaps it is our fate to never cease—rehearsing the paradoxical journeys of that tragic encounter.

We have tragic art, Segal reminds us, so "that we may not forget the dimensions of life that our structures cannot encompass. . . . Without that paradoxically pleasurable pain of tragedy, our order and our structures would become sterile, self-enclosed, solipsistic, arrogant with the hybris of their own intellectual power." [46] I believe that in the paradoxical path of the enlightenment and suffering of Toussaint Louverture, *The Black Jacobins* teaches this inspiring and unforgettable lesson.

# Epilogue

What is [the] sense of the tragic? It is, in my opinion, a sense of the inability of man in society to overcome the evil which seems inseparable from social and political organisation. To have a sense of the tragic, is to be aware of this and to judge humanity by the degree to which man is able to struggle against this overriding doom; to establish moral and psychological domination over the feeling of impotence and futility which it would otherwise impose.

I have been trying over the course of this book, above all else, to engage in a certain revisionary practice of historical criticism in the present and to do so against the background of what seems to me the deadend of the hopes that defined the futures of the anticolonial and (early) postcolonial projects. My general aim has been to make out a case for a practice of criticism that is alert to the idea that propositions are always answers to questions or interventions in a discursive context, because it seems to me that keeping this idea in view is one way of helping us to determine whether the questions we have been asking the past to answer continue to be questions worth having answers to, and whether the stories we have been telling ourselves about the past's relation to the present continue to be stories worth telling. In pursuing this concern, my specific aim has been to argue for changing the questions we ask about the colonial past as a way of beginning the work of imagining new answers for the present and new horizons for the future. I do not assume this work to be straightforward or easy.

I have been saying that, on the whole, anticolonialism has been written in the narrative mode of Romance and, consequently, has projected a distinctive image of the past (one cast in terms of what colonial power denied or negated) and a distinctive story about the relation between that past and the hoped-for future (one emplotted as a narrative of revolu-

tionary overcoming). But after Bandung, after the end of anticolonialism's promise, our sense of time and possibility have altered so significantly that it is hard to continue to live in the present as though it were a
mere transitory moment in an assured momentum from a wounded past
to a future of salvation. The horizon that made that erstwhile story so
compelling as a dynamo for intellectual and political work has collapsed.
It is now a superseded future, one of our futures past.

As I said at the beginning of this book, in my view we live in tragic
times. Not meaningless times, not merely dark or catastrophic times but
times that in fundamental ways are distressingly off kilter in the specific
sense that the critical languages in which we wagered our moral vision
and our political hope (including, importantly, the languages of black
emancipation and postcolonial critique) are no longer commensurate
with the world they were meant to understand, engage, and overcome.
And consequently, to reinvoke Raymond Williams's deeply poignant
phrase, we are living with the "slowly settling loss of any acceptable
future." It seems to me, therefore, that a tragic sensibility is a particularly apt and timely one because, not driven by the confident hubris of
teleologies that extract the future seamlessly from the past, and more
attuned at the same time to the intricacies, ambiguities, and paradoxes
of the relation between actions and their consequences, and intentions
and the chance contingencies that sometimes undo them, it recasts our
historical temporalities in significant ways.

This has been my broad preoccupation. I have routed it through
C. L. R. James's masterpiece, The Black Jacobins, because (as I hope by now
is abundantly clear) it is a book of enormous insight in many registers
simultaneously. Not only is it one of the founding anticolonial texts of
the twentieth century and a book about one of the founding anticolonial
struggles in the modern world, it is a book of profound historiographical self-consciousness. In The Black Jacobins, James is practicing effective
history. His acute sensitivity to his successive historical presents make
its composition (in the mid-1930s) an exemplary instance of anticolonialism's emplotment of the past and future in the present, and its (partial) recomposition (in the early 1960s) an uncanny intuition that this
mode of history-telling—Romance—may stand in need of displacement
by another—tragedy. I have read The Black Jacobins—in the disjuncture between its first and second editions—as opening up a discursive space
in which to explore the contrast-effect of tragedy as a mode of emplot-

ting the story of the relation between our pasts, our presents, and our possible futures.

It may be helpful, though, as a way of closing off these reflections, to set beside James another intellectual whose sense of the tragic and time was also worked out in relation to the problem of revolution and the founding of freedom.

IN THE SAME year that Vintage issued the second and revised edition of C. L. R. James's *The Black Jacobins*, 1963, another famous study of revolution was published (this one by Viking): Hannah Arendt's *On Revolution*.[1] It is a book that, however neglected it might be by contemporary students of Arendt, marks an important stage in the overall evolution of her moral and political thinking between the 1950s and 1960s. But readers of *On Revolution* will recall that Arendt brings her study to a close with a meditative and moving evocation of tragedy as a mode of remembering the spirit of the revolutionary tradition. Significantly, she invokes Sophocles's late play, *Oedipus at Colonus*, and quotes from it the memorable lines: "Not to be born prevails over all meaning uttered in words; by far the second-best for life, once it has appeared, is to go as swiftly as possible whence it came."[2] These of course are the melancholy words spoken by the chorus at one of the crucial—transfiguring—junctures in the development of the dramatic action in Sophocles's tragedy. It is that moment when the blind and broken—but also bitter and awesomely determined—Oedipus is about to be confronted by the hypocritical pleas of his son, Polynices, who is seeking to enlist his father's support for his fratricidal campaign against his brother and Thebes. Oedipus has paid his debt, and although he carries upon his person the everlasting stain of his unspeakable crime, the sign of his polluting negativity, he has begun a reversal from an object of mere pity to a subject of an elemental and prophetic power. The scene is one of poignant choral reflection on the grim and ennobling spectacle of humanity. Fully aware now of who this shattered suppliant is, what the catastrophe was that befell him, and the abject and humiliating life of wandering beggary to which he has since been subjected, the chorus offers a plaintive requiem for the helpless misery of old age and the death which is our final and inescapable release from "envy and enemies, rage and battles."[3] In contrast to the earlier Oedipus play (*Oedipus Tyrannus*), the overriding note here is of tragic reconciliation rather than tragic conflict.[4]

Hannah Arendt does not tell us this, however. Instead she simply, and somewhat enigmatically, points our attention in another—characteristically political—direction, foregrounding the great legislator Theseus rather than Oedipus. She writes: "There he [Sophocles] also let us know, through the mouth of Theseus, the legendary founder of Athens and hence her spokesman, what it was that enabled ordinary men, young and old, to bear life's burden: it was the polis, the space of men's free deeds and living words, which could endow life with splendour." This is all she says, but it is enough to encapsulate and evoke for us the consoling relation between political memory and poetic tragedy she is striving for. The resonance with *The Black Jacobins* is uncanny. *Oedipus at Colonus*, written toward the end of his own life, was Sophocles's great paean to the passing glory of Periclean Athens and its embodiment in the figure of Theseus, the mythic hero of Attic unity. With his usual solemnity, the old poet and statesman returns to the theme of Oedipus, to place his equally aging hero at yet another crossroads. The years of pain and desolation visible in his bearing, bereft of every comfort save the unceasing companionship of his faithful daughter, Antigone, Oedipus has nevertheless survived (if also survived *with*) his past. And now, on the outskirts of Athens, near the village of Colonus (where Sophocles himself was born), he has come to make a final resting place for his mortal remains and to offer himself—an embodiment of virtue—as a sacrificial blessing to his chosen city in its future time of trouble.

What Arendt means us to bear witness to here is a contrasting political ethos: the contrast between the cold machinations of Creon and Polynices (both of whom aim at luring Oedipus back to Thebes for their own instrumental purposes) and the magnanimity of Theseus who offers Oedipus a haven of hospitality. It is the contrast between the boorish authoritarianism of Thebes and Athens as the embodiment of forbearance and fellowship, gracious compassion and welcoming citizenship. Part of the virtue of the Athenian polis, Arendt seems to be saying, is that, as the birthplace of tragic thought, it was well attuned to the fact of human action's exposure to contingencies, its vulnerability to the unexpected and the unplanned-for. Because the polis was "the space of men's free deeds and living words," it was necessarily a space in which human action was at once indeterminately plural and concretely particular; therefore, it was also a space of collisions and negotiations of rival wills and intentions, one that depended for its durability upon an acute sense of human fragility and the inherent mutability of human ends.[5]

As one of her most astute readers, Judith Shklar, famously suggested shortly after Arendt's death in 1975, for Hannah Arendt there was an intimate connection between political philosophy and tragic thought.[6] I want to conclude my own reflections on *The Black Jacobins* here by exploring briefly some aspects of what James and Arendt share, and what they don't, and what the implications of this might be for connecting up tragedy, the political, and the historical memory of our postcolonial present. Hannah Arendt and C. L. R. James are particularly interesting to read with each other, I think, because of the ways in which they intersect with, and diverge from, one another. Born within a few years of each other (James in 1901, Arendt in 1906), both were passionately independent and public intellectuals formed in subordinate positions by a European tradition in political and philosophical crisis: James as a colonial and black, Arendt as a Jew and woman. Both were drawn, almost reluctantly, toward a heterodox preoccupation with, and understanding of, politics (Arendt from philosophy, James from literature); and both praised spontaneous, autonomous, and direct-participatory political action such as had occurred in the Paris Commune of 1871, the Russian soviets of 1905 and 1917, and of course the workers' councils in the Hungarian Revolution of the fall of 1956.[7] For both of them, too, their conception of politics was shaped to a considerable extent by the rise of the totalitarian regimes of Hitler and Stalin; indeed, both saw in Nazism and Soviet communism the end of the old Europe. Moreover, both James and Arendt were compelling storytellers who relied heavily on the evocative, illuminative, and revelatory power of narrative to do theoretical work (it is not insignificant that James was a published novelist and Arendt an occasional writer of unpublished poems).[8] Drawing on different intellectual traditions—Arendt from German philhellenism and James from Victorianism—both also took as their Archimedean point of literary-political reference the dramatic aesthetics of the Athenian polis. Finally, both conceived a particular admiration for the American republic. Of course, neither was an uncritical observer of social and political life in the country in which both spent formative years, but both thought they could recognize in its emblematic doctrine of freedom the hope of a new public happiness. (It is not unimportant in this regard that they were both very fond of Herman Melville, James of *Moby-Dick* and Arendt of the posthumously published short work, *Billy Budd, Sailor*.) But these are only the incidentals.

More important to my purposes here, both *The Black Jacobins* and *On*

*Revolution* are fundamentally concerned with the problem of the founding of freedom and its relation to tragedy. James and Arendt, admittedly in different ways, through different historical instances and elaborations, and with different degrees of explicitness and focus, are both concerned with the distinction between mere liberation from tyranny and oppression, on the one hand, and the political project of creating institutional conditions for the positive work of freedom, on the other. James, I think, would have agreed with Arendt when early in *On Revolution* she writes: "It may be a truism to say that liberation and freedom are not the same; that liberation may be the condition of freedom but by no means leads automatically to it; that the notion of liberty implied in liberation can only be negative, and hence, that even the intention of liberating is not identical with the desire for freedom. Yet if these truisms are frequently forgotten, it is because liberation has always loomed large and the foundation of freedom has always been uncertain, if not altogether futile."[9] Ultimately I want to suggest that both *The Black Jacobins* and *On Revolution* are informed by a tragic vision of freedom. Both Arendt and James share "a sense of the tragic" (to use James's phrase); they share a poignant sense of humanity's everlasting struggle with the ineluctable contingencies of evil that, as James puts it, are "inseparable from social and political organization" and that give rise to human suffering. Both, I think, were profoundly sensitive to the sense of futility that is so often the crushing measure of our mortal lives in the face of this evil; and both, moreover, saw tragedy as a way of thinking about the fragility of the project of founding freedom and the fact that it has, by and large, eluded the modern aspiration to revolution.

ON REVOLUTION IS sometimes thought of as the third and final volume in Hannah Arendt's trilogy on political theory. And indeed, anyone familiar with the first two, *The Origins of Totalitarianism* and *The Human Condition* (as well as the collection of essays that complements these monographs, *Between Past and Future*),[10] will easily recognize that although the mood and tone of each of these books is different—registering, in part, their different occasions and different organizing subject matter—the central preoccupations are much the same: the nature of freedom, the virtue of public action and speech, the idea of authority, the concept of politics and its distinctive realm, and so on.[11] In many ways, Arendt is pursuing an interconnected project of remarkable consistency and continuity. At the same time, however, *On Revolution* is its own profoundly original book.[12] It is, above all, Arendt's lament for what she calls the "lost treasure" of the revolutionary tradition.[13] All revolutions since the French Revolution (the constitutive point of origin of the revolutionary tradition) have been carried out in the name of freedom, but all of them, Arendt argues, have missed the opportunity to *found* freedom — that is to say, they have failed to give freedom an appropriate and durable political-institutional form. As a consequence, she maintains, the "revolutionary spirit" embodied in the principles of "public freedom, public happiness, and public spirit" (the principles that inspired and motivated the eighteenth-century revolutionaries) has faded not only from practice but even from memory. In *The Black Jacobins* too, as we have seen, James is also asking a question about the fate and the legacy of the eighteenth-century revolutionary tradition, how it shaped and how it doomed his tragic hero, Toussaint Louverture.

In *On Revolution*, Hannah Arendt offers a story about the vicissitudes of the French and American Revolutions, for her the defining revolutions of the modern age. In this account, the French Revolution began its career as a demand for nothing less than *political* freedom, but went into eclipse when, pressed by the surging multitudes of the poor, the social question displaced the political one, and as she puts it, "freedom had to be surrendered to necessity, to the urgency of the life process itself."[14] The lasting and far-reaching importance of Marx ("the greatest theorist the revolutions ever had"), Arendt argues, was to give this shift its most profound formulation. In his thought, she maintains, the preoccupation with history (the story of the objective course of events) rather than politics (the problem of the foundation of freedom) distracted the revolutionary tradition from its proper aim. With Marx, as she put it, "the abdication of freedom before the dictate of necessity" had "found its theorist."[15] He did, she says, what his teacher in revolution, Robespierre, had done before, and what Lenin, his greatest disciple, was to do after: he surrendered freedom to necessity.[16] Henceforth, "abundance" and not freedom would become the (misguided) aim of revolution. This shift is the great theme of Arendt's book.

By contrast with the French, the American Revolution has had little impact on the development of the revolutionary tradition. Or rather, such impact as it has had has been entirely negative; that is to say, it has contributed largely to an *antirevolutionary* tradition. Arendt considers this a pity because the American Revolution, she maintains, is the only revolution that directed its attention and focused its energies entirely upon the problem of the political founding of freedom. Undistracted as they were by the necessities of poverty, and therefore by the claims of the social, the American revolutionaries were able to devote themselves to the establishment of a political realm, to grounding freedom within the framework of a sovereign constitution. But the American founding fathers ultimately failed to sustain the revolutionary spirit of their institutions, Arendt argues, and they failed to do this because they failed to establish the cognitive conditions of "remembrance" of what they were originally seeking to do. As Arendt writes: "For if it is true that all thought begins with remembrance, it is also true that no remembrance remains secure unless it is condensed and distilled into a framework of conceptual notions within which it can further exercise itself." [17] She goes on, in a passage worth quoting because it captures so succinctly Arendt's political philosophy: "Experience and even the stories which grow out of what men do and endure, of happenings and events, sink back into the futility inherent in the living word and the living deed unless they are talked about over and over again. What saves the affairs of mortal men from their inherent futility is nothing but this incessant talk about them, which in its turn remains futile unless certain concepts, certain guideposts for future remembrance, and even for sheer reference, arise out of it." [18] It was the "self-forgetfulness" (the phrase belongs to Jaspers) of the Americans that doomed their revolution. Freedom in America became merely freedom *from* politics; freedom to pursue economic gain.

Consequently, the revolutionary spirit has been lost to our discussions of possible futures. Neither in the French nor in the American revolutions did that spirit of public freedom find an appropriate and secure institutional form, one that would enable it to both sustain and reproduce itself in the practices of succeeding generations. In each of these historical instances Arendt speaks of these lost opportunities as tragedies. But this loss, Arendt suggests, grave and dismaying as it is, is not—or at least, not necessarily—final. It need not lead us into pessimism and paralysis for in the end there are still the consolations of language, the resources of memory, the possibilities of speech and sharing: in a word, storytelling. If the revolutionary tradition has been lost to our political practices this can only be compensated for by the preservation of that spirit in memory and recollection; and since it is our poets who make our words and keep our memories, it is to them that we must turn for an approximation of "our lost treasure."[19] For Arendt, Sophocles is one (though not the only one) of the great poets of this treasure.[20]

THERE IS OF course much in Arendt's account of the revolutionary tradition and its fate that someone of James's background, formation, and outlook would not—indeed, could not—have shared. He would not have shared, at least not entirely, not unambiguously, her assessment of Marx, though he might well have shared, with some qualification of course, her contempt for the "absurd scholasticism of twentieth century Marxism."[21] In his often impetuous way, James may have disavowed heterodoxy, but his Marxism was—with one or two exceptions—rarely ever scholastic.[22] And however much he could have appreciated her splendid account of the relation between Rousseau and Robespierre ("If Rousseau had introduced compassion into political theory," she says, "it was Robespierre who brought it on to the market-place with the vehemence of his great revolutionary oratory"),[23] he doubtlessly would have called into question her reading of the role of the Jacobins in helping to send the French Revolution to its ultimate doom. After all, in James's view, it is the rise of the Jacobins in August 1792 and especially their decree of February 1794 (the month before Robespierre's arrest and subsequent execution) that gives impetus to the self-emancipation of the San Domingo slaves. But more than anything else what James would have found completely objectionable in Arendt's account of revolution is her curious "silencing" (as Michel-Rolph Trouillot would call it) of the Haitian Revolution, her complete elision of it and its place in the story of the revolutionary tradition and its legacy.

For Arendt there are only two eighteenth-century revolutions, the French and the American. It is a paradoxical fact that she is unsparingly contemptuous of those who, with familiar Eurocentric hubris, have "proceeded as though there never had occurred a revolution in the New World and as though there never had been any American notions and experiences in the realm of politics and government worth thinking about,"[24] when she herself proceeds as though the American Revolution were the only revolution in the New World in the eighteenth century. It was as though Thomas Jefferson and James Madison and John Adams were the only citizens of the New World who had "notions and experiences in the realm of politics and government worth thinking about," as though Toussaint Louverture were a minor or negligible figure on the world-historical stage.[25] This is precisely the kind of hubris against which The Black Jacobins is written. It is the meaning of James's boldly stated vindicationist claim in the preface that "with the single exception of Bonaparte himself no single figure appeared on the historical stage more greatly gifted than this Negro, a slave till he was 45."[26] But Arendt's oversight is all the more puzzling, and all the more disappointing, because what she is lamenting in On Revolution is precisely the failure of memory; she is in fact urging the importance of "remembrance" to sustaining the spirit of the revolutionary tradition. Perhaps in this James's fidelity to memory as a resource of criticism commands a more profound regard.

Indeed there is an unforgettable moment in The Black Jacobins in which James seems to be responding to Hannah Arendt on just this question. The year is 1797. In France royalist and proslavery colonists have made a significant comeback with the reactionary Vaublanc representing them in the newly elected legislature. They would be purged before the end of the year, but it is now clear to Toussaint that France can no longer be depended upon. In San Domingo, the Jacobin and great liberator Léger-Félicité Sonthonax names Toussaint commander-in-chief of the French republican army, but soon finds himself urged to return to France, ostensibly to assume his seat in the French legislature. For Toussaint, the game is up. He has so far played it with a resolute commitment to principle and honor. But the circle has slowly closed and he has finally come face to face with the insurmountable impossibility of simultaneously holding on to power (a power that would preserve the liberty of the former slaves) and loyalty to France. On November 5 he writes a letter to the Directory in which, while carefully disavowing suspicion of their intentions and asserting his personal faithful attachment to France, he makes clear that any attempt to reenslave the blacks will be met with determined force: "we have known how to face dangers to obtain our liberty, we shall know how to brave death to keep it." For James, this is Toussaint Louverture's finest political and diplomatic moment. If the letter is a masterpiece it is James's commentary that deserves quoting at length:

> Pericles on Democracy, Paine on the Rights of Man, the Declaration of Independence, the Communist Manifesto, these are some of the political documents which, whatever the wisdom or weakness of their analysis, have moved men and will continue to move them, for the writers, some of them in spite of themselves, strike

chords and awaken aspirations that sleep in the hearts of the majority of every age. But Pericles, Tom Paine, Jefferson, Marx and
Engels, were men of a liberal education, formed in the tradition
of ethics, philosophy, and history. Toussaint was a slave, not six
years out of slavery, bearing alone the unaccustomed burden of
war and government, dictating his thoughts in the crude words of
a broken dialect, written and rewritten by his secretaries until their
devotion and his will had hammered them into adequate shape.
Superficial people have read his career in terms of personal ambition. This letter is their answer. Personal ambition he had. But he
accomplished what he did because, superbly gifted, he incarnated
the determination of his people never to be slaves again.

Soldier and administrator above all yet his declaration is a masterpiece of prose excelled by no other writer of the revolution.
Leader of a backward and ignorant mass, he is yet in the fore-
front of the historical movement of his time. The blacks were
taking their part in the destruction of European feudalism begun
by the French Revolution and liberty and equality, the slogans of
the revolution meant far more to them than to any Frenchman.
That was why in the hour of danger Toussaint, uninstructed as
he was, could find the language of Diderot, Rousseau, and Raynal, of Mirabeau, Robespierre, and Danton. And in one respect he
excelled them all. For even these masters of the spoken and written word, owing to the class-complications of their society, had
always to pause, to hesitate, to qualify. Toussaint could defend the
freedom of the blacks without reservation, and this gave to his
declaration a strength and a single-mindedness rare in the great
documents of the time. The French bourgeoisie could not understand it. Rivers of blood were to flow before they understood that
elevated as was his tone Toussaint had written neither bombast
nor rhetoric but the simple and sober truth.[27]

This is C. L. R. James's answer to Hannah Arendt. It is a moment in which
he shows Toussaint Louverture in the incomparable role of a political
statesman and strategist, the embodiment of the *vita activa*, stepping into
the political realm and acting with brilliant and eloquent decision.

However, if in all the conventionally recognizable ways Arendt was
a Eurocentric, this is not all that she was; nor is it the only or the most
important lesson to be drawn from *On Revolution*. The story of Toussaint

Louverture in *The Black Jacobins* is, I believe, the sort of story of the tragedy of the revolutionary tradition that *On Revolution* wishes us to remember, a solemn story of the surrendering of freedom to necessity, of the political to the social. Or at least in my view one can read *The Black Jacobins* as a story about the distinction between liberation and freedom and the relation between these and tragedy. On this reading, the tragedy of Toussaint Louverture is the tragedy of a leader who (like Robespierre and Lenin) felt obliged to forgo the principles of public freedom, public happiness, and public spirit—however temporary he might have imagined the contingency to be. It is a memorable and central theme in James's narrative that the end of white domination and the tyranny of plantation slavery was one thing, the fashioning of a free black republic, the creation of a public and constitutional arena in which the newly emancipated black could *appear* and have her voice heard, quite another. All of Toussaint's later errors were committed within the conflicted space of this insurmountable conundrum. Faced with economic devastation, foreign military encirclement aiming to return the blacks to slavery, and an increasingly restless, hungry, and suspicious mass of emancipated slaves, Toussaint had precious little space within which to act. But act he had to. And when he did, he (again like Robespierre and Lenin) opted to secure the economic (necessity) over the risk of the political (freedom) on the calculated grounds that the former was at least a guarantee of the latter. Surely one of the sobering lessons of the story of the downfall of Toussaint Louverture is that nothing guarantees freedom but the political commitment to its founding—and even this, James is likely to have added, is often not enough.

WHAT THEN IS the sense of the tragic for our postcolonial time? Because tragedy has a more respectful attitude to the contingencies of the past in the present, to the uncanny ways in which its remains come back to usurp our hopes and subvert our ambitions, it demands from us more patience for paradox and more openness to chance than the narrative of anticolonial Romanticism does, confident in its striving and satisfied in its own sufficiency. The colonial past may never let go. This is a hard truth. Toussaint Louverture, James's magnificent hero, arrived at this insight by a long and difficult road and without the benefit of precedent to guide him. Nor were there second chances, the option of starting over. And Toussaint Louverture paid for the lesson of his insight with his life. The knowledge of our postcolonial selves this insight has enabled is Toussaint's gift to modernity's conscripts, and the price he paid for it is our debt to his doomed endeavor. The sense of the tragic for our postcolonial time is not the belief that we are likewise doomed, that change is futile, that in the end we are mere pawns of imperial tyranny. For *The Black Jacobins*, the sense of the tragic for our postcolonial time is an awareness of Toussaint's gift: the awareness that our own struggle for alternative futures, beginning as they do with the inheritance of what has gone before, has always to be tempered by our remembrance of his example.

# Notes

## PROLOGUE

The epigraph is taken from C. L. R. James, "Why I Wrote *The Black Jacobins*," *Small Axe* 8 (September 2000).

1 See David Scott, *Refashioning Futures: Criticism after Postcoloniality* (Princeton: Princeton University Press, 1999).

2 See Martin Carter, "A Free Community of Valid Persons," in "A Martin Carter Prose Sampler," *Kyk-Over-Al* 44 (May 1993): 30–32. This special issue was guest edited by Ian McDonald and Nigel Westmas.

3 Raymond Williams, *Modern Tragedy*, rev. ed. (London: Verso, 1979), 209.

4 Needless to say, I do not mean to suggest that *all* self-defining postcolonial theorists share exactly the same views concerning the proper approach to colonialism. For more on my worry about social constructionism, see David Scott, "The 'Social Construction' of Postcolonial Studies," in Suvir Kaul, Ania Loomba, Antoinette Burton, Matti Bunzl, eds., *Postcolonial Studies and Beyond* (Durham: Duke University Press, forthcoming, 2005).

5 See my earlier discussion of this concept in Scott, *Refashioning Futures*, 7–9.

6 Bernard Yack, *The Longing for Total Revolution: Philosophical Sources of Social Discontent from Rousseau to Marx and Nietzsche* (Berkeley: University of California Press, 1992 [1986]).

7 For a sense of Yack's political investments in a pragmatic liberalism, see the postscript to the 1992 edition of *The Longing for Total Revolution*; see also Bernard Yack, ed., *Liberalism without Illusions: Essays on Liberal Theory and the Political Vision of Judith Shklar* (Chicago: University of Chicago Press, 1996).

8 This may be as good a place as any to acknowledge that there are a number of points of contact between the disquiet that frames this book and the one that frames some other recent books concerned with colonialism and its aftermaths. I am thinking here of Uday Mehta, *Liberalism and Empire: A Study in Nineteenth-Century British Liberal Thought* (Chicago: University of Chicago Press, 1999); Dipesh Chakrabarty, *Provincializing Europe: Postcolonial Thought and Historical Difference* (Princeton: Princeton University Press, 2000); and Achille Mbembe, *On the Postcolony* (Berkeley: University of California Press, 2001). What brings them together with my concerns, I think (however much we diverge in the directions of our respective arguments), is their sense of the intransigence of the postcolonial

present, its resistance to the forms of critical rationality once thought adequate to its deconstruction.

9    Talal Asad, "Conscripts of Western Civilization," in Christine Gailey, ed., *Dialectical Anthropology: Essays in Honor of Stanley Diamond*, vol. 1, *Civilization in Crisis* (Gainesville: University Press of Florida, 1992), 333–51.

10   See Stanley Diamond, *In Search of the Primitive: A Critique of Civilization* (New Brunswick, N.J.: Transaction Books, 1974). "In this anthropological 'experiment' which we initiate," Diamond wrote in a classically Boasian formulation, "it is not they who are the ultimate objects but ourselves. We study men, that is, we reflect on ourselves studying others, because we must, because man in civilization is the problem. Primitive peoples do not study man. It is unnecessary; the subject is given" (100).

11   Diamond, "The Uses of the Primitive," in ibid., 204. Also quoted in Asad, "Conscripts of Western Civilization," 333.

12   Asad, "Conscripts of Western Civilization," 333.

13   See David Scott, "The Tragic Sensibility of Talal Asad," in David Scott and Charles Hirschkind, eds., *Powers of the Secular Modern: Talal Asad and his Interlocutors*, forthcoming.

14   C. L. R. James, *The Black Jacobins: Toussaint L'Ouverture and the San Domingo Revolution* (New York: Penguin, 2001).

15   *American Civilization* was written at the end of the 1940s but only published posthumously by Blackwell in 1993. *Mariners, Renegades, and Castaways: Herman Melville and the World We Live In* was written in 1952 while James was being held on Ellis Island, New York, pending a decision on his immigration case. It was self-published in 1953. *Beyond a Boundary* was first published in London by Hutchinson in 1963. The essay on Hamlet, "Notes on Hamlet," was written around 1953, and is collected in *The C. L. R. James Reader*, edited by Anna Grimshaw and published by Blackwell in 1992.

16   See Charles Segal, *Tragedy and Civilization: An Interpretation of Sophocles* (Norman: University of Oklahoma Press, 1999); Martha Nussbaum, *The Fragility of Goodness: Luck and Ethics in Greek Tragedy and Philosophy* (New York: Cambridge University Press, 1986); J. Peter Euben, *The Tragedy of Political Theory: The Road Not Taken* (Princeton: Princeton University Press, 1990); Christopher Rocco, *Tragedy and Enlightenment: Athenian Political Thought and the Dilemmas of Modernity* (Berkeley: University of California Press, 1997); and Jean-Pierre Vernant and Pierre Vidal-Naquet, *Myth and Tragedy in Ancient Greece*, trans. by Janet Lloyd (New York: Zone Books, 1990).

17   Vernant and Vidal-Naquet, *Myth and Tragedy in Ancient Greece*, 45.

18   Perhaps this is the place to comment briefly on Terry Eagleton's recent book, *Sweet Violence: The Idea of the Tragic* (Oxford: Blackwell, 2003), which appeared just as I was completing this manuscript. There are both points of contact as well as points of divergence in what we are doing in our respective uses of tragedy.

I share, to some extent, Eagleton's worry that "postmodern" forms of historicism (which I characterize as "social constructionism") often misconstrue the
relationship between contingency and human action (though I don't share Eagleton's typically disdainful way of discussing postmodernism). And I agree with
him that the left by and large has adopted a disapproving attitude to what it takes
to be tragedy's lack of historical perspective. With Eagleton I think that, to the
contrary, tragedy is not lacking in a particular understanding of history (this
book is concerned precisely with this question). But I do not share Eagleton's
left-wing/right-wing scale of political value and his desire to read tragedy into
the narrative of socialism.

19   See, for example, Paul Buhle, C. L. R. James: The Artist as Revolutionary (London:
     Verso, 1988); Anthony Bogues, Caliban's Freedom: The Early Political Thought of C. L. R.
     James (London: Pluto, 1997); Kent Worcester, C. L. R. James: A Political Biography
     (Albany: State University of New York Press, 1996); Aldon Lynn Nielsen, C. L. R.
     James: A Critical Introduction (Jackson: University of Mississippi Press, 1997).

20   Needless to say I do not mean to suggest that there has been no recent critical
     discussion of it. See, for instance, A. W. Singham, "C. L. R. James on the Black
     Jacobin Revolution in San Domingo: Notes Towards a Theory of Black Politics,"
     Savacou 1, no. 1 (1970): 82–96; F. M. Birbalsingh, "The Literary Achievement of
     C. L. R. James," Journal of Commonwealth Literature 19, no. 1 (1984): 108–21; Robert
     Hill, "In England, 1932–1938," in Paul Buhle, ed., C. L. R. James: His Life and Work
     (London: Allison and Busby, 1986), 61–80; Brian Meeks, "Re-reading The Black
     Jacobins: James, the Dialectic and the Revolutionary Conjuncture," Social and Eco-
     nomic Studies 43, no. 3 (September 1994): 75–103; and Stuart Hall (interviewed by
     Bill Schwarz), "Breaking Bread with History: C. L. R. James and The Black Jacobins,"
     History Workshop Journal 46 (autumn 1998): 17–31.

21   See, for example, David Geggus, Slavery, War and Revolution: The British Occupation
     of Saint Domingue, 1793–1798 (Oxford: Clarendon Press, 1982); Geggus, "Slave Re-
     sistance Studies and the Saint Domingue Slave Revolution: Some Preliminary
     Considerations," Occasional Papers Series, no 4. (Miami: Florida International
     University, 1983); and most recently, Geggus, Haitian Revolutionary Studies (Bloom-
     ington: Indiana University Press, 2002); Carolyn Fick, The Making of Haiti: The Saint
     Dominigue Revolution from Below (Knoxville: University of Tennessee Press, 1990);
     and Fick, "Dilemmas of Emancipation: From the San Domingo Insurrection to
     the Emerging Haitian State" History Workshop Journal 46 (autumn 1998): 1–15; and
     Alex Dupuy, Haiti in the World Economy: Class, Race, and Underdevelopment since 1700
     (Boulder, Colo.: Westview Press, 1989).

22   See Michel-Rolph Trouillot, Silencing the Past: Power and the Production of History
     (Boston: Beacon Press, 1995), especially chapters 2 and 3.

23   George Lamming, The Pleasures of Exile (London: Michael Joseph, 1960).

24   Here is Lamming on James: "We will not raise the question of James's relation
     to the colonial bureaucracy; for the author of Black Jacobins is too great a man to

be dragged into such marginal disputes. We will not involve in such polemics the sharpest mind that the British Caribbean has produced in three centuries of learning. I have chosen his classic study *Black Jacobins* for summary in a later chapter. After re-reading this history of the Haitian Revolt it is clear to me that, level for level, generation for generation, there was no British intellectual of the 'thirties who had a finer mind than James" ( ibid., 47). See also David Scott, "The Sovereignty of the Imagination: An Interview with George Lamming," *Small Axe* 12 (September 2002): 134–45, 162–66.

25  Lamming, *The Pleasures of Exile*, 118–19.

26  For a recent discussion of Lamming's Caliban, see Jonathan Goldberg's 2001 Garnett Sedgewick Memorial Lecture, *The Generation of Caliban* (Vancouver: Ronsdale Press, 2002). I'm much obliged to Jonathan Goldberg for sharing this work with me.

27  See Kara M. Rabbitt, "C. L. R. James's Figuring of Toussaint-Louverture: *The Black Jacobins* and the Literary Hero," in Selwyn R. Cudjoe and William E. Cain, eds., *C. L. R. James: His Intellectual Legacies* (Amherst: University of Massachusetts Press, 1995). I would like to pay tribute to this exceptional essay. If I disagree here and there with it, I have also been much inspired and stimulated by it.

28  Ibid., 120.

29  Ibid.

30  Ibid., 121.

31  Ibid., 128.

32  Ibid.


I FUTURES PAST

The epigraph is taken from C. L. R. James, *The Black Jacobins: Toussaint L'Ouverture and the San Domingo Revolution* (London: Secker and Warburg, 1938), vii–ix.

1  William Wordsworth, preface to the *Lyrical Ballads* (London: Routledge, 1991 [1800]). "I have said that Poetry is the spontaneous overflow of powerful feelings: it takes its origin from emotion recollected in tranquillity: the emotion is contemplated till by a species of reaction the tranquillity gradually disappears, and an emotion, similar to that which was before the subject of contemplation, is gradually produced, and does itself actually exist in the mind. In this mood successful composition generally begins, and in a mood similar to this it is carried on" (266). I would like to thank Robert Hill who, many years ago, alerted me to this implicit reference to Wordsworth. It will be clear to the reader how far situating James among the Romantics (and, as we will see, the *Victorian* Romantics more specifically) is important to my reading of *The Black Jacobins*.

2  In the "fever and the fret" there is an allusion to Keats's "Ode to a Nightingale": "Fade far away, dissolve, and quite forget / What thou among the leaves hast never known, / The weariness, the fever, and the fret." See John Keats, *The Col-*

lected *Poems* (New York: Penguin, 1973), 346-48. It is an interesting fact that James alludes to these two Romantic poets, Wordsworth and Keats, one a poet of self-affirmation, and the other a poet of self-negation. But both are, quintessentially, Romantic poets (of the first and second generation, respectively) for whom the imagination was a faculty that enabled the artist to reach beyond the boundaries of his or her self.

3   See C. L. R. James, *Beyond a Boundary* (Kingston: Sangster, 1963), 59, 71. Indeed we also know about James's familiarity with the Romantics from some of his earlier writing too. See, for example, his article on his meeting with Edith Sitwell shortly after his arrival in London in 1932. Originally published in the Port of Spain *Gazette* on June 21, 1932, it was subsequently published as "Bloomsbury: An Encounter with Edith Sitwell," in Anna Grimshaw, ed., *The C. L. R. James Reader* (Oxford: Blackwell, 1992), 43-48, and most recently as "The Bloomsbury Atmosphere," in C. L. R. James, *Letters from London*, Nicholas Laughlin, ed. (Port of Spain: Prospect Press, 2003), 18-34.

4   Compare James's 1938 use of Wordsworth's preface here to that in his 1969 essay on the great Barbadian cricketer, Garfield Sobers. There he quotes favorably Wordsworth's sense of the civilizational crisis through which he was living and to which his — and Coleridge's — poetry in the *Lyrical Ballads* constituted a poetic alternative. "That was the period," says James, "and those the circumstances in which modern cricket was born. In its own way it did what Wordsworth was trying to do." See C. L. R. James, "Garfield Sobers," in his collection *Cricket*, edited by Anna Grimshaw (London: Alison and Busby, 1986), 227.

5   The conflict galvanized many British writers and intellectuals, among them Stephen Spender, Cecil Day-Lewis, Christopher Isherwood, Cyril Connolly, and W. H. Auden. Not all went to Spain, however, and fewer saw actual battle. See the very interesting account in Noel Annan, *Our Age: English Intellectuals between the Wars — A Group Portrait* (New York: Random House, 1990); and James K. Hopkins, *Into the Heart of the Fire: The British in the Spanish Civil War* (Stanford, Calif.: Stanford University Press, 1998).

6   George Orwell, *Homage to Catalonia* (London: Secker and Warburg, 1938). Legend has it that Orwell began writing *Homage to Catalonia* in the trenches in February 1937. As one of his biographers has written: "He composed *Homage to Catalonia* — 'the best [book] I have written' — in a state of white-hot anger. Disgusted by the lies he read in the English newspapers, he was determined to tell the truth about what really happened in Spain." See Jeffrey Meyers, *Orwell: Wintry Conscience of a Generation* (New York: Norton, 2000), 173. Orwell reviewed a number of books on the Spanish conflict, including Franz Borkenau's *The Spanish Cockpit*, Mary Low and Juan Breá's *Red Spanish Notebook*, and Arthur Koestler's *Spanish Testament*. See George Orwell, *Collected Essays, Journalism, Letters*, vol. 1, *An Age Like This, 1920-1940* (Boston: Nonpareil Books, 1968).

7   C. L. R. James, preface to Mary Low and Juan Breá's *Red Spanish Notebook: The First*

*Six Months of the Revolution and the Civil War* (London: Secker and Warburg, 1937), vi. In his review of this book, Orwell remarks on James's preface without comment: "Mr. C. L. R. James, author of that very able book *World Revolution*, contributes an introduction." See Orwell, *An Age Like This*, 288. James and Orwell were at least acquaintances. They had both been introduced to their publisher, Frederic Warburg, by Fenner Brockway, leader of the Independent Labour Party. For a lively and intimate account of this period with vivid portraits of both James and Orwell, see Warburg's memoir, *An Occupation for Gentlemen* (London: Hutchinson, 1959).

8 See W. H. Auden, "Spain 1937," in *The Collected Poetry of W. H. Auden* (New York: Random House, 1945), 181–85. Auden had himself gone to Spain in January 1937, ostensibly to drive an ambulance. The poem's dramatic ending is worth remembering: "The stars are dead; the animals will not look: / We are left alone with our day, and the time is short and / History to the defeated / May say Alas but cannot help or pardon." The poem was written after his return from Spain in March 1937 and first published that May.

9 Eric Hobsbawm, *Age of Extremes: The Short Twentieth Century, 1914–1991* (New York: Abacus, 1994), 160. This work is especially helpful in situating this crisis in the unfolding years between the Great War of 1914–18 and the 1939–45 war, as also is his wonderful memoir, *Interesting Times: A Twentieth-Century Life* (London: Allen Lane, 2002), chapter 8. Similarly, Annan writes: "No one can have a glimmering of the feelings of the intelligentsia of the left in the pre-war years who does not recognize that the Spanish Civil War obsessed them. For that generation Guadalajara and Teruel sounded as mournful as the Somme and Ypres to their fathers. They thought no one could dispute that it was a war in which justice was solely on one side, perhaps the only such war ever known in history" (*Our Age*, 183–84).

10 For a description of the trials, see Robert Conquest, *The Great Terror: A Reassessment* (New York: Oxford University Press, 1990). Before turning to his historical work, Conquest was one of the Movement poets of the 1950s deeply influenced by Orwell. It is hard to forget, too, the picture drawn by Arthur Koestler in *Darkness at Noon*, published in 1941. Koestler, also the author of a work on Spain, *Spanish Testament*, was a figure of some note in the London circles James would have been familiar with in the 1930s.

11 C. L. R. James, *World Revolution, 1917–1936: The Rise and Fall of the Communist International* (London: Secker and Warburg, 1937), 199. In 1938 Franz Borkenau published his account of the International, *The Communist International* (London: Faber and Faber, 1938). It is an interesting fact that Orwell reviews this book but not James's earlier one (though he mentions it). See Orwell, *An Age Like This*, 348–51.

12 Some sense of the scope of this movement is given in Robert Alexander's compendious *International Trotskyism, 1929–1985: A Documented Analysis of the Movement* (Durham: Duke University Press, 1991). "During the first four years of Trotsky's efforts after 1929 to organize an international movement he and his followers

regarded themselves as an 'opposition' faction of the Communist International which was for reasons beyond its control temporarily outside of the formal ranks of the CI [Communist International]. After the collapse of the German Communist Party in the face of the Nazis in 1933, Trotsky and his supporters declared their objective to be the establishment of a Fourth International (FI). In September 1938 at a conference held outside of Paris, that Fourth International was formally declared to exist" (20). C. L. R. James attended one of the preparatory conferences for the founding of the Fourth International, the famous "Geneva" meetings (actually held in Paris), 26–31 July 1936.

13  C. L. R. James, "Why I Wrote *The Black Jacobins*," *Small Axe* 8 (September 2000): 68–69.

14  It is an interesting fact that it was the representative of the British section of the Communist International, J. T. Murphy, who proposed the expulsion of Trotsky in September 1927. On the British Trotskyist movement in the 1930s, see Sam Bornstein and Al Richardson, *Against the Stream: A History of the Trotskyist Movement in Britain, 1924–38* (London: Socialist Platform, 1986); and Robert Alexander, "Trotskyism in Great Britain: The Early Years of British Trotskyism," in *International Trotskyism*, 437–51. On the ILP see Robert E. Dowse, *Left in the Centre: The Independent Labour Party, 1893–1940* (London: Longmans, 1966), especially chapters 12 and 13. It is curious that Dowse nowhere mentions James's participation in the ILP even when he discusses the divisive ideological controversy provoked by Mussolini's October 1935 invasion of Abyssinia (195–96).

15  See Al Richardson, Clarence Chrysostom, and Anna Grimshaw, *CLR James and British Trotskyism: An Interview* (London: Socialist Platform, 1987), 1.

16  See also Bornstein and Richardson, *Against the Stream*, especially chapters 6 through 10. James's *World Revolution* was dedicated "To the Marxist Group." See also the very curious but very fascinating "personal" account of the Marxist Group by Louise Cripps Samoiloff, *C. L. R. James, Memories and Commentaries* (New York: Cornwall Books, 1997), in particular, part 1, Memories. In *An Occupation for Gentlemen*, Warburg writes of James, his *World Revolution*, and the Marxist Group in the following revealing way: "One of the first authors introduced to me by Brockway was C. L. R. James, and his book *World Revolution*, became a kind of Bible of Trotskyism. We published it in April 1937. It was dedicated to the Marxist Group. How many members composed this group at the time I don't know, probably less than fifty, for it was a quality of Trotskyist groups to break into two, like amoeba when reproducing itself, and to continue doing so until the fission process had reduced the group to a mere handful. Trotskyism in fact resembled a corps of guerilla fighters, partisans—and how partisan they were!—harassing the communist enemy, to whom they were linked by a burning and ambivalent emotion" (211).

17  On Harold Moody and the League of Coloured Peoples, see Imanuel Geiss, *The*

Pan-African Movement: A History of Pan-Africanism in America, Europe and Africa, trans. by Ann Keep (New York: Africana Publishing House, 1974), chapter 17. See also the very useful Roderick J. Macdonald, "Introduction to The Keys," in the reprint of The Keys: The Official Organ of the League of Coloured Peoples (New York: Kraus-Thomson, 1976).

18  See Robert G. Weisbord, "British West Indian Reaction to the Italian-Ethiopian War: An Episode in Pan-Africanism," Caribbean Studies 10, no. 1 (April 1970): 34–41; and Weisbord, "Black America and the Italian-Ethiopian Crisis: An Episode in Pan-Negroism," The Historian 34, no. 2 (February 1972): 230–41.

19  C. L. R. James, The Life of Captain Cipriani (Nelson: Cartmel and Co., 1932). A shorter version of this work was published in Britain the following year under the title The Case for West-Indian Self Government (London: Hogarth Press, 1933).

20  C. L. R. James, "Abyssinia and the Imperialists," The Keys 3, no. 3 (January–March 1936): 40.

21  These troubles were widely reported in Britain at the time. See R. O. Thomas, "Revolt in the West Indies," The Keys 3, no. 3 (January–March 1936): 37–38.

22  In 1971 James said: "Now, what did I have in mind when I wrote this book? I had in mind writing about the San Domingo Revolution as the preparation for the revolution that George Padmore and all of us were interested in, that is, the revolution in Africa." See James, "Why I Wrote The Black Jacobins," 72. In an interview in the United States on the newly emerging field of black studies James reflected: "In those times [the 1930s] not many people were concerned about black studies. Some people were interested. My book was published, The Black Jacobins. It resulted from the studies I was making with George Padmore, my old friend from school days." "The Black Scholar Interviews: C. L. R. James," The Black Scholar 2, no. 1 (September 1970): 35. It should also be remembered that James first wrote a play entitled "Toussaint L'Ouverture" which was produced by Peter Godrey at the Westminster Theatre in London in March 1936. It was, in part, a response to the crisis in Abyssinia. The play was subsequently retitled "Black Jacobins." See "Black Jacobins" in Grimshaw, The C. L. R. James Reader. A short but favorable review signed "G. M." was carried in The Keys 3, no. 4 (April–June 1936): 68–69. A review of the book The Black Jacobins signed "K. A." was carried in The Keys 6, no. 2 (October–December 1938): 12–13.

23  There is a story waiting to be told about the actual writing of this book, the way the research was carried on, the people James depended upon, and so on.

24  Reinhart Koselleck, Futures Past: On the Semantics of Historical Time, trans. by Keith Tribe (Cambridge, Mass.: MIT Press, 1985).

25  See David Scott, "Introduction: Criticism after Postcoloniality," in Refashioning Futures: Criticism after Postcoloniality (Princeton: Princeton University Press, 1999).

26  I borrow the phrase "selfconscious narrative presence" from Linda Orr, whose work on Michelet's preface I have found stimulating. See Linda Orr, "Intimate

Images: Subjectivity and History—Staël, Michelet and Tocqueville," in Frank
Ankersmit and Hans Kellner, eds., *A New Philosophy of History* (Chicago: University
of Chicago Press, 1995), 89.

27   James, *The Black Jacobins*, vii.

28   Ibid.

29   Ibid.

30   Ibid., vii–viii.

31   See J. B. Bury, "The Science of History," in his *Selected Essays*, ed. by Harold Tem-
perley (Cambridge: Cambridge University Press, 1930), 3–22. This was Bury's
inaugural lecture at Cambridge University delivered on January 26, 1903. Following Lord Acton as much in his views as in his chair, Bury expressed his worry
that while a "revolution" in historical discourse had occurred (partly through the
example of Leopold van Ranke), it was not yet secure and needed to be underlined and emphasized. "History," he declared, "has really been enthroned and
ensphered among the sciences; but the particular nature of her influence, her
time-honoured association with literature, and other circumstances, have acted
as a sort of vague cloud, half concealing from men's eyes her new position in the
heavens" (5). G. M. Trevelyan's, "Clio, A Muse," in *Clio, A Muse and Other Essays
Literary and Pedestrian* (London: Longmans, Green and Company, 1913), 1–55, was
something of a response to the view held by Bury. In the splendid opening of this
riposte, he wrote: "The last fifty years have witnessed great changes in the man-
agement of Clio's temple. Her inspired prophets and bards have passed away and
been succeeded by the priests of an established church; the vulgar have been ex-
cluded from the Court of the Gentiles; doctrine has been defined; heretics have
been excommunicated; and the tombs of the aforesaid prophets have been duly
blackened by the new hierarchy. While these changes were in process the statue
of the Muse was seen to wink an eye. Was it in approval, or in derision?" (1). For a
useful discussion, see Richard T. Vann, "Turning Linguistic: History and Theory
and *History and Theory*, 1960–1975," in Ankersmit and Kellner, *A New Philosophy
of History*, 41–42. For a survey of this debate see for example, H. Stuart Hughes,
*History as Art and as Science* (New York: Harper, 1964).

32   James, *The Black Jacobins*, viii.

33   The art and science distinction was a matter of considerable preoccupation for
James. One has the sense that his discovery of Marx enabled him to draw them
together into a productive tension. See, by contrast, the article "A Visit to the
Science and Art Museums," originally published in the Port of Spain *Gazette* on
May 22, 1932, and recently reproduced in James, *Letters from London*. Contrasting
the airplanes of the Science Museum (in particular the one in which Lieutenant
Stanforth won the Scheider Trophy) with Rodin's *John the Baptist* in the Victo-
ria and Albert Museum, James suggests that whereas scientific inventions are
marked by time, artistic creations are timeless. He writes:

Three thousand years from now, some wanderer from the West Indies
will walk down Exhibition Road. He will go into the Science Museum and
see the latest thought-plane. (That vanished type of conveyance, aircraft,
will be represented by models.) Will he see Lieutenant Stanforth's plane?
Only as one of a crowd of obsolete designs.

But in the Art Museum he will see the statue of the man walking. It will
be to him as it is to me. It cannot grow old. It cannot go out of date. It
is timeless, made materially of bronze but actually, as has been said of
great literature, the precious life-blood of a master spirit.

That is why though I shall sometimes visit the Museum of Science it
will always be on my way to the Museum of Art. (14)

A few years later, the preface to *The Black Jacobins* imagines a more complicated
relation between art and science.

34   James, *The Black Jacobins*, viii.
35   Michael Oakeshott, "Present, Future and Past," in *On History and Other Essays*
     (Indianapolis: Liberty Fund, 1999), 8.
36   Ibid., 9.
37   The reference here is to Michel Foucault, *Discipline and Punish: The Birth of the Prison*,
     trans. by Alan Sheridan (New York: Pantheon, 1979), 31.
38   Koselleck, *Futures Past*, xxiii.
39   For a discussion of the specificity of *Begriffsgeschichte* see Koselleck, "Begriffsge-
     schichte and Social History," in *Futures Past*; "On the Need for Theory in the Disci-
     pline of History," and "Social and Conceptual History," in *The Practice of Concep-
     tual History: Timing History, Spacing Concepts* (Stanford: Stanford University Press,
     2002). And for a helpful discussion of the project of "the history of concepts"
     that Koselleck and his colleagues have been engaged in, see Melvin Richter, *The
     History of Political and Social Concepts: A Critical Introduction* (New York: Oxford Uni-
     versity Press, 1995); as well as Hartmut Lehmann and Melvin Richter, eds., *The
     Meaning of Historical Terms and Concepts: New Studies on Begriffsgeschichte* (Wash-
     ington, D.C.: German Historical Institute, 1996).
40   Koselleck, " 'Space of Experience' and 'Horizon of Expectation': Two Histori-
     cal Categories," in *Futures Past*, 270. For more on "experience" and "expectation"
     see "Transformations of Experience and Methodological Change: A Historical-
     Anthropological Essay" in *The Practice of Conceptual History*.
41   Koselleck, " 'Space of Experience,' " 271.
42   Ibid., 273.
43   Ibid.
44   Ibid., 277.
45   Ibid. It may be worth remarking here, also, that Koselleck does not take either
     "experience" or "expectation" to be *transparent grounds* of anything. If they seem
     ontological it is because Koselleck is trying to formulate a version of what Ian

Hacking might call a specifically *historical* ontology (see Hacking, *Historical Ontology* [Cambridge, Mass.: Harvard University Press, 2002]). Koselleck is, after all, a historian of concepts. What concerns him are the distinctive concepts and conceptual ensembles in which "experience" and "expectation" are organized and formulated.

46  Koselleck, "On the Need for Theory in the Discipline of History," 7.

47  This is not to say that there has been no mutual recognition of the adjacency of their respective preoccupations. Hayden White has written a warmly appreciative foreword to Koselleck's *The Practice of Conceptual History*, and in one of the chapters in this book, "Introduction to Hayden White's *Tropics of Discourse*," Koselleck marks the significance of White's tropological theory.

48  Hayden White, "Literary Theory and Historical Writing," in *Figural Realism: Studies in the Mimesis Effect* (Baltimore: Johns Hopkins University Press, 1999), 4.

49  Ibid., 4.

50  Hayden White, *Metahistory: The Historical Imagination in Nineteenth Century Europe* (Baltimore: Johns Hopkins University Press, 1973). The books published subsequently are *Tropics of History: Essays in Cultural History* (Baltimore: Johns Hopkins University Press, 1978); *The Content of the Form: Narrative Discourse and Historical Representation* (Baltimore: Johns Hopkins University Press, 1987); and most recently, *Figural Realism*. There is now a good deal of critical work on White, both positive and negative. For an excellent early discussion that places *Metahistory* in the context of White's prior work (especially on humanism), see Hans Kellner, "A Bedrock of Order: Hayden White's Linguistic Humanism," *History and Theory* 19 (1980): 1–29. See also the helpful article by Wulf Kansteiner, "Hayden White's Critique of the Writing of History," *History and Theory* 32, no. 3 (1993): 273–95; Michael Roth, "Politics of Cultural Criticism," in *The Ironist's Cage* (New York: Columbia University Press, 1995); and F. A. Ankersmit, "Hayden White's Appeal to the Historians," in *Historical Representation* (Stanford: Stanford University Press, 2001).

51  White, *Metahistory*, 7.

52  See Northrop Frye, *Anatomy of Criticism: Four Essays* (Princeton: Princeton University Press, 1957). White has acknowledged a great debt to Frye and argued for his centrality in contemporary debates about cultural and historical theory. Indeed it is from Frye that White takes the term "metahistory." See his "Frye's Place in Contemporary Cultural Studies," in Alvin A. Lee and Robert D. Denham, eds., *The Legacy of Northrop Frye* (Toronto: University of Toronto Press, 1994).

53  White, *Metahistory*, 8–9.

54  Ibid., 9.

55  Ibid.

56  Ibid.

57  Ibid., xii.

58    See, for example, Carlo Ginzburg, "Just One Witness," in Saul Friedlander, ed.,
      *Probing the Limits of Representation: Nazism and the Final Solution* (Cambridge, Mass.:
      Harvard University Press, 1992), 82–96.

59    See, for example, Maurice Mandelbaum, "The Presuppositions of Metahistory,"
      *History and Theory* 19 (1980): 47–48.

60    See White, "Historical Emplotment and the Problem of Truth in Historical Rep-
      resentation," in *Figural Realism*.

61    Ibid., 30.

62    Ibid., 41.

63    See, for comments, Kansteiner, "Hayden White's Critique of the Writing of His-
      tory," 291–93.

64    Hayden White, "The Burden of History," in *Tropics of Discourse: Essays in Cultural
      Criticism* (Baltimore: Johns Hopkins University Press, 1978), 49.

65    In what follows I develop ideas set out in my introduction to *Refashioning Futures*.

66    R. G. Collingwood, *The Idea of History* (Oxford: Oxford University Press, 1956),
      215. There are, of course, numerous other statements, more or less clear, of this
      idea scattered throughout this book, but it is given special attention in the now
      controversial part 5, the "Epilegomena." For a critical assessment of the posthu-
      mous assembly of *The Idea of History* by Collingwood's student T. M. Knox, see
      W. J. van der Dussen's introduction to Oxford's 1993 revised edition. William H.
      Dray and van der Dussen have more recently edited the manuscript (long pre-
      sumed lost) of *The Principles of History* (Oxford: Oxford University Press, 1999).
      For a discussion of the usefulness of the new Collingwood materials, see Stefan
      Collini, "When the Goose Cackled," *TLS* 27 August 1999, 3–6.

67    One thinks of such work as Louis O. Mink, *Mind, History, and Dialectic: The Philoso-
      phy of R. G. Collingwood* (Bloomington: Indiana University Press, 1969), and chap-
      ters 11 and 12 of *Historical Understanding* (Ithaca: Cornell University Press, 1987);
      W. J. van der Dussen, *History as a Science: The Philosophy of R. G. Collingwood* (The
      Hague: Martinus Nijhoff, 1981); and William H. Dray, *History as Re-enactment: R. G.
      Collingwood's Idea of History* (Oxford: Oxford University Press, 1995).

68    See Collingwood, *An Autobiography* (Oxford: Oxford University Press, 1939), chap-
      ter 5.

69    See Mink, *Mind, History, and Dialectic*, 8.

70    See Dray, *History as Re-enactment*, 48.

71    See Skinner's interesting account of this influence in "An Interview with Quentin
      Skinner," *Cogito* 11, no. 2 (November 2002): 73.

72    Most of these essays have usefully been brought together in James Tully, ed.,
      *Meaning and Context: Quentin Skinner and His Critics* (Princeton: Princeton Univer-
      sity Press, 1988). They have more recently been revised and published in Quentin
      Skinner, *Visions of Politics*, vol. 1., *Regarding Method* (Cambridge: Cambridge Uni-
      versity Press, 2002).

73  See, of course, J. L. Austin, *How to Do Things with Words* (Cambridge, Mass.: Harvard University Press, 1962).

74  Melvin Richter has initiated a fascinating and rewarding discussion on the relation between Koselleck's *Begriffsgeschichte* and the methodological approach to the history of the languages of politics associated with Quentin Skinner and J. G. A. Pocock. See Richter, "Pocock, Skinner and the *Geschichtliche Grundbegriffe*," *History and Theory* 29 (1990): 38–70; Richter, *The History of Political and Social Concepts*, chapter 6; and Richter, "Appreciating a Contemporary Classic: The *Geschichtliche Grundbegriffe* and Future Scholarship," in Lehmann and Richter, *The Meaning of Historical Terms and Concepts*. See also Kari Palonen, "The History of Concepts as a Style of Political Theorizing: Quentin Skinner's and Reinhart Koselleck's Subversion of Normative Political Theory," *European Journal of Political Theory* 1, no. 1 (2002): 91–106.

75  Rather, in his view there can only be histories of the various *uses* of concepts in argument. See Skinner, "Reply to My Critics," in Tully, *Meaning and Context*, 283. The point, of course, is the Wittgensteinian one that the meaning of a concept comprises the range of things that can actually be done with it. Part of the unresolved disagreement between Koselleck on the one hand and Skinner and Pocock on the other turns on just what each side means by "concepts" and their understanding of the relation between "concepts" and larger units of language such as "discourse" or "ideology." Both Skinner and Pocock seem to think that Koselleck has too isolationist or atomistic a notion of concepts. For Skinner's view, see Richter, *History of Political and Social Concepts*, 134–35. For his part, Pocock considers that the difference between Koselleck and himself may well be "cultural"; he maintains that he sees "the history of concepts as a feature of, and as exhibited within, an ongoing history of discourses." See Pocock, "Concepts and Discourses: A Difference in Culture? Comment on a Paper by Melvin Richter," in Lehmann and Richter, *The Meaning of Historical Terms and Concepts*, 58. In his reply to Pocock and others in the same volume, Koselleck denied any such isolationism or atomism and demonstrated a more discourse-embedded idea of concepts than Pocock allows him. As he says at one point: "Although basic concepts always function within a discourse, they are pivots around which all arguments turn. For this reason I do not believe that the history of concepts and the history of discourse can be viewed as incompatible and opposite. Each depends inescapably on the other. A discourse requires basic concepts in order to express what it is talking about. And analysis of concepts requires command of both linguistic and extra-linguistic contexts, including those provided by discourses" (65). It seems to me that this is a potentially very fruitful debate and can only benefit from more considered comparisons and engagements.

76  Skinner, "Reply to my Critics," 274–75, and "Interpretation and the Understanding of Speech Acts," in *Regarding Method*, 115.

77　Skinner, *Reason and Rhetoric in the Philosophy of Hobbes* (Cambridge: Cambridge University Press, 1996), 7–8. Wittgenstein's aphorism, offered parenthetically, is from *Philosophical Investigations*, trans. by G. E. M. Anscombe (New York: Macmillan, 1958), para. 256.

78　See James Tully, "The Pen Is a Mighty Sword: Quentin Skinner's Analysis of Politics," in Tully, *Meaning and Context*.

79　See especially Skinner, "Language and Political Change," in Terrence Ball, James Farr, and Russell L. Hanson, eds., *Political Innovation and Conceptual Change* (Cambridge: Cambridge University Press, 1989).

80　Indeed some of his sympathizers see his work very much in terms of its relevance to the question of the present. James Tully, for example, is keen to see parallels drawn between Michel Foucault and Quentin Skinner and sees Skinner's magisterial two-volume study, *The Foundations of Modern Political Thought* (Cambridge: Cambridge University Press, 1978), as offering a "genealogy" of the modern state comparable, in many ways, to Foucault's genealogies. As he says, Skinner is not "solely concerned with history and method, but also with using both to throw light on the present." See his "The Pen Is a Mighty Sword," 7. Skinner himself has paid tribute to Foucault but is less explicit about his relation to his work.

81　Quentin Skinner, *Liberty before Liberalism* (Cambridge: Cambridge University Press, 1998), 117. See also *Reason and Rhetoric*, 15.

82　Skinner, *Liberty before Liberalism*, 116.

83　Ibid., 118, 119. Nietzsche notwithstanding, I find the metaphor regrettable. See Friedrich Nietzsche, preface, *On the Genealogy of Morality*, trans. by Carol Diethe (Cambridge: Cambridge University Press, 1994), 10.

84　Skinner, *Liberty before Liberalism*, 118.

85　See also Skinner, *Reason and Rhetoric*, 15–16.

86　This is what I have been calling a "strategic" practice of criticism. See my *Refashioning Futures*, especially the introduction.


## 2　ROMANTICISM AND ANTICOLONIAL REVOLUTION

The epigraph is taken from C. L. R. James, *The Black Jacobins: Toussaint L'Ouverture and the San Domingo Revolution* (London: Secker and Warburg, 1938), vii; *The Black Jacobins: Toussaint L'Ouverture and the San Domingo Revolution*, 2nd ed. rev. (New York: Vintage, 1963), ix.

1　James, *The Black Jacobins* (London: Secker and Warburg, 1938), viii. Hereafter references to this book are abbreviated BJ in parenthesis in the body of the text; page numbers to the 1963 edition are given in brackets.

2　For a very useful discussion of the relation between Romanticism and historical discourse, see Stephen Bann, *Romanticism and the Rise of History* (New York: Twayne, 1995).

3　See, for example, Jerome McCann, *The Romantic Ideology: A Critical Investigation*

(Chicago: University of Chicago Press, 1983); and Marilyn Butler, *Romantics, Rebels, and Reactionaries: English Literature and Its Background, 1760–1830* (Oxford: Oxford University Press, 1981).

4   Alan Richardson and Sonia Hofkosh, introduction to Alan Richardson and Sonia Hofkosh, eds., *Romanticism, Race, and Imperial Culture* (Bloomington: Indiana University Press, 1996), 2. See also Tim Fulford and Peter Kitson, eds., *Romanticism and Colonialism* (Cambridge: Cambridge University Press, 1998). In the early 1940s two studies of Romanticism focused on the presence of blacks. See Eva Beatrice Dykes, *The Negro in English Romantic Thought: A Study of Sympathy for the Oppressed* (Washington, D.C.: Associated Publishers, 1942); and Wylie Sypher, *Guinea's Captive Kings: British Anti-Slavery Literature of the XVIIIth Century* (Chapel Hill: University of North Carolina Press, 1942).

5   Mary Louise Pratt, *Imperial Eyes: Travel Writing and Transculturation* (New York: Routledge, 1992), 138.

6   On this case, see Peter Fryer, *Staying Power: Black People in Britain since 1504* (Atlantic Highlands, N.J.: Humanities Press, 1984), 120–26; and James Walvin, *Black Ivory: Slavery and the British Empire*, 2nd ed. (Oxford: Blackwell, 2001), 12–14. The popular view was that with the ruling in favor of Somerset, Mansfield had outlawed slavery in Britain. But as Walvin says, he had done no such thing. Mansfield had refused to take a stand on the principle of the matter. Indeed, Mansfield's own slave, Elizabeth Dido Lindsay, was only freed in his will drawn up in 1782 (14).

7   See Fryer, *Staying Power*, 127–30; and Walvin, *Black Ivory*, 14–17.

8   Wordsworth arrived in Paris on November 30, 1791, and began taking a tour of the city, taking in the ruins of the Bastille, the Jacobin Club, the Legislative Assembly, and other landmarks of the moment. For a fascinating account of Wordsworth's time in France and especially his relation with Jacques-Pierre Brissot, see Kenneth Johnston, *The Hidden Wordsworth: Poet, Lover, Rebel, Spy* (New York: Norton, 1998), chapter 13.

9   On Duncan Wu's account in *Wordsworth's Reading, 1770–1799* (Cambridge: Cambridge University Press, 1993), Wordsworth "became a Godwinian after Robespierre's execution in July 1794, though he must have read *Political Justice* by June" (66). It did not last long, however. Soon after receiving a copy of the second edition of Godwin's book we see him writing condemning the preface. As Wu says, Wordsworth's "condemnation of the 'barbarous' writing of the preface is the first sign of a reaction against Godwin" (67).

10  The question of the shifts in Wordsworth's political sympathies has been a topic of some discussion among scholars of the English Romantic poets. Disputing claims to the contrary, E. P. Thompson wrote, "In my view, Wordsworth remained an 'odious democrat' until after the Peace of Amiens [1815], and his poems of national independence and liberty are often criticisms of the course of the French Revolution from the 'left,' for its own self-betrayal." See E. P. Thompson, *The Romantics: England in a Revolutionary Age* (New York: New Press, 1997), 94.

11  See the very informative discussion of Wordsworth's relation to the antislavery cause in Helen Thomas, *Romanticism and Slave Narratives: Transatlantic Testimonies* (Cambridge: Cambridge University Press, 2000), chapter 3; and in Debbie Lee, *Slavery and the Romantic Imagination* (Philadelphia: University of Pennsylvania Press, 2002), chapter 8. Particularly noteworthy is the episode involving the widow of the Haitian King, Henri Christophe, and her two daughters, who Thomas Clarkson had invited in 1822 to his house after Christophe committed suicide. Wordsworth refused to meet them and sent Clarkson a ridiculing poem, "Queen and Negress."

12  Coleridge was the author of "Lecture on the Slave Trade" delivered in Bristol in 1795. Southey had written an important antislavery poem, "To the Genius of Africa." On Coleridge and Southey, see Thomas, *Romanticism and Slave Narratives*, 89–95. Indeed, between 1795 and 1797, Wordsworth lived rent-free at Racedown Lodge, a house owned by a prominent Bristol slave trader, John Pinney. See Johnston, *The Hidden Wordsworth*, chapter 19; and Lee, *Slavery and the Romantic Imagination*, 201–2. At the same time, in 1807, after Parliament outlawed the slave trade, he dedicated a sonnet to Thomas Clarkson, "To Thomas Clarkson, On the final passing of the Bill for the Abolition of the Slave Trade, March 1807." The poem, not surprisingly, is less about the slave trade than about Clarkson's heroic labor: "Clarkson! it was an obstinate Hill to climb; / How toilsome, nay how dire it was, by Thee / Is know, — by none, perhaps so feelingly." See Wordsworth, *Poems, Two Volumes and Other Poems, 1800–1807*, ed. by Jared Curtis (Ithaca: Cornell University Press, 1983), 246–47.

13  "To Toussaint L'Ouverture" was first published in the London *Morning Post* on February 2, 1803. It was subsequently collected from 1815 onward among the "Poems Dedicated to National Independence and Liberty."

14  There is a significant literature on Equiano. See James Walvin, *An African's Life: The Life and Times of Olaudah Equiano, 1745–1797* (London: Cassell, 1998); Thomas, *Romanticism and Slave Narratives*, chapter 8; and Sonia Hofkosh, "Tradition and the Interesting Narrative: Capitalism, Abolition, and the Romantic Individual," in Richardson and Hofkosh, *Romanticism, Race, and Imperial Culture*, 330–43.

15  For an excellent discussion of Wedderburn, see Ian McCalman, introduction to Ian McCalman, ed., *The Horrors of Slavery and Other Writings by Robert Wedderburn* (Kingston: Ian Randle, 1991). Anyone seeking an understanding of the wider political context of Wedderburn's political underground should consult Ian McCalman, *Radical Underworld: Prophets, Revolutionaries, and Pornographers in London, 1795–1840* (Cambridge: Cambridge University Press, 1988). On Wedderburn, see also Thomas, *Romanticism and Slave Narratives*, chapter 9.

16  McCalman suggests that Wedderburn "was probably the first English plebian radical to make substantial use of the St Domingo (Haitian) revolution of the 1790s which was simultaneously inspiring subject blacks across the Atlantic"

(19–20). It should be remembered, however, that Equiano was also a member of a Jacobin organization shortly before he died in 1797, Thomas Hardy's London Corresponding Society. On the contrast between Equiano and Wedderburn, see McCalman, introduction to *The Horrors of Slavery*, 3–7.

17  I think Peter Linebaugh is up to the same suggestion in his essay, "What If C. L. R. James Had Met E. P. Thompson in 1792?" in Paul Buhle, ed., *C. L. R. James: His Life and Work* (London: Allison and Busby, 1986).

18  See especially David Scott, "Revolution/Theory/Modernity: Notes on the Cognitive-Political Crisis of Our Time," *Social and Economic Studies* 44, nos. 2 and 3 (1995): 1–23; and Scott, "Fanonian Futures?" in *Refashioning Futures: Criticism after Postcoloniality* (Princeton: Princeton University Press, 1999).

19  James has paid tribute to Michelet and Trotsky in many places, for example, in his 1971 lectures on the writing of *The Black Jacobins*. See C. L. R. James, "Why I Wrote *The Black Jacobins*," *Small Axe* 8 (September 2000): 67, 77. In my view, James was considerably more indebted to Michelet for his historiographical poetics than he was to Trotsky. Indeed in some accounts of the making of *The Black Jacobins* he makes mention of Michelet but not Trotsky (though of course his political persuasion was guided more by the latter's revolutionary Marxism than the former's militant liberalism). See, for example, James's remark in the foreword to *The Black Jacobins* (London: Allison and Busby, 1980): "above all, Michelet" (vi).

20  See the interesting psychohistorical study by Arthur Mitzman, *Michelet, Historian* (New Haven: Yale University Press, 1990), xv.

21  Hayden White, *Metahistory: The Historical Imagination in Nineteenth-Century Europe* (Baltimore: Johns Hopkins University Press, 1978), 140; and Mitzman, *Michelet, Historian*, xv. On Michelet and Vico generally, see Edmund Wilson, *To the Finland Station: A Study in the Writing and Acting of History* (New York: Noonday, 1972 [1940]), 3–6. The subsequent chapters on Michelet's history are equally valuable, as indeed is the work as a whole. As H. Stuart Hughes has suggested, it is in Wilson's *Finland Station* that, in the Anglo-American world at least, Michelet is "rehabilitated" and first situated as "the precursor of historical writing harnessed to revolutionary ends." See Hughes, *The Obstructed Path: French Thought in the Years of Desperation, 1930–1960* (New York: Harper and Row, 1968), 21. See also Hughes's "The Sweep of the Narrative Line" in *History as Art and as Science: Twin Vistas on the Past* (New York: Harper and Row, 1964), 78.

22  Jules Michelet, *History of the French Revolution*, trans. by Charles Cocks (Chicago: University of Chicago Press, 1967). Hereafter references to this book will be abbreviated HFR in parenthesis in the text. I am indebted to Linda Orr's study, *Jules Michelet: Nature, History, and Language* (Ithaca: Cornell University Press, 1976), one of the earlier works on Michelet to take Hayden White seriously.

23  As Arthur Mitzman has remarked, "anyone reading hurriedly the first ten pages of Michelet's introduction to his book on the Revolution might think he had

stumbled by mistake into a theological treatise." See Mitzman's "Romanticism and Revolution: The Vision of Jules Michelet," in Max Blechman, ed., *Revolutionary Romanticism* (San Francisco: City Lights, 1999), 90.

24 Leon Trotsky, *The History of the Russian Revolution*, 3 vols., trans. by Max Eastman (New York: Simon and Schuster, 1932, 1933). Hereafter references to this book will be abbreviated HRR in parenthesis in the text.

25 H. Stuart Hughes, *Consciousness and Society: The Reorientation of European Social Thought, 1890–1930* (New York: Knopf, 1958).

26 White, *Metahistory*, 152.

27 Northrop Frye, *The Anatomy of Criticism: Four Essays* (Princeton: Princeton University Press, 1957), 186.

28 Prior to his study of Toussaint Louverture, James had written a study of Captain A. A. Cipriani, *The Life of Captain Cipriani* (Nelson: Cartmel and Co., 1932), and he subsequently wrote one of Herman Melville, *Mariners, Renegades and Castaways: The Story of Herman Melville and the World We Live In* (New York: James, 1953), and then of Kwame Nkrumah, *Nkrumah and the Ghana Revolution* (London: Allison and Busby, 1977). At various times in his life he planned to write biographical treatments of Shakespeare, George Padmore, and Eric Williams. It is a curious and interesting fact that he was never able to write the biography of himself. For some useful remarks, see F. M. Birbalsingh, "The Literary Achievement of C. L. R. James," *Journal of Commonwealth Literature* 19, no. 1 (1984): 108–21.

29 See Walter E. Houghton's useful *The Victorian Frame of Mind, 1830–1870* (New Haven: Yale University Press, 1957), chapter 12. "The great need of the age," as Houghton says, "was a whole series of biographies" (318).

30 See Thomas Carlyle, "On History" in *Critical and Miscellaneous Essays*, vol. 2 (London: Chapman and Hall, 1899), 83–95.

31 Karl Marx, *The Eighteenth Brumaire of Louis Bonaparte* (New York: International Publishers, 1963 [1852]), 15.

32 For James's only explicit reference to *The Eighteenth Brumaire*, see *The Black Jacobins*, 32 [44].

33 See Houghton, *The Victorian Frame of Mind*, 306. Houghton goes on to write: "When the Victorian period began, all the prerequisites for hero worship were present: the enthusiastic temper, the conception of the superior being, the revival of Homeric mythology and medieval ballad, the identification of great art with the grand style, the popularity of Scott and Byron, and the living presence of Napoleonic soldiers and sailors. But traditions die without nourishment, and this one throve. For it answered, or it promised to answer, some of the deepest needs and problems of the age. In the fifty years after 1830 the worship of the hero was a major factor in English culture" (310).

34 G. W. F. Hegel, *The Philosophy of History*, trans. by J. Sibree (New York: Dover, 1956), 30. Hegel went on in a passage worth quoting at length:

Such individuals had no consciousness of the general Idea they were un-folding, while prosecuting those aims of theirs; on the contrary they were practical, political men. But at the same time they were thinking men, who had an insight into the requirements of the time—what was ripe for development. This was the very Truth for their age, for their world; the species next in order, so to speak, and which was already formed in the womb of time. It was theirs to know this nascent principle; the neces-sary, directly sequent step in progress, which their world was to take; to make this their aim, and to expend their energy in promoting it. World-historical men—the Heroes of an epoch—must, therefore, be recognized as its clear-sighted ones; their deeds, their words are the best of that time (30).

35  See the very interesting early study by Charles Frederick Harrold, *Carlyle and Ger-man Thought: 1819–1834* (New Haven: Yale University Press, 1934), especially chap-ter 7, "Carlyle and Heroes." And for a discussion of German Romanticism, see Frederick C. Beiser, *Enlightenment, Revolution, and Romanticism: The Genesis of Modern German Political Thought, 1790–1800* (Cambridge: Harvard University Press, 1992).

36  I am referring, of course, to his "Occasional Discourse on the Negro Question," *Fraser's Magazine* 40 (December 1849), and reissued as a pamphlet in 1853 with the revised title, "Occasional Discourse on the Nigger Question," *Critical and Miscellaneous Essays*, vol. 4 (London: Chapman and Hall, 1899), 348–83. On Car-lyle's relation to Caribbean matters, see Bernard Semmel, *Jamaican Blood and Victo-rian Conscience: The Governor Eyre Controversy* (Boston: Houghton Mifflin, 1963); and Catherine Hall, "Competing Masculinities: Thomas Carlyle, John Stuart Mill and the Case of Governor Eyre," in *White, Male and Middle Class: Explorations in Femi-nism and History* (New York: Routledge, 1992), 255–95, and Hall, *Civilising Subjects: Metropole and Colony in the English Imagination, 1830–1867* (Chicago: University of Chicago Press, 2002), 347–53.

37  See Carlyle, "Democracy," in *Past and Present* (London: Chapman and Hall, 1897 [1843]).

38  Thomas Carlyle, *On Heroes, Hero Worship and the Heroic in History* (Lincoln: Univer-sity of Nebraska Press, 1966 [1841]). Hereafter references to this book will be abbreviated H in parenthesis in the body of the text.

39  See J. W. Burrow, *A Liberal Descent: Victorian Historians and the English Past* (Cam-bridge: Cambridge University Press, 1981). Burrow writes:

In some more famous accounts, notably Hegel's, the successive phases of the spirit's incarnation become moments of a developmental sequence, successively more adequate and comprehensive embodiments of univer-sal reason. There is little or nothing of this in Carlyle. . . . Essentially in Carlyle there is not sequence but only the cyclic assurance of the retribution that waits for forms from which the spirit has departed, and the endless self-renewal of the latter. If there is an Absolute Reality it is immanent, as an ever-present possibility of sudden, blinding, life-changing illumination, an immediate access to grace. It is not an historical terminus. Carlyle's conception of history was apocalyptic and messianic, but pluralist; not a consummation (253–54).

40 On the other side, Michelet had a very unfavorable view of Robespierre and the Jacobin dictatorship, which, he felt, had eliminated the hope of a transformation of the classical or political revolution into a social and religious revolution. See Mitzman, "Romanticism and Revolution," 93; and Mitzman, *Michelet, Historian*, 120.

41 See Mitzman, *Michelet, Historian*, 117. It might be remembered that his 1846 study, *The People*, turned precisely on a preoccupation with the idea of forms of fraternity or collective solidarity.

42 In this context it is hard to forget that while his admiration for Lenin was real there had been an important difference between them between the first congress of the Social Democratic Party in 1903 and the Revolution in 1917.

43 Indeed it is interesting that looking back from 1971 James says that he might have followed Michelet (and Lefebvre) more closely in diminishing the role of the individual hero. See C. L. R. James, "How I Would Re-Write *The Black Jacobins*," *Small Axe* 8 (September 2000): 104–7. But perhaps in 1938 the most compelling way to vindicate the black in history was to figure him or her as a historical hero.

44 The names here are well-enough known. One thinks, for instance, of the West Indians, Edward Blyden, John Jacob Thomas, and Theophilus Scholes; the African Americans, Alexander Crummell, Frederick Douglass, and Martin Delaney; and the West African, J. E. Casley Hayford—each, in his way, a black vindicationist. So far as the West Indians are concerned, on Blyden, see Hollis Lynch, *Edward Wilmot Blyden: Pan-Negro Patriot, 1832–1912* (New York: Oxford University Press, 1967); on John Jacob Thomas, see Faith Smith, *Creole Recitations: John Jacob Thomas and Colonial Formation in the Late Nineteenth Century Caribbean* (Charlottesville: University of Virginia Press, 2002); on Theophilus Scholes, see Patrick Bryan, "Black Perspectives in Late Nineteenth Century Jamaica: The Case of Dr Theophilus E. S. Scholes," in Rupert Lewis and Patrick Bryan, eds., *Garvey: His Work and Impact* (Kingston: ISER, 1988).

45 Robert A. Hill, "C. L. R. James: The Myth of Western Civilization," in George Lamming, ed., *Enterprise of the Indies* (Port of Spain: Trinidad and Tobago Institute of the West Indies, 1999), 255–59.

46 C. L. R. James, "The Intelligence of the Negro: A Few Words with Dr. Harland," *The Beacon* 1, no. 5 (August 1931): 6–10. For some contextual discussion of the significance of *The Beacon* to James's generation of West Indian writers, see Reinhard W. Sander, *The Trinidad Awakening: West Indian Literature of the Nineteen Thirties*

(Westport, Conn.: Greenwood Press, 1988), 27–46 and 91–114. James's essay was subsequently anthologized in the selection from *The Beacon* brought together in Reinhard W. Sander, ed., *From Trinidad: An Anthology of Early West Indian Writing* (New York: Africana, 1978). On the educational background that James would have brought to this essay, and on the importance of the Imperial College of Tropical Agriculture where Harland was a senior member of the faculty, see Carl C. Campbell, *The Young Colonials: A Social History of Education in Trinidad and Tobago, 1834–1939* (Kingston: University Press of the West Indies, 1996).

47   Sidney C. Harland, "Race Admixture," *The Beacon* 1, no. 4 (July 1931): 25–29. I am grateful to Patricia Saunders for procuring this and James's article from the library at the University of the West Indies, St. Augustine. For some context see Sander, *The Trinidad Awakening*, 31. Note that in his own article Harland's first name is spelled "Sidney" whereas in James's rebuttal it is "Sydney."

48   Harland, "Race Admixture," 25.

49   Ibid., 26.

50   Francis Galton, *Hereditary Genius: An Inquiry into Its Laws and Consequences* (London: Macmillan, 1892 [1869]). Harland erroneously refers to this book as being published in 1892. This was its *second* edition, brought out again, the author says, because of demand. "I propose to show in this book," Galton wrote in the opening sentence of the introductory chapter, "that a man's natural abilities are derived by inheritance, under exactly the same limitations as are the forms and physical features of the whole organic world" (1). Galton, however, was not without his critics. Frank Constable was one of them. In his book *Poverty and Hereditary Genius: A Criticism of Mr. Francis Galton's Theory of Hereditary Genius* (London: Fifield, 1905), Constable set out an environmentalist critique. Of Galton's conclusions regarding race, and Toussaint Louverture in particular, Constable writes that "when he relies on achievement as a measure of natural ability, he introduces the very great influence of environment. Buonaparte himself, with the environments of Toussaint l'Ouverture, could have probably achieved no more than the negro did" (118).

51   Harland, "Race Admixture," 27.

52   Ibid.

53   James, "Intelligence of the Negro," 7.

54   Ibid., 8.

55   Ibid.

56   Percy Waxman, *The Black Napoleon: The Story of Toussaint L'Ouverture* (New York: Harcourt, Brace and Company, 1931). See James's peremptory remark — "A superficial book" — in the bibliography of *The Black Jacobins*, 322 [388]. I think this remark is somewhat disingenuous. Not a profound book, it is true (essentially it lacks the complexity of James's understanding of historical action and social relations), yet it would be easy to show what James's figuring of Toussaint shares with Waxman's. The very contrast in the titles is worth observing.

57 James, "Intelligence of the Negro," 8–9.

58 Ibid., 10. In Sander's anthology he renders James's "touchous" as "touchy," assuming, one supposes, a typo in the original. According to the *Oxford English Dictionary* (online version), however, "touchous" means "easily offended, sensitive, touchy." The first known use is 1867. Interestingly, we are told that "[In the Caribbean] an overly sensitive person is 'touchous,' not touchy." At the end of James's article the editor of *The Beacon* appended the following note: "Dr. Harland is at present out of the island. But he took away with him a type-written copy of Mr. James's article and has promised to send his reply" (10).

59 Hill, "C. L. R. James," 259.

60 There are a variety of ways into this problem. See Christine Bolt's useful *The Victorians and Race* (London: Routledge and Kegan Paul, 1971); Douglas A. Lorimer, *Class, Colour, and the Victorians: English Attitudes to the Negro in the Mid-Nineteenth Century* (Leicester: Leicester University Press, 1978); Patrick Brantlinger, *Rule of Darkness: British Literature and Imperialism, 1830–1914* (Ithaca: Cornell University Press, 1988); Simon Gikandi, *Maps of Englishness: Writing Identity in the Culture of Colonialism* (New York: Columbia University Press, 1996); Thomas C. Holt, *The Problem of Freedom: Race, Labor, and Politics in Jamaica and Britain, 1832–1938* (Baltimore: Johns Hopkins University Press, 1992); and Catherine Hall, *Civilising Subjects*.

61 See George W. Stocking Jr.'s useful *Victorian Anthropology* (New York: Free Press, 1987).

62 See, for example, Bolt, *The Victorians and Race*, chapter 1; and Lorimer, *Class, Colour, and the Victorians*, chapter 7.

63 I have in mind, of course, Anthony Trollope, *The West Indies and the Spanish Main* (London: Chapman and Hall, 1859); Charles Kingsley, *At Last, a Christmas in the West Indies* (London: Macmillan, 1871); and James Anthony Froude, *The English in the West Indies; or, the Bow of Ulysses* (London: Longmans, Green, and Company, 1888). James would doubtlessly have been acquainted with these books. Their place in the imagination of West Indian intelligentsia of the nineteenth century has been fascinatingly discussed in Smith, *Creole Recitations*.

64 For some consideration of the place of Haiti in the imagination of the West, see Michel-Rolph Trouillot, *Silencing the Past: Power and the Production of History* (Boston: Beacon Press, 1995).

65 Wilson Jeremiah Moses, *The Golden Age of Black Nationalism, 1850–1925* (New York: Oxford University Press, 1978), 44.

66 James Theodore Holly, "A Vindication of the Capacity of the Negro Race for Self-Government, and Civilized Progress, as Demonstrated by Historical Events of the Haytian Revolution; and the subsequent acts of that people since their National Independence" (1857) in Howard H. Bell, ed., *Black Separatism and the Caribbean, 1860* (Ann Arbor: University of Michigan Press, 1970). Hereafter references to this book will be abbreviated "VNR" in parenthesis in the body of the text.

67 James, *The Black Jacobins*, 237 [283].

68 Reinhart Koselleck, "Historical Criteria of the Modern Concept of Revolution," in *Futures Past: On the Semantics of Historical Time*, trans. by Keith Tribe (Cambridge, Mass.: MIT Press, 1985); Hannah Arendt, *On Revolution* (New York: Penguin, 1963).

69 Arendt, *On Revolution*, 21. Or as Koselleck writes in "Historical Criteria of the Modern Concept of Revolution": "what distinguishes earlier usage [of the term "revolution"] from our own is the consciousness of a return, indicated by the syllable 're' in the word *revolutio*. It was in this sense that Hobbes described the twenty-year period, from 1640 to 1660, following the end of the great English Revolution: 'I have seen in this revolution a circular motion' " (42).

70 Arendt, *On Revolution*, 21.

71 Koselleck, "Historical Criteria of the Modern Concept of Revolution," 43.

72 Bernard Yack, *The Longing for Total Revolution: Philosophic Sources of Social Discontent from Rousseau to Marx and Nietzsche* (Berkeley: University of California Press, 1992 [1986]).

73 Arguably this too forms part of Koselleck's interest. See Melvin Richter, *The History of Political and Social Concepts: A Critical Introduction* (New York: Oxford University Press, 1995), 43.

74 Yack, *The Longing for Total Revolution*, 6.

75 Ibid., 7.


### 3  CONSCRIPTS OF MODERNITY

The epigraph is taken from C. L. R. James, "From Toussaint L'Ouverture to Fidel Castro," in *The Black Jacobins: Toussaint L'Ouverture and the San Domingo Revolution*, 2nd ed. rev. (New York: Vintage, 1963), 391–92.

1 C. L. R. James, *The Black Jacobins* (London: Secker and Warburg, 1938), 16; *The Black Jacobins* (New York: Vintage, 1963), 24–25. In the following notes, page numbers to the latter edition appear within brackets.

2 On the abbé Raynal, see David Brion Davis, *The Problem of Slavery in Western Culture* (Ithaca: Cornell University Press, 1966), 13–17; and Robin Blackburn, *The Overthrow of Colonial Slavery, 1776–1848* (New York: Verso, 1988), 53–54.

3 "In France Liberalism was still an aspiration and 'trusteeship,' its fig-leaf, was as yet unknown. But on the tide of humanitarianism rising on the bourgeois revolt against feudalism, Diderot and the Encyclopaedists had attacked slavery. 'Let the colonies be destroyed rather than be the cause of so much evil,' said the Encyclopaedia in its article on the slave-trade. But such outbursts neither then nor now have carried much weight. And wordy attacks against slavery drew sneers from observers which were not altogether undeserved. The authors were compared to doctors who offered to a patient nothing more than invectives against

the disease which consumed him." James, *The Black Jacobins*, 16 [24]. There is no indication that James knew about the relation between Raynal and Diderot who, it has been argued, had a substantial impact on the *Philosophical and Political History*. See, for example, J. H. M. Salmon, "Liberty by Degrees: Raynal and Diderot on the British Constitution," *History of Political Thought* 20, no. 1 (spring 1999): 87–106. Salmon writes: "As *Two Indies* chronicled the savagery and rapine of the colonizing powers, and as its scope expanded through the three principal editions of 1770, 1774 and 1780 to include comment on the American Revolution, the influence of Diderot radicalized the work until it became an outspoken assault on despotism, imperialism, slavery and superstition" (89).

Peter Gay concurs with James's view on the philosophes' attitudes to slavery. In *The Science of Freedom*, vol. 2 of *The Enlightenment: An Interpretation* (New York: Norton, 1969), Gay writes: "The philosophes' views on slavery are predictable and anything but systematic: they are generally exclamations, rarely thoroughgoing analyses. Well-meaning, often vague, they read rather like an automatic response to human misery that speaks well for the philosophe's intentions but hardly amounts to a crusade; indeed, advocates of slavery sometimes borrowed the philosophe's imprecise pronouncements or deliberately misread their sarcasms for their own purposes. In general, though, the men of the Enlightenment helped to change men's thinking on the subject; early in the field and eloquent in their revulsion, they swelled antislavery sentiment from a trickle to a respectable stream of opinion that would grow, at the end of the century, with their help, into the torrent of abolitionism" (410).

4  Abbé Raynal, *Philosophical and Political History of the Settlement and Trade of the Europeans in the East and West Indies*, 3 vols. (Glasgow: D. McKenzie, 1812 [1770]), 2:311.

5  Ibid., 312.

6  Quoted in James, *The Black Jacobins*, 16–17 [25]. Michel-Rolph Trouillot has disputed the historical veracity of the claim that Toussaint was acquainted with Raynal. He does allow, however, that the question of its historical truth may be less important than the mythical image it projects of Toussaint. See his "An Unthinkable History: The Haitian Revolution as a Non-Event," in *Silencing the Past: Power and the Production of the Past* (Boston: Beacon, 1997), 84–85, 170, n22.

7  It may be useful to have Raynal's words from the *Philosophical and Political History*:

> But, what am I saying? Let the ineffectual calls of humanity be no longer
> pleaded with the people and their masters; perhaps they have never been
> consulted in any public transactions. If then, ye nations of Europe, inter-
> est alone can exert its influence over you, listen to me once more: Your
> slaves stand in no need either of your generosity or of your counsels,
> in order to break the sacrilegious yoke which oppresses them. Nature
> speaks a more powerful language than philosophy, or interest. Some
> white people, already massacred, have expiated a part of our crimes; al-

ready have two colonies of fugitive negroes been established, to whom treaties and power give a perfect security from your attempts. Poison hath at different times been the instrument of their vengeance. Several have eluded your oppression by a voluntary death. These enterprises are so many indications of the impending storm; and the negroes only want a chief, sufficiently courageous to lead them on to vengeance and slaughter.

Where is this great man to be found, whom Nature, perhaps, owes to the honour of the human species? Where is this new Spartacus, who will not find a Crassus? Then will the black code be no more; and the white code will be dreadful, if the conqueror only regards the right of reprisals.

Till this revolution take place, the negroes will groan under the yoke of oppression, the description of which cannot but interest us more and more in their destiny (2:316–17).

8   In James's play, "Toussaint L'Ouverture [Black Jacobins]" there is a marvelous scene in the prologue in which Madame L'Ouverture is urging Toussaint to come to bed, and he answers: "I can't sleep. There is something frightening in the air. And I have just opened my Raynal to read an even more frightening thing. The book just opened and I looked. The Abbe is saying: 'A courageous chief only is wanted.' I have read it a thousand times before, but it is as if I had seen it for the first time." In Anna Grimshaw, ed., *The C. L. R. James Reader* (Oxford: Blackwell, 1992), 71.

9   These criticisms have often been articulated in terms of the generation of a radical black intellectual tradition in which C. L. R. James is situated as a seminal figure whose vision, in the end, was limited by its dependence on Europe. For one recent version of this disquiet, see Paget Henry, *Caliban's Reason: Introducing Afro-Caribbean Philosophy* (New York: Routledge, 2000), chapter 2. For an earlier one, see Cedric Robinson, *Black Marxism: The Making of the Black Radical Tradition* (Chapel Hill: University of North Carolina Press, 2000 [1983]), chapter 10.

10  In an interview of very complex insight into James and *The Black Jacobins*, and to which I return in this chapter, Stuart Hall also offers a criticism that runs in this direction: "But inevitably there is something that this narrative misses, and that might be thought [of] as the African dimension. Of course, I don't mean to suggest that he is unaware that these are African slaves: that is how he opens his narrative, insisting upon the African connection. Yet I suspect that the early insurrection had more to do with the ruptured continuities embedded in the lived African cultures in the slave quarters, with what remained of African religions, customs, beliefs and languages. This James does not investigate with the same care and depth. . . . This African presence, for James, remains a kind of silence." See Stuart Hall (interviewed by Bill Schwarz), "Breaking Bread with History: C. L. R. James and *The Black Jacobins*," *History Workshop Journal* 46 (autumn 1998): 25.

11   It is not irrelevant to remember that in August 1933, the year following James's
     arrival in Britain, there were centenary celebrations in the city of Hull memorial-
     izing the role of William Wilberforce in the abolition of British colonial slavery.

12   See, for example, James, The Black Jacobins, 206 [246].

13   Ibid., 66 [85–86].

14   See, for example, ibid., 206 [246].

15   For example, the prologue in which, with biting ridicule, James writes, "The
     Spaniards, the most advanced Europeans of their day, annexed the island, called
     Hispaniola, and took the backward natives under their protection. They intro-
     duced Christianity, forced labour in the mines, murder, rape, blood-hounds,
     strange diseases, and artificial famine (by the destruction of cultivation to starve
     the rebellious). These and other requirements of the higher civilisation reduced
     the native population from between one and three million to 60,000 in 15 years."
     The Black Jacobins, xv [3–4].

16   See, for example, ibid., 227 [271].

17   See the famous tracing of this colonial self-fashioning in C. L. R. James, Beyond
     a Boundary (London: Hutchinson, 1963). But see also Stuart Hall's remarks: "I
     always think in relation to James that our contemporary attitude of postcolonial
     intellectuals towards Europe is by now so primitive compared to his, for we must
     either ditch it or kill it, love it or mimic it. Of course there are elements of mimicry
     in him. . . . He could adopt the pose of a Victorian gentleman out of place. And
     he did indeed possess a commitment to charm, manners and propriety. But he's
     not in that sense someone who sold out to Europe. He understood Europe his-
     torically, rather than it being something which simply won his allegiance." Hall,
     "Breaking Bread with History," 24–25.

18   C. L. R. James, "How I Would Rewrite The Black Jacobins," Small Axe 8 (September
     2000): 99–112. The other two lectures in the series, published in the same issue
     of Small Axe, are "How I Wrote The Black Jacobins" (65–82) and "The Black Jacobins
     and Black Reconstruction: A Comparative Analysis" (83–98). For a sense of the occa-
     sion of these lectures and the significance of the Institute of the Black World,
     see Robert Hill's preface to them (61–64).

19   James, "How I Wrote The Black Jacobins," 99. Justin Girod-Chantrans (1750–1841)
     was the author of Voyage d'un Suisse dans différentes colonies d'Amérique pendant la der-
     nière guerre, avec une table d'observations météorologiques faites à Saint-Domingue (1785).

20   It is important to remember that it is in the context of the civil rights and Black
     Power movements that James was able to return to the United States for the first
     time after his immigration-enforced departure in 1953.

21   James, The Black Jacobins (New York: Vintage, 1963), 338 n. 39. James is refer-
     ring here to Lefebvre's La Fuite du Roi [The Flight of the King], mimeographed lec-
     tures delivered at the Sorbonne that James had picked up in Paris in 1956. There
     is a story waiting to be written about James and Lefebvre. That story would
     also have to take into account the transformations in the historiography of the

French Revolution, especially the shifts away from a "social" to a "political" understanding associated with Francois Furet and *Interpreting the French Revolution* (Cambridge: Cambridge University Press, 1981), and in many ways exemplified in Keith Michael Baker, *Inventing the French Revolution* (Cambridge: Cambridge University Press, 1990).

22  James, "How I Would Rewrite *The Black Jacobins*," 108.

23  See, for example, Anthony Bogues, "Afterword," *Small Axe* 8 (September 2000): 113–17.

24  Edward [Kamau] Brathwaite, *The Development of Creole Society in Jamaica, 1770–1820* (Oxford: Clarendon Press, 1971); and Brathwaite, *Folk Culture of the Slaves in Jamaica* (London: New Beacon Books, 1970); Monica Schuler, "Afro-American Slave Culture," in Michael Craton, ed., *Roots and Branches: Current Directions in Slave Studies* (Toronto: Pergamon Press, 1979); John W. Blassingame, *The Slave Community: Plantation Life in the Antebellum South* (New York: Oxford University Press, 1972); Lawrence W. Levine, *Black Culture and Black Consciousness: Afro-American Folk Thought from Slavery to Freedom* (New York: Oxford University Press, 1977); and Albert Raboteau, *Slave Religion* (New York: Oxford University Press, 1978).

25  See David Scott, *Refashioning Futures: Criticism after Postcoloniality* (Princeton: Princeton University Press, 1999), chapter 5.

26  The suggestive phrase, "questioning slavery," is James Walvin's. See his *Questioning Slavery* (New York: Routledge, 1996). It turns precisely on the kind of problematic that seems to me in need of revision.

27  See David Scott, "That Event, This Memory: Notes on the Anthropology of African Diasporas in the New World," *Diaspora* 1, no 3 (1991): 261–84.

28  John Thornton, *Africa and Africans in the Making of the Atlantic World, 1400–1800*, 2nd ed. (Cambridge: Cambridge University Press, 1998).

29  See, for example, John Thornton, "African Soldiers in the Haitian Revolution," *Journal of Caribbean History* 25 (1993): 58–80. Since Melville Herskovits, of course, Haiti has been one crucial conceptual-ideological terrain for the substantiation of the thesis of the agency of African cultural resistance.

30  Interestingly, Thornton is an "Atlantic" historian influenced by Fernand Braudel. His thesis bears a considerable resemblance to that of the "new Cambridge" school of historians of modern India such as Christopher Bayly and David Washbrook. See, for example, Bayly, *Indian Society and the Making of the British Empire* (Cambridge: Cambridge University Press, 1988); and Bayly, *Imperial Meridian: The British Empire and the World, 1780–1830* (London: Longman, 1989). For one trenchant criticism of this line of argument, see Partha Chatterjee, *The Nation and Its Fragments* (Princeton: Princeton University Press, 1993), chapter 2.

31  Thornton, *Africa and Africans*, 6.

32  Ibid., 6–7.

33  Sidney W. Mintz and Richard Price, *An Anthropological Approach to the Afro-American Past: A Caribbean Perspective* (Philadelphia: Institute for the Study of Human Issues,

1976). This classic was subsequently reissued with a new preface as *The Birth of African-American Culture: An Anthropological Perspective* (Boston: Beacon, 1992). All references will be to the latter edition.

34  Mintz and Price, *The Birth of African-American Culture*, 81.

35  See also Sidney Mintz, "Afro-Caribbeana: An Introduction," in his *Caribbean Transformations* (Chicago: Aldine, 1974), 7–8.

36  Mintz and Price, *The Birth of African-American Culture*, 14. See also Mintz, "Afro-Caribbeana," 11–12.

37  Mintz and Price, *The Birth of African-American Culture*, 17.

38  Ibid., 19.

39  Thornton is not, of course, the only critic of Mintz's and Price's essay. For some remarks on the reception of the work, see the preface to the 1992 Beacon edition, vii–xiv.

40  Thornton, *Africa and Africans*, 162.

41  Ibid., 182.

42  Ibid., 320.

43  I have tried to demonstrate the kind of investigation into the formation of conceptual objects this would be in my "That Event, This Memory."

44  Mintz and Price, *The Birth of African-American Culture*, 83. Or, Mintz, "Afro-Caribbeana": "The glory of Afro-Americana inheres in the durable fiber of humanity, in the face of what surely must have been the most repressive epoch in world history" (14).

45  A good deal of scholarship has been expended on the conceptual salience of the problem of modernity. See, for example, the introduction to and the essays collected in Bruce M. Knauft, ed., *Critically Modern: Alternatives, Alterities, Anthropologies* (Bloomington: Indiana University Press, 2002).

46  See, for example, Robin Blackburn, *The Making of New World Slavery: From the Baroque to the Modern, 1492–1800* (London: Verso, 1997). One of the most consistent and impressive arguments in this direction has of course been that embodied in the work of Sidney Mintz. In "Afro-Caribbeana" he wrote: "New World plantation organization during the sixteenth century and the subsequent two centuries, though of course agricultural, had a very modern — even industrial — cast for its time. . . . The relatively highly developed industrial character of the plantation system meant a curious sort of 'modernization' or 'westernization' for the slaves — an aspect of their acculturation in the New World that has too often been missed because of the deceptively rural, agrarian, and pseudo-manorial quality of the slave-based plantation production" (9). And further: "Thus, the growth of slave-based economies in the New World was an integral part of the rise of European commerce and industry, while European factory workers were in a position structurally parallel to that occupied by the enslaved and forced labor strata of New World colonial societies" (10). See also Mintz, *Sweetness and Power: The Place of Sugar in Modern History* (New York: Penguin, 1985); and Michel-Rolph Trouillot,

"The Otherwise Modern: Caribbean Lessons from the Savage Slot" in Knauft, *Critically Modern.*

47  Charles Taylor, "Modernity and Difference," in Paul Gilroy, Lawrence Grossberg, and Angela McRobbie, eds., *Without Guarantees: In Honour of Stuart Hall* (New York: Verso, 2000); and Taylor, "Two Theories of Modernity," *Public Culture* 11 (1999): 153–74. See also S. N. Eisenstadt, "Multiple Modernities," *Daedalus* 129, no. 1 (2001): 1–31.

48  Taylor, "Modernity and Difference," 366.

49  Ibid., 367.

50  Ibid.; emphasis in original.

51  Ibid., 368.

52  Ibid.

53  Books like Paul Gilroy's *The Black Atlantic: Modernity and Double Consciousness* (Cambridge, Mass.: Harvard University Press, 1993) tell this story in new but recognizable ways.

54  Talal Asad, "Are There Histories of Peoples without Europe? A Review Article," *Comparative Studies in Society and History* 29, no. 3 (1987): 607. Eric Wolf's book, *Europe and the People without History* (Berkeley: University of California Press, 1982), is "epigrammatic" because it is one of the early and defining instances of the modernity-and-difference arguments.

55  Asad, "Are There Histories of Peoples without Europe?" 603.

56  Ibid., 607.

57  In a fascinating discussion that bears on the kind of paradigm shift I am referring to here, Arthur Danto talks about the displacement of the form of question that was shaped by the conceptual world of C. G. Hempel: "Hempel's theory in fact strikes me still as true. It just stopped being relevant, the way the whole philosophy of history it defined stopped being. It was replaced with a different set of questions, a world in effect, into which it no longer fit." See Arthur C. Danto, "The Decline and Fall of the Analytical Philosophy of History," in Frank Ankersmit and Hans Kellner, eds., *A New Philosophy of History* (Chicago: University of Chicago Press, 1995), 85. Again the connection to Collingwood's logic should be apparent.

58  Asad, "Are There Histories of Peoples without Europe?" 607.

59  Ibid.

60  Talal Asad, "Conscripts of Western Civilization," in Christine Gailey, ed., *Dialectical Anthropology: Essays in Honor of Stanley Diamond*, vol. 1, *Civilization in Crisis* (Gainesville: University Press of Florida, 1992), 333. Though published in the early 1990s this essay was written in the middle 1980s.

61  See David Scott, "Fanonian Futures?" in *Refashioning Futures.*

62  See Asad's very useful discussion in the introduction to his *Genealogies of Religion: Discipline and Reasons of Power in Christianity and Islam* (Baltimore: Johns Hopkins University Press, 1993), 1–24.

63  See the introduction to Scott, *Refashioning Futures.*

64  See also Talal Asad, "Afterword: From the History of Colonial Anthropology to the Anthropology of Western Hegemony," in George W. Stocking Jr., ed., *Colonial Situations: Essays on the Contextualization of Ethnographic Knowledge* (Madison: University of Wisconsin Press, 1991), 314–24.

65  Along with Herbert Aptheker's *American Negro Slave Revolts* (New York: Columbia University Press, 1943), *The Black Jacobins* helped to inaugurate the study of New World slave resistance and revolt.

66  This is a chapter of slave responses to slavery that builds on a prior chapter that traces out a "continuum" of resistance: from passive resistance to active revolt.

67  Eugene Genovese, *From Rebellion to Revolution: Afro-American Slave Revolts in the Making of the Modern World* (Baton Rouge: Louisiana State University Press, 1979), 82.

68  Genovese's indebtedness to Eric Hobsbawm's work is clear, especially his seminal work on premodern European rebellions, *Primitive Rebels: Studies in Archaic Forms of Social Movement in the Nineteenth and Twentieth Centuries* (New York: Praeger, 1963), and the first volume of his great history of the modern world, *The Age of Revolution, 1789–1848* (London: Weidenfeld and Nicolson, 1962).

69  Genovese, *From Rebellion to Revolution,* 88.

70  Michael Craton, *Testing the Chains: Resistance to Slavery in the British West Indies* (Ithaca: Cornell University Press, 1982), 99.

71  Ibid.

72  Ibid., 249.

73  Ibid., 252.

74  Ibid.

75  David Patrick Geggus has a long and impressive list of publications; some of the more important for my purposes here are: "Slave Resistance Studies and the Saint Domingue Slave Revolt: Some Preliminary Considerations," Occasional Paper Series, Latin American and Caribbean Center, Florida International University, 1983; "The French and Haitian Revolutions, and Resistance to Slavery in the Americas: An Overview," *Revue Français d'Histoire d'Outre-Mer* 56 (1989): 107–24; "Slavery, War and Revolution in the Greater Caribbean, 1789–1815," in David Barry Gaspar and David Patrick Geggus, eds., *A Turbulent Time: The French Revolution and the Greater Caribbean* (Bloomington: Indiana University Press, 1997). See also David P. Geggus, ed., *The Impact of the Haitian Revolution in the Atlantic World* (Columbia: University of South Carolina Press, 2001).

76  Geggus, "Slave Resistance Studies," 20.

77  Ibid., 21. See also David Geggus, "Toussaint Louverture and the Slaves of Bréda Plantations," *Journal of Caribbean History* 20 (1985/86): 30–48.

78  See David Geggus's long-awaited and very impressive *Haitian Revolutionary Studies* (Bloomington: Indiana University Press, 2003).

79  Genovese, *From Rebellion to Revolution,* xiii.

80  Craton, *Testing the Chains,* 242.

81   George Lamming, who had met and grown close to James soon after the latter's
     return to London in 1953, records his astonishment at the absence of a continu-
     ous memory of James's work. A famous chapter in his book *The Pleasures of Exile*
     (London: Michael Joseph, 1960), "Caliban Orders History," is devoted to rehears-
     ing James's story in *The Black Jacobins*, a book that, as Lamming says, "should be
     Bible-reading for every boy who would be acquainted with the period in ques-
     tion" (119). On Lamming's relation to James, see David Scott, "The Sovereignty of
     the Imagination: An Interview with George Lamming," *Small Axe* 12 (September
     2002): 134–45.

82   C. L. R. James, *The Black Jacobins*, 2nd ed. rev. (New York: Vintage, 1963), 391–418.

83   James, "From Toussaint L'Ouverture to Fidel Castro," in ibid., 402. In the pref-
     ace to the second edition of *The Black Jacobins* James writes: "The Appendix, 'From
     Toussaint L'Ouverture to Fidel Castro,' attempts for the future of the West Indies,
     all of them, what was done for Africa in 1938" (unpaginated page).

84   Ibid., 402.

85   Ibid., 391.

86   Ibid.

87   See, for example, C. L. R. James, *Party Politics in the West Indies* (Port of Spain:
     James, 1962). Quoting from his report to Eric Williams of June 1957 and remark-
     ing on the distinctiveness of the Caribbean, James says: "India, Burma, Ceylon
     and Africa have an indigenous civilization and culture. They adapt and modern-
     ise this, but in the period of transition this serves as a rallying-point and a basis
     of solidarity. West Indians have nothing of the kind" (13). And further, "Day in
     and day out Nkrumah sings on the need for developing the 'African personality.'
     It is a grand phrase. He has here the inestimable advantage of an African back-
     ground, language, religion, law, institutions, culture. We have to make our own
     way, dominated by language, institutions, culture, which are in essence similar
     to Britain and the still more powerful United States" (100).

88   James, "From Toussaint L'Ouverture to Fidel Castro," 405.

89   Ibid., 391–92, emphasis added.

90   Ibid., 392, emphasis added.

91   James, *The Black Jacobins*, 5 [12].

92   Among the many essays that could be cited here, see Michel Foucault, "The Sub-
     ject and Power," in Hubert Dreyfus and Paul Rabinow, *Michel Foucault: Beyond Struc-
     turalism and Hermeneutics* (Chicago: University of Chicago Press, 1982).

93   In a very illuminating passage discussing this aspect of *The Black Jacobins*, Stuart
     Hall remarks: "James does not represent Caribbean peoples as an old African
     people, a traditional people, decimated by plantation slavery and the experi-
     ence of forced migration, free—when abolition arrived—to go back to the old
     ways. James understood well enough that the history of modernity revolutionizes
     everything. Nothing could be turned back. Everything is transformed. Thus the
     people of the Caribbean—fortuitously, paradoxically—had been transformed

into a kind of prototypical, modern people, no longer rooted in a traditional, religious or particularistic way of understanding the world. They had had—James argued—their own traditions transformed, fractured and violently inserted into the most advanced ideas of the time, into the very syntax of the declaration of the rights of man and into the dawn of a new world." Hall, "Breaking Bread," 23.

94 James, *The Black Jacobins*, 66 [85-86].

95 Asad, "Conscripts of Western Civilization," 340.

96 James, "From Toussaint L'Ouverture to Fidel Castro," 418.


## 4 TOUSSAINT'S TRAGIC DILEMMA

The epigraph is taken from C. L. R. James, *The Black Jacobins: Toussaint L'Ouverture and the San Domingo Revolution*, 2nd ed. rev. (New York: Vintage, 1963), 291.

1 George Steiner, *The Death of Tragedy* (New Haven: Yale University Press, 1996 [1961]), 130.

2 Ibid., 128.

3 I'm thinking here of Walter Kaufman, *Tragedy and Philosophy* (New York: Doubleday and Company, 1968), 43-44. The view that tragedies, by definition, end badly, end in misfortune, is of course both old and controversial. It comes first and foremost from chapter 13 of Aristotle's *Poetics*, trans. by Malcolm Heath (New York: Penguin, 1996), in which he praises *Oedipus* as the play with the best sort of plot. But since Aristotle, in chapter 14 of the *Poetics*, also praises Euripides's *Iphigenia*, a play with a happy ending, there is room for considerable debate. For a fascinating discussion of this question and of the variety of ways of understanding tragedy from Greek antiquity to the Middle Ages, see Henry Ansgar Kelly, *Ideas and Forms of Tragedy from Aristotle to the Middle Ages* (Cambridge: Cambridge University Press, 1993).

4 Hayden White, *Metahistory: The Historical Imagination in Nineteenth-Century Europe* (Baltimore: John Hopkins University Press, 1978), 8-10.

5 James arrived in New York in October 1938 at the invitation of the Socialist Workers Party leader, James Cannon, intending to lecture for a few months. He stayed fifteen years. In 1948 the Immigration and Naturalization Service began proceedings against him. In 1953, in order to avoid actual deportation James returned to Britain. The story of the years in between is told in varying detail in several places. See, for example, Anna Grimshaw, "C. L. R. James: A Revolutionary Vision for the Twentieth Century," introduction to Anna Grimshaw, ed., *The C. L. R. James Reader* (Oxford: Blackwell, 1992); Anna Grimshaw and Keith Hart, "*American Civilization*: An Introduction," in C. L. R. James, *American Civilization*, ed. by Anna Grimshaw and Keith Hart (Oxford: Blackwell, 1993); Scott McLemee, "American Civilization and World Revolution: C. L. R. James in the United States, 1938-1953 and Beyond," in Scott McLemee and Paul Le Blanc, eds., *C. L. R. James*

and *Revolutionary Marxism: Selected Writings of C. L. R. James, 1939–1949* (Atlantic Highlands, N.J.: Humanities Press, 1994).

6 For a discussion of the swp and the larger context of Trotskyism in the United States, see Paul Buhle, *Marxism in the United States: Remapping the History of the American Left* (New York: Verso, 1987).

7 On these famous discussions, see C. L. R. James, "Discussions with Trotsky," in *At the Rendezvous of Victory* (London: Allison and Busby, 1984); and James, "Preliminary Notes on the Negro Question" and "Notes following the Discussions" in Scott McLemee, ed., *C. L. R. James on the "Negro Question"* (Jackson: University Press of Mississippi, 1996).

8 Besides James (J. R. Johnson), the central figures in the group were Raya Dunyayevskaya (Freddie Forest) and Grace Lee (Ria Stone). Of the emergence of the name of the Tendency, Scott McLemee, "American Civilization and World Revolution," 235, n21, writes: "The group was known simply as 'the minority' throughout most of the period it existed in the Workers party [wp]. The tendency's first public appearance under the name 'Johnson-Forest' seems to have been during the 'interim period' of 1947 between leaving the wp and joining the swp. Inside the swp, they were called 'the Johnsonites.'" Robert A. Hill, in his "Literary Executor's Afterword" to *American Civilization*, puts the date when the group "formally became known as the 'Johnson-Forest Tendency'" at 1945 (304). For a firsthand account by principal members, see Grace Lee Boggs, *Living for Change: An Autobiography* (Minneapolis: University of Minnesota Press, 1998), chapter 3; and Martin Glaberman, introduction to Martin Glaberman, ed., *Marxism for Our Time: C. L. R. James on Revolutionary Organization* (Jackson: University Press of Mississippi, 1999), xi–xxvii.

9 This thesis eventually appeared in its full dimensions as an internal discussion document coauthored with Raya Dunyayevskaya and Grace Lee within the Socialist Workers Party and was later published as *State Capitalism and World Revolution* (Chicago: Charles H. Kerr, 1986 [1950]).

10 See C. L. R. James, *Notes on Dialectics: Hegel, Marx, Lenin* (Westport, Conn.: Lawrence Hill, 1980 [1948]).

11 See James, *Beyond a Boundary* (Kingston: Sangster, 1963), 149.

12 The story of James's relation to Trotsky's ideas is of course a complicated one. "As early as 1941," James writes in *Beyond a Boundary*, "I had begun to question the premises of Trotskyism. It took nearly a decade of incessant labour and collaboration to break with it and reorganize my Marxist ideas to cope with the postwar world. That was a matter of doctrine, of history, of economics and politics" (149). The break itself is not uncontroversial. See Paul Le Blanc, introduction to McLemee and Le Blanc, *C. L. R. James and Revolutionary Marxism*, 12–19.

13 See, for example, "Education, Propaganda, Agitation: Post-War America and Bolshevism," in Glaberman, *Marxism for Our Time*. "'To Bolshevize America,'" James

wrote, "*it is necessary to Americanize Bolshevism*" (16, his emphasis). See also Scott
McLemee, "American Civilization and World Revolution," 221–24.

14  Interestingly, James eschewed the characterization of "heterodoxy." "Please,"
James asked, breaking into an interviewer's attempt to pose a question, "what
is a 'heterodox form of Marxism'? Because that statement implies a regulation,
a normal form of Marxism." "An Audience with C. L. R. James," *Third World Book
Review* 1, no. 2 (1984): 7. The remark is fascinating for what it suggests about
James's nondogmatic attitude to Marx and Marxism.

15  The late 1940s and early 1950s are also a period of the theorization of "personality" across and between a number of theoretical fields, most prominently anthropology and psychology (the whole debate about "culture and personality" belongs here). But perhaps the most famous work on personality of these years was
T. W. Adorno et al., *The Authoritarian Personality* (New York: Harper and Row, 1950).

16  In this period—1949 to 1952—James gave lectures on tragedy.

17  The manuscript, originally bearing the provisional title "Notes on American Civilization," was apparently drafted at speed between late 1949 and early 1950. For
some discussion about its genesis, see Grimshaw and Hart, "*American Civilization*:
An Introduction"; and Hill, "Literary Executor's Afterword."

18  See, for example, *Beyond a Boundary* (Kingston: Sangster, 1963), in which James
writes: "Perhaps for one reason, because of my colonial background, I always
saw it [the United States] for what it was and not for what I thought it ought to
be" (52).

19  James was a "civilizational" thinker. His admiration of Oswald Spengler's thesis
in *The Decline of the West* is worth remembering here. On Spengler's influence on
a wide spectrum of intellectuals of James's generation, see H. Stuart Hughes,
*Oswald Spengler: A Critical Estimate* (New York: Scribner, 1952).

20  James, *American Civilization*, 36; emphasis in original.

21  Ibid., 149.

22  Ibid., 153.

23  Ibid., 153–54.

24  Ibid., 154.

25  The *Windrush* was the name of the ship that brought the first West Indian immi-
grants to Britain in 1948. See the useful book by Mike Phillips and Trevor Phillips,
*Windrush: The Irresistible Rise of Multi-Racial Britain* (London: HarperCollins, 1998).

26  Louise Bennett, "Colonisation in Reverse," in *Jamaica Labrish* (Kingston: Sangster, 1966).

27  He looked, Lamming said, like a "vagrant." "It's very odd. First of all, James
was not in very good physical condition. When he said 'Lamming' and I said
'Yes,' I was very excited and a little shocked when he told me who he was." See
David Scott, "The Sovereignty of the Imagination: An Interview with George
Lamming," *Small Axe* 12 (September 2002): 134.

28   "Once in a blue moon, i.e. once in a lifetime," James wrote in *Beyond a Boundary*, "a writer is handed on a plate a gift from heaven. I was handed mine in 1958. I had just completed a draft of this book up to the end of the previous chapter when I returned to the West Indies in April 1958, after twenty-six years of absence. I intended to stay three months, I stayed four years" (217).

29   See Ivar Oxaal, *Black Intellectuals Come to Power: The Rise of Creole Nationalism in Trinidad and Tobago* (Cambridge, Mass.: Schenkman, 1968), chapter 7. It is likely that James's going to Trinidad to assist Williams was on the cards well before 1958. On James's account, in 1956 Williams went to London and had discussions with him on the formation of a paper for the newly formed People's National Movement. See James, *Party Politics in the West Indies* (Port of Spain: James, 1962), 99.

30   For a description of these, see O. Nigel Bolland, *On the March: Labour Rebellions in the British Caribbean, 1934–39* (Kingston: Ian Randle, 1995).

31   C. L. R. James, *The Life of Captain Cipriani: An Account of British Government in the West Indies* (Nelson: Cartmel and Co., 1932).

32   On the expulsion of the Marxist Left from the People's National Party in 1952, see Trevor Munroe, *The Cold War and the Jamaican Left, 1950–1955: Re-Opening the Files* (Kingston: Kingston Publishers, 1992); and David Scott, "Memories of the Left: An Interview with Richard Hart," *Small Axe* 3 (March 1998): 65–114. The story of the overthrow of the Jagan regime is told in Cheddi Jagan, *Forbidden Freedom: The Story of British Guiana* (London: Lawrence and Wishart, 1954).

33   For James's account of this period in Trinidad, see his *Party Politics in the West Indies*. Of the middle class he wrote with barely concealed contempt: "The job, the car, the fridge, the trip abroad, preferably under government auspices and at government expense, these seem to be the beginning and end of their preoccupation" (135).

34   See James, *Party Politics in the West Indies*, 109. Needless to say, James's relationship with Eric Williams is notoriously complex. And *Party Politics* is a slim book of profound—and very often moving and disturbing—complexity. For in it James not only sketches a description of the specific relationship between the *Nation* and the PNM as well as an insightful analysis of the general problem of the nationalist party and what one might call its ideological apparatuses; it is also an attempt to explain and justify the personal predicament in which he found himself vis-à-vis the pettiness, narrow-mindedness, and philistinism of the PNM leadership and Williams. For a fascinating review of this book see Roy Augier, "Something to Discuss," *New World Quarterly* 2, no. 1 (1965): 84–91.

35   James, *Party Politics in the West Indies*, 163.

36   Anna Grimshaw and Keith Hart, on the one hand, and Robert A. Hill, on the other, argue in their respective introduction and afterword that *American Civilization* ought to be seen as a bridge between James's "early" work of the 1930s (principally, *The Black Jacobins*) and the "later" work of the 1950s (principally, *Be-*

*yond a Boundary*). I don't disagree with this assessment, but I want to urge that the central formulation here has to do with tragedy and that James seeks to rejoin these moments in the revised edition of *The Black Jacobins* in 1963.

37   George Lamming tells a fascinating story about his relation to the publication of this book. See Scott, "The Sovereignty of the Imagination," 110.

38   James, *Beyond a Boundary*, 149.

39   Ibid., 149–50.

40   Ibid., 151: "The conjunction hit me as it would have hit few of the students of society and culture in the international organization to which I belonged. Trotsky had said that the workers were deflected from politics by sports. With my past I simply could not accept that. I was British and the history of those decades in Britain was very familiar to me, both the politics and the sport."

41   Ibid., 152: "The first task was to get Greece clear."

42   Ibid., 153.

43   Ibid.

44   Ibid., 154–55.

45   Ibid., 155.

46   Ibid.

47   Ibid., 192.

48   Ibid., 192–93.

49   James of course always insisted that the book was written for the African, not the Caribbean, anticolonial struggle. See James, "Preface to the Vintage Edition" of *The Black Jacobins*.

50   James, *The Black Jacobins*, 231 [275].

51   The words are from the poem, "Winding up," in Derek Walcott, *Sea Grapes* (New York: Farrar, Straus and Giroux, 1976).

52   James, *The Black Jacobins*, 241 [288].

53   Ibid.

54   Friedrich Nietzsche, *On the Genealogy of Morality* (Cambridge: Cambridge University Press, 1994 [1887]), 77.

55   James, *The Black Jacobins*, 2nd ed., 289–92.

56   C. L. R. James, "Letters to Literary Critics," in Anna Grimshaw, ed., *The C. L. R. James Reader* (Oxford: Blackwell, 1992), 220. In the same year, Herman Melville would also be included in this pantheon. "Except for Aristotle, writing nearly 2500 years ago," James wrote in *Mariners, Renegades and Castaways: The Story of Herman Melville and the World We Live In* (New York: James, 1953), "and Hegel who wrote a generation before Melville, no critic of literature has written so profoundly of the art of great writing" (81).

57   James, "Preface to Criticism," in Grimshaw, *The C. L. R. James Reader*, 255.

58   Ibid., 256. This essay was written around 1955. James is responding in part here to the revolution in literary criticism occurring on both sides of the Atlantic that sought a more "scientific" or "objective" criticism. In Britain this movement was

associated with formalist practices introduced at Cambridge University in the 1920s by I. A. Richards and others; in the United States it was associated with the New Critics of the 1940s onward. In general these critics were contemptuous of what they perceived to be the naive belletristic criticism of the Victorians. F. R. Leavis (influenced by Richards) was the most prominent and formidable literary critic in Britain in the first half of the twentieth century. L. C. Knights was a Shakespeare critic and author of, among other books, *How Many Children Had Lady Macbeth?* (Cambridge: Minority Press, 1933). Both Leavis and Knights were fierce antagonists of the criticism of A. C. Bradley, whose work we will meet in a moment. It is not insignificant that James's arrival in Britain in the spring of 1932 corresponds with the debut of Leavis's magazine, *Scrutiny*. By the time James returned to literary criticism in the 1950s, the revolution in criticism had become the norm. For a discussion of the new intellectual professionalism and the influence of Leavis, see Francis Mulhern's excellent *The Moment of 'Scrutiny'* (London: New Left Books, 1979).

59 James, "Preface to Criticism," 256.

60 Ibid., 257.

61 Aristotle, *Poetics*, chapter 13, section 7:2.

62 For instructive discussions of Greek tragedy see Malcolm Heath, *The Poetics of Greek Tragedy* (Stanford, Calif.: Stanford University Press, 1987); and Simon Goldhill, *Reading Greek Tragedy* (Cambridge: Cambridge University Press, 1986).

63 Aristotle, *Poetics*, chapter 13, section 7:2.

64 Kaufman, *Tragedy and Philosophy*, is inclined to limit the importance of the concept altogether, urging that it will be noticed just "how very little Aristotle says about *hamartia* and how little he does with it" (62).

65 Aristotle, *Poetics*, chapter 13, section 7:2.

66 See Malcolm Heath, introduction to Aristotle, *Poetics* (London: Penguin, 1996), xxxiii. For a useful collection of essays discussing hamartia, see Douglas V. Stump, James A. Arieti, Lloyd Goson, and Eleonore Stump, eds., *Hamartia: The Concept of Error in the Western Tradition* (New York: Edmin Mellen Press, 1983).

67 James, *The Black Jacobins*, 241 [288].

68 I owe a significant debt here to Stuart Hall. In the spring of 1999, in the early stages of my thinking about *The Black Jacobins* and the tragedy of colonial modernity, he remarked to me, in his inimitable way, and in the unlikely setting of Baltimore, that James's conception of tragedy was Hegelian. He left it there like an unopened gift. Only later did I grasp the full import (and still, no doubt, imperfectly) of this characteristically sparing yet incisive insight of Stuart Hall's.

69 It is also interesting that of the ancient tragic poets it is Aeschylus that James mentions here and not, say, Sophocles or Euripides. Aeschylus, the oldest of the three great fifth-century tragedians, was often thought of as the least intellectual and most passionate. As is well known, Sophocles was Aristotle's favorite, and *Oedipus* was for him the best example of the construction of the tragic effect of

fear and pity. But for James, it is Aeschylus who is the surpassing ancient tragedian. Of the *Oresteia* he says that it is "the greatest play of ancient times"; and he
was particularly engaged by the prototypical status of the fire-stealing Prometheus in *Prometheus Bound*. See *Mariners, Renegades and Castaways* (New York: James,
1953), 65, 139–40, respectively.

70 Peter Szondi, *An Essay on the Tragic*, trans. by Paul Fleming (Stanford, Calif.: Stanford University Press, 2002), 1.

71 Interestingly, tragedy as such is not explicitly central to *The Phenomenology of Spirit*
(1807), the place where the structure of the dialectic achieves its mature form;
it is discussed in the late subsection, "The spiritual work of art." At the same
time, as Szondi argues, it is clear that in the *Phenomenology* tragedy shapes Hegel's
conception of the dialectic as a process of self-division and sacrifice.

72 See A. C. Bradley, "Hegel's Theory of Tragedy," in *Oxford Lectures on Poetry* (London:
Macmillan, 1965 [1909]).

73 See, for example, Kaufman, *Tragedy and Philosophy*, 200, 211, 283. In Kaufman's
view, however, "Hegel breached the framework Aristotle had laid down in chapter 13 of the *Poetics*" (202).

74 Szondi, *An Essay on the Tragic*, 16. For a similar "genealogy of the tragic" in Hegel,
see also Miguel de Beistegui, "Hegel: Or the Tragedy of Thinking," in Miguel de
Beistegui and Simon Sparks, eds., *Philosophy and Tragedy* (New York: Routledge,
2000). For a fascinating discussion that seeks to restore the centrality of comedy
to Hegel's overall conception of history and drama, see Rudolphe Gasché, "Self-
Dissolving Seriousness: On the Comic in the Hegelian Concept of Tragedy," in
de Beistegui and Sparks, *Philosophy and Tragedy*. "Even though one would likely
not find the tragic to be comic," writes Gasché, "tragic fate nevertheless hinges
on a possibility that is specifically of the order of the comic" (50).

75 G. W. F. Hegel, *Aesthetics: Lectures on Fine Art*, trans. by T. M. Knox (Oxford: Clarendon, 1975), 2:1198.

76 Ibid., 2:1194.

77 Ibid., 2:1218.

78 Ibid., 2:1217–18.

79 Ibid., 2:1206.

80 Ibid., 2:1225–26.

81 Andrew Cecil Bradley (1851–1935) came from a family of intellectuals. His elder
brother was the equally famous philosopher, Francis Herbert Bradley (1846–
1924), one of the leaders of the Oxford philosophical movement known as the
British Idealists.

82 Bradley, "Hegel's Theory of Tragedy," 71. It is not of course the case that Bradley
dismissed Aristotle. To the contrary, he made much use of the latter's ideas of
the dramatic effect of fear and pity on audiences. His lecture on Hegel begins
with a salutation to Aristotle: "Since Aristotle dealt with tragedy, and, as usual,
drew the main features of his subject with those sure and simple strokes which

no later hand has rivaled, the only philosopher who has treated it in a manner both original and searching is Hegel" (69).

83  A. C. Bradley, *Shakespearean Tragedy: Lectures on Hamlet, Othello, King Lear, Macbeth* (New York: St Martin's Press, 1957 [1904]).

84  Ibid., 6–7. For some critical and contextualizing discussion of Bradley's contribution to modern Shakespeare studies, see Katherine Cooke's very useful *A. C. Bradley and His Influence on Twentieth Century Shakespeare Criticism* (Oxford: Clarendon Press, 1972), and more recently, Harry Levin's "Critical Approaches to Shakespeare from 1660 to 1904," Kenneth Muir's "Twentieth Century Shakespeare Criticism: The Tragedies," and Terrence Hawkes's "Shakespeare and New Critical Approaches," all in Stanley Wells, ed., *The Cambridge Companion to Shakespeare Studies* (Cambridge: Cambridge University Press, 1986).

85  As Bradley writes in *Shakespearean Tragedy*: "The dictum that with Shakespeare, 'character is destiny' is no doubt an exaggeration, and one that may mislead . . . but it is the exaggeration of a vital truth" (8). On Bradley as a Victorian "character-chaser" see Cooke, *A. C. Bradley and His Influence*, especially chapter 6. For a fascinating discussion of the question of character in Shakespeare, one much indebted to Bradley, see Bert States, *'Hamlet' and the Concept of Character* (Baltimore: Johns Hopkins University Press, 1992).

86  Bradley, *Shakespearean Tragedy*, 7.

87  Ibid., 9, emphasis in the original.

88  James in fact mentions Bradley on a number of occasions, though so far as I can tell he has no explicit, substantive engagement with his work. See, for example, James, "Letters to Literary Critics," 236; and "Preface to Criticism," 255. But I want to suggest a deeper relation between Bradley's and James's Hegelianism. There is an allusive connection between James and the Oxford Hegelian moral philosopher T. H. Green, in James's remark, quoted in chapter 1, regarding the writing of history. It is interesting and suggestive, I think, that Bradley was not only an admirer and associate of Green's, but after Green's death in 1882, Bradley edited his unfinished *Prolegomena to Ethics*. On this relation, see Cooke, *A. C. Bradley and His Influence*, 21–24, 29, 31; and Melvin Richter, *The Politics of Conscience: T. H. Green and His Age* (Cambridge, Mass.: Harvard University Press, 1964), 13–14, 149.

89  James, "Letters to Literary Critics," 231. Jay Leyda was the author, among other things, of a book on Herman Melville that James had a great deal of regard for, namely, *Melville Log* (New York: Harcourt, Brace and Co., 1951).

90  James, "Letters to Literary Critics," 231.

91  Ibid., 236. See also James, "Preface to Criticism," 259.

92  C. L. R. James, "Notes on *Hamlet*," in Grimshaw, *The C. L. R. James Reader*, 243. James's essay was written around 1953.

93  James, *Mariners, Renegades and Castaways*, 140.

94  James, "Notes on *Hamlet*," 243–44.

95  Victor Kiernan, *Eight Tragedies of Shakespeare* (London: Verso, 1996), 73.

96 For a recent and fascinating discussion of the ghost of Hamlet's father, see Stephen Greenblatt, *Hamlet in Purgatory* (Princeton: Princeton University Press, 2001).

97 Kiernan, *Eight Tragedies of Shakespeare*, 80.

98 James, "Notes on *Hamlet*," 244.

99 Ibid., 245.

100 Kiernan makes a similar observation in *Eight Tragedies of Shakespeare*. Hamlet, he says, is a "born in intellectual, one of the first in modern literature. Men like him belong oftenest to times when the air is full of a confused onrush of new thinking, as yet only half making sense. They are not the ones who know how to make profitable use of ideas, but people who are seized and as it were made use of by ideas seeking entry into the world" (65). For a discussion of the relation between intellectuals and modernity, see Zygmunt Bauman, *Legislators and Interpreters: On Modernity, Post-Modernity, and Intellectuals* (Ithaca: Cornell University Press, 1987).

101 This may be as good a place as any to simply note Marx's own fascination with Shakespeare and with *Hamlet* in particular. Especially after he moved to England in 1849 Marx devoted himself to reading Shakespeare (indeed the entire Marx family was involved in a virtual Shakespeare ritual). Marx was keenly interested in the figure of the ghost of old Hamlet and of the haunting of the past in the present. *The Eighteenth Brumaire of Louis Bonaparte* is perhaps the best-known instance of this interest. Here the revolution itself is imagined through the ghost as "still journeying through purgatory." See *The Eighteenth Brumaire* (New York: International Publishers, 1963 [1852]), 121. For a discussion, see Peter Stallybrass, " 'Well grubbed, old mole': Marx, *Hamlet*, and the (Un)Fixing of Representation," in Jean E. Howard and Scott Cutler Shershow, eds., *Marxist Shakespeares* (London: Routledge, 2001).

## 5 THE TRAGEDY OF COLONIAL ENLIGHTENMENT

The epigraph is taken from C. L. R. James, *The Black Jacobins: Toussaint L'Ouverture and the San Domingo Revolution* (London: Secker and Warburg, 1938), 241; *The Black Jacobins: Toussaint L'Ouverture and the San Domingo Revolution*, 2nd ed. rev. (New York: Vintage, 1963), 288. In the 1963 edition, the last sentence was omitted.

1 C. L. R. James, *The Black Jacobins*, 2nd ed. rev. (New York: Vintage, 1963), 291. Hereafter references to *The Black Jacobins* are abbreviated BJ in parentheses in the body of the text; page numbers to the 1938 edition are given first, with those from the 1963 edition given in brackets.

2 Shelley, preface to "Prometheus Unbound: A Lyrical Drama in Four Acts," in *Shelley's Poetry and Prose*, ed. Donald H. Reiman and Sharon B. Powers (New York: Norton, 1977), 133.

3 One influential site for the articulation of this argument is John Gray, *Enlightenment's Wake: Politics and Culture at the Close of the Modern Age* (New York: Rout-

ledge, 1995). In Gray's view, the Enlightenment is an unmitigated disaster and its project of universal civilization is now reaping the whirlwind of its hubris. "We live today," writes Gray with considerable eloquence in the last chapter of the book, "amid the dim ruins of the Enlightenment project, which was the ruling project of the modern period. If, as I believe, the Enlightenment project has proved to be self-destroying, then that fact signals the close of the modern period, of which we are the heirs. Our patrimony is the disenchantment which the Enlightenment has bequeathed to us—a disenchantment all the more profound since it encompasses the central illusions of the Enlightenment itself" (145).

4   See David Scott, *Formations of Ritual: Colonial and Anthropological Discourses on the Sinhala Yaktovil* (Minneapolis: University of Minnesota Press, 1994), and *Refashioning Futures: Criticism after Postcoloniality* (Princeton: Princeton University Press, 1999).

5   See J. G. A. Pocock, "Enthusiasm: The Antiself of Enlightenment," in Lawrence E. Klein and Anthony J. La Vopa, eds., *Enthusiasm and Enlightenment in Europe, 1650–1850* (San Marino, Calif.: Huntington Library, 1998), 7. Pocock urges that we give up the idea of "the Enlightenment" understood as a "unitary and universal phenomenon with a single history to be either celebrated or condemned" and understand it rather as "a family of discourses arising about the same time in a number of European cultures." This thinking of course frames Pocock's magisterial work on Edward Gibbon in which he urges the plurality of Enlightenments and argues the distinctiveness of the eighteenth-century English Enlightenment. See J. G. A. Pocock, *Barbarism and Religion*, 2 vols. (New York: Cambridge University Press, 1999). On the "demonology" of Enlightenment, see James Schmidt, "What Enlightenment Project?" *Political Theory* 28, no. 6 (2000): 734–57; and Schmidt, "Civility, Enlightenment, and Society: Conceptual Confusions and Kantian Remedies," *American Political Science Review* 92, no. 2 (June 1998): 419–27. See also the essays collected in Keith Michael Baker and Peter Hanns Reill, eds., *What's Left of Enlightenment: A Postmodern Question?* (Stanford, Calif.: Stanford University Press, 2001).

6   Not the least of those puzzled by Foucault's turn to Enlightenment has been Jürgen Habermas. See in particular his memorial address, "Taking Aim at the Heart of the Present: On Foucault's Lecture on Kant's *What Is Enlightenment?*" in *The New Conservatism: Cultural Criticism and the Historian's Debate*, trans. by Shierry Weber Nicholsen (Cambridge, Mass.: MIT Press, 1991). Following a subtle summary of Foucault's discussion of Kant's "What Is Enlightenment?" and *Conflict of the Faculties* (1798), Habermas raises the question of how "such an affirmative understanding of modern philosophizing" comports with Foucault's "unyielding critique of modernity." "Wouldn't every line of Kant's philosophy of history, his speculations about a constitution of freedom, about world-citizenship and perpetual peace, his interpretation of revolutionary enthusiasm as a sign of historical progress toward the better—wouldn't every line of all this provoke the

scorn of Foucault the theoretician of power?" (176). In the end Habermas sees an insoluble contradiction. "Of the circle of those in my generation engaged in philosophical diagnoses of the times, Foucault has had the most lasting effect on the Zeitgeist, not least of all thanks to the earnestness with which he perseveres in productive contradictions. Only complex thought produces instructive contradictions. Kant became entangled in an instructive contradiction of this kind when he explained revolutionary enthusiasm as a historical sign that allowed an intelligible disposition in the human race to appear within the phenomenal world. Equally instructive is the contradiction in which Foucault becomes entangled when he opposes his critique of power, disabled by the relevance of the contemporary moment, to the analytic of the true in such a way that the former is deprived of the normative standards it would have to derive from the latter. Perhaps it is the force of this contradiction that drew Foucault, in this last of his texts, back into the sphere of influence he had tried to blast open, that of the philosophical discourse of modernity" (178–79).

7  See, for example, James Schmidt and Thomas E. Wartenburg, "Foucault's Enlightenment: Critique, Revolution, and the Fashioning of the Self," in Michael Kelly, ed., *Critique and Power: Recasting the Foucault/Habermas Debate* (Cambridge, Mass.: MIT Press, 1994). Bringing their fascinating discussion to a close, the authors write: "Foucault's 'What Is Enlightenment?' should not be read as a deathbed conversion. His interest in Kant spanned his career and he had been concerned with Kant's essay on the question of enlightenment for at least the last decade of his life. Through it all, his stance toward the enlightenment remained a good deal more nuanced and complex than his critics would lead us to believe. It was never, for him, a question of deciding 'for' or 'against' the enlightenment— as if we could somehow manage to disavow an event which has, in fundamental ways, defined how we think about ourselves" (303–4).

8  See Immanuel Kant, "An Answer to the Question: What Is Enlightenment?" in James Schmidt, ed., *What Is Enlightenment? Eighteenth Century Answers and Twentieth Century Questions* (Berkeley: University of California Press, 1996). See especially Schmidt's excellent introduction: "What Is Enlightenment? A Question, Its Context, and Some Consequences" (1–44). See also Schmidt, "The Question of Enlightenment: Kant, Mendelssohn, and the *Mittwochsgesellschaft*," *Journal of the History of Ideas* 50, no. 2 (1989): 269–91; and Schmidt, "What Enlightenment Was: How Moses Mendelssohn and Immanuel Kant answered the *Berlinische Monatsschrift*," *Journal of the History of Philosophy* 30, no. 1 (1992): 77–101.

9  The three essays of Foucault's are "What Is Critique?" in Schmidt, *What is Enlightenment?*; "Kant on Enlightenment and Revolution," *Economy and Society* 15, no. 1 (1986): 88–96; and "What Is Enlightenment?" in Paul Rabinow, ed., *The Foucault Reader* (New York: Pantheon, 1984). For another discussion of these essays, see Colin Gordon, "Questions, Ethos, Event: Foucault on Kant and Enlightenment,"

*Economy and Society* 15, no. 1 (1986): 71–87; and Michael Meranze, "Critique and Government: Michel Foucault and the Question 'What Is Enlightenment?'" in Baker and Reill, *What's Left of Enlightenment?*

10  Foucault, "What Is Enlightenment?" 43.

11  Ibid., 42.

12  Ibid., 34.

13  In the opening sentence of his essay Kant writes: "*Enlightenment is mankind's exit from its self-incurred immaturity. Immaturity* is the inability to make use of one's own understanding without the guidance of another. *Self-incurred* is this inability if its cause lies not in the lack of understanding but rather in the lack of the resolution and the courage to use it without the guidance of another. *Sapere aude!* Have the courage to use your own understanding! is thus the motto of enlightenment." In Kant, "What Is Enlightenment?" 58 (italics in original).

14  Foucault, "What Is Enlightenment?" 46.

15  Ibid., 47.

16  Charles Segal, *Tragedy and Civilization: An Interpretation of Sophocles* (Norman: University of Oklahoma Press, 1981).

17  Ibid., 2.

18  "Sophoclean tragedy's ample, yet austere, form could concentrate issues of enormous moment into remarkably small compass. Its climactic structure, building up from crisis to peripety to resolution, made it the ideal vehicle for exploring reversals and inversions in the situations and emotions of men, in language, in values. Sophocles especially made irony, paradox, and conscious ambiguity his stock-in-trade" (ibid., 9).

19  Ibid., 207. See also Charles Segal, *Oedipus Tyrannus: Tragic Heroism and the Limits of Knowledge* (New York: Oxford University Press, 2001).

20  See Martha C. Nussbaum, *The Fragility of Goodness: Luck and Ethics in Greek Tragedy and Philosophy* (Cambridge: Cambridge University Press, 1986).

21  Ibid., 34–35.

22  For a brief but useful as well as dissenting discussion of Kant's place and significance in the history of moral theorizing in the West, see Alasdair MacIntyre, *A Short History of Ethics* (New York: Macmillan, 1966). MacIntyre writes: "For many who have never heard of philosophy, let alone Kant, morality is roughly what Kant said it was" (190).

23  For a critical discussion of this constructionism, see Ian Hacking, *The Social Construction of What?* (Cambridge, Mass.: Harvard University Press, 1999), 46–47. "All construct-isms," Hacking writes further, "dwell in the dichotomy between appearance and reality set up by Plato, and given a definitive form by Kant. Although social constructionists bask in the sun they call postmodernism, they are really very old-fashioned" (49). This work of Hacking's has been very useful in my thinking about the influence of constructionism in the study of the postcolo-

nial world. See David Scott, "The 'Social Construction' of Postcolonial Studies," in Suvir Kaul, Ania Loomba, Antoinette Burton, Matti Bunzl, eds., *Postcolonial Studies and Beyond* (Durham: Duke University Press, forthcoming).

24 See the introduction to J. Peter Euben, ed., *Greek Tragedy and Political Theory* (Berkeley: University of California Press, 1986).

25 See, for example, Kevin Schilbrack, ed., *Thinking through Myths: Philosophical Perspectives* (New York: Routledge, 2002).

26 Euben, *Greek Tragedy and Political Theory*, 9. See also Nussbaum, *The Fragility of Goodness*, especially part 2. In her compelling discussion, she contrasts different moments in the development of Plato's ethics. Where in the early period, represented by the *Protagoras*, for instance, we see Plato responding to some of the same preoccupations of the tragedians and mobilizing some of their strategies for managing contingency, in his middle period, in the *Republic* most famously, we see him more resolutely taking steps to eliminate the intrusive force of chance and developing a form of dialogue that might be conceived as an *alternative* to tragedy. In later work, represented by the *Phaedrus*, we see Plato revising and modifying this conception of the good. And see Segal, *Oedipus Tyrannus*: "Plato, who writes his dialogues in dramatic form, is in a sense the successor to the tragedians in a postmythical age" (22).

27 Euben, *The Tragedy of Political Theory: The Road Not Taken* (Princeton: Princeton University Press, 1990), 5.

28 The remark, quoted by Euben in *The Tragedy of Political Theory* (19), is of course from Foucault's *Discipline and Punish*, 217.

29 Euben, *The Tragedy of Political Theory*, 25.

30 Ibid., 29–30.

31 Ibid., 30.

32 See Christopher Rocco, *Tragedy and Enlightenment: Athenian Political Thought and the Dilemmas of Modernity* (Berkeley: University of California Press, 1997).

33 Ibid., 36.

34 Ibid., chapter 2.

35 Max Horkheimer and Theodor W. Adorno, *Dialectic of Enlightenment*, trans. by John Cumming (New York: Continuum, 1972). For a different discussion of this work than Rocco provides, but one nevertheless that is very valuable, see James Schmidt, "Language, Mythology, and Enlightenment: Historical Notes on Horkheimer and Adorno's *Dialectic of Enlightenment*," *Social Research* 65, no. 4 (winter 1998): 807–38.

36 Rocco, *Tragedy and Enlightenment*, 31.

37 Ibid., 32.

38 Ibid., 174.

39 Ibid., 176.

40 Segal, *Tragedy and Civilization*, 10.

41 For a fascinating discussion of Henri Christophe, see Michel-Rolph Trouillot,

"The Three Faces of Sans Souci," in his *Silencing the Past: Power and the Production of History* (Boston: Beacon, 1995), chapter 2.

42 Interestingly, in the play, James suggests that Toussaint and Madame Bayou de Libertas (there, Madame Louis Bullet) were intimately involved. See "The Black Jacobins," in Anna Grimshaw, ed., *The C. L. R. James Reader* (Oxford: Blackwell, 1992), 93–94.

43 For a useful discussion of this question, see Alex Dupuy, "Toussaint-Louverture and the Haitian Revolution: A Reassessment of C. L. R. James's Interpretation," in Selwyn R. Cudjoe and William E. Cain, eds., *C. L. R. James: His Intellectual Legacies* (Amherst: University of Massachusetts Press, 1995).

44 There is a splendid imaginative description of this entire episode in Madison Smartt Bell's remarkable novel *Master of the Crossroads* (New York: Pantheon, 2000), 667. This is the sequel to his equally remarkable *All Souls Rising* (New York: Penguin, 1995). Together these two novels recount the story of the Haitian Revolution.

45 Aimé Césaire, *Discourse on Colonialism*, trans. by Joan Pinkham (New York: Monthly Review, 1972), 24.

46 Segal, *Tragedy and Civilization*, 42.


EPILOGUE

The epigraph is taken from C. L. R. James, Letter to Maxwell Geismar, April 11, 1961, in Anna Grimshaw, ed., *The C. L. R. James Reader* (Oxford: Blackwell, 1992), 278.

1 Hannah Arendt, *On Revolution* (New York: Viking, 1963). In 1963 another book of Arendt's—a much more famous and vastly more controversial book—was also published, *Eichmann in Jerusalem: A Report on the Banality of Evil* (New York: Viking, 1963). The book grew out of her coverage of the 1961 war crimes trial of Adolf Eichmann in Jerusalem for *The New Yorker*.

2 Arendt, *On Revolution*, 281. This is Arendt's own translation. Robert Fagles's translation in the Penguin Classics edition, *Sophocles: The Three Theban Plays* (New York: Penguin, 1984), is somewhat different: "Not to be born is best / when all is reckoned in, but once a man has seen the light / the next best thing, by far, is to go back / back where he came from, quickly as he can" (358).

3 Sophocles, "Oedipus at Colonus," in *Sophocles: The Three Theban Plays* (New York: Penguin, 1984), 358, 1395.

4 For a splendid reading of *Oedipus at Colonus* (as indeed of everything by Sophocles), see Charles Segal, *Tragedy and Civilization: An Interpretation of Sophocles* (Norman: University of Oklahoma Press, 1981), chapter 11. "In moving from feeble exile to heroized savior, Oedipus reverses the pattern of his earlier play, with its movement from king to beggar, godlike authority to pollution and misery. By returning to this figure whose life contains the most extreme of tragic reversals,

Sophocles seems to be consciously reflecting upon and transcending the tragic pattern which he did so much to develop. . . . At the end of the Colonus Oedipus sums up and visually enacts the tragic road of life, now traveled to an incomprehensible end, through and beyond tragedy to a virtual apotheosis" (406).

5  While not explicitly connecting it to tragedy, Arendt had of course developed this idea of action, political freedom, and the polis in The Human Condition (Chicago: University of Chicago Press, 1958).

6  Judith Shklar, "Hannah Arendt's Triumph," The New Republic (December 27, 1975). "Political Philosophy," Shklar wrote, "is tragic thought. Without a dramatic sense of fate and mutability no rational intelligence would turn to this subject" (10). Shklar was one of Arendt's most perceptive readers. See also Shklar's "Rethinking the Past," Social Research 44, no. 1 (1977): 80–90, which also makes a number of insightful remarks about Arendt and tragedy. There are a few students of Arendt's work who have followed up on Shklar's early insight on the work of tragedy in Arendt's thought, but none with the systematicity recently brought to bear by Robert C. Pirro in his full-length treatment, Hannah Arendt and the Politics of Tragedy (DeKalb: Northern Illinois University Press, 2001). In this fascinating book, Pirro sets out to consider "how an unacknowledged theory of Greek tragedy—inherited by Arendt from her philhellenic predecessors in the German tradition of philosophy and letters—shaped her understanding of storytelling and its relevance to democratic citizenship in a disenchanted world" (9).

7  Indeed, both James and Arendt wrote exultantly and significantly of the Hungarian worker's councils. See C. L. R. James, "The Worker's Councils," in C. L. R. James, Grace C. Lee, and Pierre Chaulieu, Facing Reality (Detroit: Correspondence Publishing Company, 1958), 7–19; and Hannah Arendt, "Totalitarian Imperialism," Journal of Politics 20 (February 1958): 5–43.

8  I have discussed James's self-consciousness of narrative in chapter 1 of this book. There are now a number of useful discussions of the work of storytelling and narrative in Arendt. See, for example, Elisabeth Young-Bruehl, "Hannah Arendt's Storytelling," Social Research 44, no. 1 (1977): 183–90; Melvyn A. Hill, "The Fictions of Mankind and the Stories of Men," in Melvyn A. Hill, ed., Hannah Arendt: The Recovery of the Public World (New York: St. Martin's Press, 1979); Seyla Benhabib, "Hannah Arendt and the Redemptive Power of Narrative," in Lewis Hinchman and Sandra Hinchman, eds., Hannah Arendt: Critical Essays (Albany: State University of New York Press, 1994); and Pirro, Hannah Arendt and the Politics of Tragedy, chapter 1.

9  Arendt, On Revolution, 29. For an instructive discussion of the contrasting problem of "founding" in Arendt and Derrida, see Bonnie Honig, "Declarations of Independence: Arendt and Derrida on the Problem of Founding a Republic," American Political Science Review 85 (March 1991): 97–113. See also Pirro, Hannah Arendt and the Politics of Tragedy, chapter 3.

10  Hannah Arendt, The Origins of Totalitarianism (New York: Harcourt, Brace and Co.,

1951); and Arendt, *Between Past and Future: Eight Exercises in Political Thought* (New York: Viking, 1961).

11  See Elisabeth Young-Bruehl, *Hannah Arendt: For Love of the World* (New Haven: Yale University Press, 1982), for some of the backgrounds and connections among these books. It is an interesting fact that of all of them it is *The Origins of Totalitarianism* that has seemed to many in our time the most pertinent and that has received the most systematic attention. See, for example, the recent issue of *Social Research* 69, no. 2 (summer 2002), devoted to "Hannah Arendt: *The Origins of Totalitarianism*: Fifty Years Later."

12  Perhaps the most perceptive and sympathetic commentator on *On Revolution* was Arendt's mentor, Karl Jaspers. In his warmly appreciative letter to Arendt of May 16, 1963, Jaspers wrote: "I'm still far from having finished it. But I have grasped the basic thrust of your intention. I think that it is a book that is the equal of, if not perhaps superior to, your book on totalitarianism in the profundity of its political outlook and the masterly quality of its execution. I sense nothing artificial in it, no forced rational arguments; I find no superfluous digressions. Your presentation of a single idea is a powerful current that pulls me along. Your insight into the nature of political freedom and your courage in loving the dignity of man in this arena are wonderful." Lotte Kohler and Hans Saner, eds., *Hannah Arendt/Karl Jaspers Correspondence, 1926–1969*, trans. by Robert Kimber and Rita Kimber (New York: Harcourt Brace Jovanovich, 1992), 504. Jaspers, moreover, discerned the centrality of tragedy to Arendt's thinking: "Ultimately, the whole is your vision of a tragedy that does not leave you despairing: an element of the tragedy of humankind" (505). As Pirro reminds us, Jaspers had himself published a book on tragedy (*Tragedy Is Not Enough*) a little more than a decade before. See *Hannah Arendt and the Politics of Tragedy*, 28–33.

13  It is an interesting fact that one of the inspirations for *On Revolution* was Rosa Luxemburg, with whom Arendt formed a strong identification and whose book *The Russian Revolution* she read while teaching at the University of California, Berkeley, in the middle 1950s. See Young-Bruehl, *Hannah Arendt*, 294. Many historians— Eric Hobsbawm among them—found *On Revolution* wanting in the way of proper social history. It was short, or misinformed, on the facts. But as Elisabeth Young-Bruehl has written: "Hannah Arendt discussed revolutions not in order to outline their histories or distinguish their types but in order to present an ideal for practice" (406). For a discussion of responses to *On Revolution*, see Young-Bruehl, *Hannah Arendt*, 402–6.

14  Arendt, *On Revolution*, 60.

15  Ibid., 61.

16  Hannah Arendt had a very complicated relationship to Marx's work. After completing *The Origins of Totalitarianism* (published in 1951), she set out to write a book devoted to locating the significance of Marx's teaching and to understanding how a body of thought so deeply embedded in the Western philosophical tradi-

tion could, nevertheless, be made use of by totalitarianism. This book, of course, was never finished, and her reflections on Marx found their way into other books, *On Revolution* among them. See the previously unpublished fragment of Arendt's writing on Marx: "Karl Marx and the Tradition of Western Political Thought," *Social Research* 69, no. 2 (summer 2002): 273–319.

17  Arendt, *On Revolution*, 220.

18  Ibid.

19  Ibid., 280.

20  The other poet Arendt quotes in this connection is René Char, one of the great poets of the French Resistance during World War II. See *On Revolution*, 215, 280. She had previously used the same paradoxical quote—"our inheritance was left to us by no testament"—as the opening to her preface of *Between Past and Future*, 3.

21  Arendt, *On Revolution*, 61.

22  On James's disavowal of heterodoxy in Marxism, see "An Audience with C. L. R. James," *Third World Book Review* 1, no. 2 (1984): 7. Perhaps the only scholastic piece of Jamesian Marxism is to be found in his *Notes on Dialectics: Hegel, Marx, Lenin* (Westport, Conn.: Lawrence Hill, 1980 [1948]).

23  Arendt, *On Revolution*, 81.

24  Ibid., 216.

25  It is not that blacks are invisible to Arendt. Though the question is far from adequately developed she is aware of the conundrum of race and black misery in the problem of the American Revolution. See *On Revolution*, 71–72. For some sense of her ambivalent relation to the Black Power movement of the 1960s, see Young-Bruehl, *Hannah Arendt*, 417–19.

26  C. L. R. James, *The Black Jacobins* (London: Secker and Warburg, 1938), vii; *The Black Jacobins*, 2nd ed. rev. (New York: Vintage, 1963), x.

27  Ibid., 162–63 [197–98].

# Acknowledgments

In April 1999 I was invited to give a lecture in the Department of African-American Studies at Northwestern University in Evanston, Illinois. I presented a paper entitled, somewhat ambitiously: "Conscripts of Political Modernity: C. L. R. James' Toussaint Louverture and the Making of the Caribbean." This book grew out of the years of wrestling with what I was tenuously and sketchily trying to get at in that lecture. I am grateful to my hosts at Northwestern University and especially to Michael Hanchard for his perceptive and encouraging remarks on that occasion. Somewhat more developed versions of that early paper were read as lectures at the University of Michigan, Ann Arbor, the University of Iowa, Iowa City, and the University of Minnesota, Minneapolis, in February, March, and April 2000, respectively. I should like to thank my hosts at each of these universities for so generously providing me with occasions on which to try out my still-fledgling ideas. In particular, I wish to thank Pradeep Jeganathan who invited me to Minneapolis and who pressed me to think harder than he found me doing about disaster and suffering. On that memorable occasion too Qadri Ismail urged me with subtle questions to consider more carefully than I was Marxism's relation to time and narrative. Needless to say, I remain ever in their debt.

In the years that followed these lectures I tended to withdraw my thinking about modernity, tragedy, and the criticism of the postcolonial present away from these sorts of formal public occasions and sought instead to try and sort out more clearly for myself what I was after and why it seemed to me that C. L. R. James's *The Black Jacobins*—a book I first read as a schoolboy, and every few years since then—was so exemplary a stage for my preoccupations. As this internal dialogue began to resurface informally, no one was more helpful and supportive than my friend Robert Hill with whom I have spent many wonderful hours in searching conversations about James and his intellectual sources. Hill is James's literary executor, and there can't be many with a more intimate acquaintance with the textual layers that constitute the complexity of *The Black*

*Jacobins*. The intellectual debt I owe to Talal Asad and Stuart Hall is, as it has always been, warmed by a friendship that by now is impossible to define or measure. Their work and their advice, and above all their example, have been a constant inspiration down the many avenues of uncertainty writing this book has carried me. That they both read the entire manuscript and offered instructive criticisms and helpful suggestions on the whole of the argument is the least of their contributions to the shape of this book and the thought at work in it.

Finally, Ritty Lukose, who likewise read the manuscript in its entirety and with an acute attention to my attempt to think about the temporality of the present, attuned me to ways of honoring the past without succumbing to its temptations. I can't say that I succeeded—indeed I much doubt that I have—but I can say that I have been enriched and consoled by her wisdom and her patience.

# Index

Abyssinia, 27

Adorno, T. W., 139, 140, 178; *Dialectic of Enlightenment*, 188–89, 190

Aeschylus, 12, 140–41, 156, 158, 160–61, 168, 182; Prometheus, 151, 173–74, 176; *Prometheus Bound*, 173, 191; *Oresteia*, 173; *Agamemnon*, 183

*Africa and Africans in the Making of the Atlantic World, 1400–1800* (Thornton), 108–11, 114

*Age of Extremes, The* (Hobsbawm), 25–26

*American Civilization* (James), 12, 14, 139, 145, 148

American Revolution, 21, 85, 215–16

anticolonialism, 6, 7, 9, 14, 18–19, 29–30, 34, 64, 94, 102, 118, 144, 172, 209; anticolonial vindicationism, 55

Arendt, Hannah, 21, 64; *On Revolution*, 21, 211, 214–15, 218–19; revolution viewed by, 88–89; on tragedy, 211–13

Aristotle, 16, 152–53, 156, 162, 182; hamartia and, 153–54, 167; *Poetics*, 153–54

Arnold, Matthew, 70

Asad, Talal, 8–9, 19, 107, 115–19, 129

Auden, W. H., 25

Austin, J. L., 52, 64

Bandung, 1, 30, 57, 210

*Begriffsgeschichte* (conceptual history), 42, 45

Bennett, Louise, 143

*Beyond a Boundary* (James), 12, 14, 145, 148

*Billy Budd, Sailor* (Melville), 213

black historiography, 14

*Black Jacobins, The* (James), 9–12, 14–19, 23, 29, 58; revised edition of, 10, 13–14, 16, 19, 123, 132, 145, 147–49, 152, 163, 165–66; as Penguin classic, 11; *Tempest* and, 15–16; problem of history and, 18, 22, 31–32, 34, 36–37, 39, 40; Romanticism and, 18, 19, 55, 59, 96; Michelet and, 18, 68; Trotsky and, 19; enlightenment and, 20, 170–71, 175; *On Revolution* and, 21, 213–14, 218–20; sovereignty and, 22; tragedy and, 22, 51, 133–35, 150–53, 175; English Romantics and, 24, 61–62; anticolonialism and, 30, 56–57; Marxism and, 38; emplotment and, 50; as Romance, 50, 59, 70, 96; as kind of linguistic action, 53, 55; slavery and, 64, 92–96, 106, 127–29; myth of the hero and, 71, 74, 78–79; biography and, 71; vindicationism and, 84, 87; idea of revolution and, 88–89, 92–96; image of Africa and, 102, 104–5, 108; modernity and, 114, 123, 125–29; African decolonization and, 124; West Indian identity and, 124; as tragedy of enlightenment, 176, 182, 190, 206–8, 221

*Black Napoleon, The* (Waxman), 81

black Romanticism, 55

Black Spartacus, 100

Blassingame, John, 104

New World slavery. *See* slavery

Nietzsche, Friedrich, 149, 187

Nussbaum, Martha, 12, 21, 182, 183, 184, 266 n. 26

Oakeshott, Michael, 40–41

*Occupation for Gentlemen, An* (Warburg), 229 n. 16

"Ode to a Nightingale" (Keats), 24, 226 n. 2

Oedipus, 154, 172, 176, 181, 211–12

*Oedipus Tyrannus*, 20, 172, 181, 188–91, 211

*On Liberty* (Mill), 82

*On Revolution* (Arendt), 21, 211, 214–15, 218–19

Orwell, George, 25, 227 n. 7

Padmore, George, 28, 87, 124, 230 n. 22

*Philosophical and Political History* (Raynal), 98–101, 107, 129, 193, 196, 246–47 n. 7

Plato, 182, 186, 203; *Republic*, 186

*Poetics* (Aristotle), 153–54

Price, Richard, 109–11, 114, 117

problem-space, 4, 7, 30, 34, 53, 57, 64, 79, 81, 97, 104, 111, 117–19

question and answer method, 5, 51, 53, 55

Rabbitt, Kara, 16–18

Raboteau, Albert, 104

"Race Admixture" (Harland), 80–81

racism, Victorian, 64

Rawls, John, 184–85

Raynal, Guillaume-Thomas-François, 98–101, 107, 129, 193, 196, 246–47 n. 7

*Red Spanish Notebook* (Low and Breá), 25

*Refashioning Futures* (Scott), 2, 4

*Republic* (Plato), 186

revolution: concept of, 64, 65; modern idea of, 88–89

Robespierre, Maximilien, 39, 191, 217, 220

Rocco, Christopher, 12, 21, 185, 188–90

Romance: story potential of, 7, 32; as mode of emplotment, 47, 56, 64, 70, 131, 135; Romantic longing and, 64; mythos of, 66, 70, 81

Romanticism: poetic, 18; materialist, 19, 69–70; vindicationist, 19, 55; revolutionary, 59; English, 59, 60, 173; Eurocentrism and, 59; anticolonial, 63

Romantics: English, 24; Victorian, 71

Rousseau, Jean-Jacques, 91–92, 100, 199, 217

Russian Revolution, 25, 39, 65, 68, 73

San Domingo Revolution (Haitian Revolution), 9, 15, 21, 28, 30, 34, 36–37, 39, 50, 57–59, 63, 85, 101, 104, 121, 123, 128, 134, 166, 192, 217

Sartre, Jean-Paul, 139

Schuler, Monica, 104

Segal, Charles, 12, 181, 188, 190, 208

Selassie, Haile, 28

Shachtman, Max, 137–38

Shakespeare, William, 12, 20, 77, 134, 136, 153, 156–58, 161, 163, 168

Sharpe, Granville, 60

Shelley, Percy Bysshe, 24, 173, 174

Shklar, Judith, 213

Skinner, Quentin, 5, 9, 33, 51–54, 56–57, 63, 79, 90, 96, 235 n. 75

slave emancipation, 29, 60, 82, 105, 133

slavery, 9, 14, 19, 43, 59, 64, 82, 92–96, 98, 102–4, 108–9, 111, 119, 164; as structure of power, 106, 110, 111; modernity and, 106, 112, 126–28, 135, 168

Société des Amis des Noirs, 99

David Scott is a professor of anthropology at Columbia University. He is the author of *Refashioning Futures:
Criticism after Postcoloniality* (1999) and *Formations of Ritual:
Colonial and Anthropological Discourse on the Sinhala Yaktovil*
(1994). He is also editor of the journal *Small Axe*.

Library of Congress Cataloging-in-Publication Data
Scott, David
Conscripts of modernity :
the tragedy of colonial enlightenment / David Scott.
p. cm.    Includes bibliographical references and index.
ISBN 0-8223-3433-X (cloth : alk. paper)
ISBN 0-8223-3444-5 (pbk. : alk. paper)
1. James, C. L. R. (Cyril Lionel Robert), 1901–
Black Jacobins. 2. Toussaint Louverture, 1743?–1803.
3. Postcolonialism—History. 4. Historiography.
5. History—Philosophy. 6. History—Periodization.
7. Literature and history. I. Title.
F1923.S36 2004    320.9′045—dc22
2004013139